Anonymous

Psalms Hymns & Spiritual Songs of the Old and New Testament

Anonymous

Psalms Hymns & Spiritual Songs of the Old and New Testament

ISBN/EAN: 9783337126285

Printed in Europe, USA, Canada, Australia, Japan

Cover: Foto ©Lupo / pixelio.de

More available books at **www.hansebooks.com**

THE
PSALMS
Hymns & Spiritual Songs
OF THE
Old and New TESTAMENT,
Faithfully tranflated into
Englifh Metre.

Being the NEW-ENGLAND Pfalm-Book *Revifed* and *Improved*: By an Endeavour after a yet nearer Approach to the *infpired Original*, as well as to the Rules of Poetry.

With an *Addition* of Fifty other HYMNS on the *moft important Subjects* of *Chriftianity*; with their *Titles*, placed *in Order*, from—*The Fall of Angels and Men*, to—*Heaven after the General Judgment.*

The SECOND EDITION.

Col. iii. 16. Let the Word of CHRIST dwell in you richly in all Wifdom; teaching and admonifhing one another in Pfalms and Hymns, and Spiritual Songs; Singing with Grace in your Hearts to the LORD.
Eph. v. 19. Speaking to yourfelves in Pfalms, and Hymns, and Spiritual Songs, finging and making Melody in your Hearts to the LORD.
James v. 13. Is any among you afflicted? let him Pray. Is any merry? let him fing Pfalms.

BOSTON, NEW-ENGLAND:
Printed by THOMAS and JOHN FLEET,
At the *Heart* and *Crown* in Cornhill, 1773.

The PREFACE.

SECTION I. *History of the* NEW-ENGLAND Psalm-Book.

THE *First Settlers* of the NEW-ENGLAND-Colonies; who came to *Plymouth* in 1620; to *Salem*, with *three Ministers* for the *Massachusetts*, and *one* for *Plymouth*, in 1629; and with the *Massachusetts* Charter, Governour, Deputy-Governour, Assistants, *four Ministers*, and 1500 People, to *Boston* and the Neighbouring Towns in 1630; were esteem'd in ENGLAND, as some of the most eminent for Scripture-Knowledge, Piety and strict Adherence to the WORD of GOD, as any in their Day. They wisely made the DIVINE ORACLES the ONLY *Rule* of their *Religion*: and their great and noble Design was to spread the holy Kingdom of CHRIST in its *Scripture-Purity*, Light and Power in this NEW WORLD; and to set up *Churches* for their Matter, Form, Worship, Liberty, Watch, Government and Discipline, as near as possible to what they were, under the Conduct of Inspiration, in the *Apostles Days*.

By 1636 there were come over hither near *thirty* pious and learned *Ministers*, educated in the *Universities* of ENGLAND: and from the same exalted Principle of *Scripture Purity* in *Religious Worship*, they set themselves to translate the *Psalms* and *other Scripture Songs* into *English Metre*, as near as possible to the *inspir'd Original*. They committed this Work especially to the Rev. Mr. *Richard Mather* of *Dorchester*; the Rev. Mr. *Thomas Weld*, and the Rev. Mr. *John Eliot* of *Roxbury*; well acquainted with the *Hebrew*, in which the *Old* Testament, and with the *Greek*, in which the *New* were *originally* written. They finished the *Psalms* in 1640: which were first Printed by Mr. *Day*, that Year, at our *Cambridge*; and had the Honour of being the *First Book* printed in NORTH-AMERICA, and as far as I find, in *This whole* NEW WORLD.

a 2   I

I have seen another Edition in 1647 (and I conclude at *Cambridge* too, there being no other Prefs in *New-England* then) with some Amendments. But for a further Improvement, it was committed to the Rev. Mr. *Henry Dunstar*, President of *Harvard College*, one of the greatest Masters of the oriental Languages that has been known in these Ends of the Earth: who was helped as to the *Poetry*, by Mr. *Richard Lyon*, an ingenious Gentleman, probably brought up at one of the Universities in *England*, sent over by Sir *Henry Mildway* as a Tutor to his Son at *Harvard College*, and resided in Mr. *Dunstar*'s House. By an *original Manuscript* of Heads of Sermons written after Mr. *Lyon* in 1650, I find He us'd to take his Turn with the *President* to preach to the Congregation at *Cambridge* in the Interval between Mr. *Shepard*'s Death, and Mr. *Mitchel*'s Ordination: And in those Heads appear the Traces both of Experimental Piety and Ingenuity.

In *two* or *three Years* they seem to have compleated it, with the Addition of the other *Songs in Scripture*: And they not only had the Happiness of approaching *nearer* to the *inspired Original* than *all other Versions* in *English Rhyme*, but in many Places of excelling them in Simplicity of Style, and in affecting Terms, being *the Words* of GOD which more strongly touch the Soul. On which Accounts I found in *England* it was by some eminent Congregations prefer'd to all *Others* in their *Publick Worship*, even down to 1717, when I last left that Part of the *British* Kingdom.

It seems a thousand Pities then, that such a *Version*, which has more of *Inspiration*, and therefore of Divine Authority and Influence on the Heart than others, should on Account of the Flatnesses in diverse Places, be wholly laid aside, and not rather mended and preserved in our Churches; as has been earnestly desired by many of refined Taste and Judgment: and especially since the learned and ingenious will by an accurate Examination find, that the nearer we come to the true Sentiment and Spirit of the admirable *Original*; the more full of Substance, Life and Majesty, and the more

moving

moving will the Verſion be: i. e. I mean when we find out Words rightly repreſenting the Sentiments of Inſpiration, and range them in a proper Order.

SECT. II. *An Account of this Improvement.*

My *great Deſign*, at the Deſire of many, therefore is—a Labour to preſerve the *Subſtance* of our NEW-ENGLAND *Verſion* in our Churches, by Reviſing and Improving it; riſing and keeping as near as poſſible to the exalted Sentiments of the *Original*, and expreſſing them in the cleareſt Style, and agreable to the Rules of Poetry. And for this—It was my Duty, *Firſt* to look to the *Divine Inſpirer*, to purify my Heart, enlighten my Mind, lead me into his own Intentions, and direct me in repreſenting them.

But then the *Method* I purſued was this——

I. I collected all the different Verſions in *Engliſh Metre* I could find, which are above 30, and I think all but 2: and comparing the 1ſt Pſalm in them, both with the *Proſe* Verſion in our *Engliſh* Bibles and with the *Hebrew*, I found about 20 took too great a liberty to vary from the *Original*; and ſelected 12, including the *New-England*—as keeping nearer; to which I added *another*, chiefly for ſome of the Poetry.

II. My Endeavour then was to gain *all* the *Sentiments*, eſpecially the great, ſublime and moſt important, in the *Original*. And in order to This—1ſt. I read over the *whole Pſalm* in our *Engliſh Bible*, with the inſtructive *Margin*. 2d. I labour'd to put my ſelf in the ſame external Circumſtance and internal Caſe, and to have the ſame Senſations and Views with the Pſalmiſt. 3d. I read every verſe (1) in the ſaid *Engliſh Bible*: and having the *Polyglot Bible* before me, (2) in the *Hebrew* with *Montanus's Interlineary*; (3) the *Septuagint*; (4) the *Chaldee*; (5) the *ancient Latin*; (6 & 7) the *Latin Verſions* of the *Syriack* and *Arabick*; (8) *Caſtalio*; (9) *Tremelius* & *Junius*; (10) *Ainſworth*; (11) *De Muis*. 4. When I met with *Difficulty*, I ſearch'd the following famous *Lexicons*, (1) *Avenarius*, (2) *Schindler*, (3) *Pagnine* and *Mercer*, (4 & 5) *Buxtorf's* 2 Lexicons, viz. *Hebrew*
and

and *Chaldaick*, &c. (6) *Leigh*, (7) *Castellus*, (8) *Bythner*, (9) *Martin Albert* As also the Interpretations of *Moller, Tremelius, Glassius, Ainsworth, DeMuis, Hammond, Pool's Synopsis, Patrick*, and Others.

All this—only to gain the *Sentiments*—And then
III. I look'd into the *New-England* as the Groundwork, and then into the 12 other *Metrical Versions* in their Order: and comparing them;—in Honour to the Word of God which demands the Best, I tho't it my Duty to use the *best Words* or *Lines* in them so far as they give the *nearest Sense* of the *Original*, and are *most musical*; and where they fail in *either*, to endeavour a further Improvement.

And avoiding *Additions* which are not plainly implied in the *Hebrew*, on the one Hand, and *Omissions* on the other; I keep as near as possible to the *Original*: Only whereas the *Hebrew* above all other Languages I know, is so wondrously *full* of *Sense*, that *Avenarius* observes, even the copious *Greek* must in many Cases use *several Words* to express the *full Sense* of a *single Word* in *Hebrew*: Where the *Original* therefore *plainly signifies* or *hints* at *Sentiments* which are not seen in our *English* Bible, I venture to give them, citing my Authorities: And tho' the Reader may be apt to think that in many Places I *add* to the *Original*; yet if he duly searches into the *Hebrew*, He will doubtless see, as I have often seen with Surprise, the Sentiments. I have only endeavoured to rise into and give the grand, exalted and lively *Sentiments* and *Hints* of *Inspiration*.

And *this IMPROVEMENT differs* from *other Poetical Versions* in *these* Particulars—

I. Whereas in *others*, by the meer Reading, we can never tell where GOD or LORD is in the *Original* or not: For they often, not only put *One* for the *Other*, but also insert them where they are not, and leave them out where they are:—In this Revisal (1) As JAH is a glorious Name peculiar to the Supreme Being, *Psal.* lxviii. 4; wherever it is in the *Original* I preserve it. (2) Wherever is the Word JEHOVAH, another Name peculiar to Him, *Psal.* lxxxiii. 18. and sounds with surpassing

The PREFACE.

passing Grandeur and Solemnity; I always write either JEHOVAH, especially where his Greatness or Majesty is represented, or LORD in Capitals. (3) Wherever is the Word *Adonai*, whose natural Signification seems to be—*Lord*; there I insert *Lord* in *Italick*. (4) Whereever is the Word ÆLOHIM, which is a famous Name of GOD in the *Plural* Number, and the *first us'd* in *Scripture*, as in *Gen.* i. 1; tho' it *sometimes figuratively* signifies *Mighty Men* and *Angels*; There I always write GOD or GODS in Capitals. (5) For the other Names of GOD, as ÆL and *its Derivatives*, I always write God in *Roman* Character, but not in Capitals. I think *Divine Inspiration* cannot be too exactly represented; and where the Wisdom of Inspiration makes a Difference, we should do so too.

II. Wherever is the famous Word HALLELUJAH, whose Signification is—*Praise* JAH; as well as the Word *Amen*, whose Signification is—*So be it;* I carefully preserve them.

III. Wherever is the Name MESSIAH in *Hebrew*, which signifies *The Anointed;* I either keep the Word MESSIAH or insert the Name CHRIST, which is the Word in *Greek, Latin* and *English*, of the same Signification.

IV. Consistent, as I apprehend, with the Latitude of the *Hebrew* Language; the Passages which are express'd by our Poets in the Form of *Curses*, or *revengeful Wishes*, I always chuse to express, agreeable to the *Prophetick* SPIRIT of *Inspiration*, and the Graces of the same SPIRIT, *not* in the Form of *Wishes* in the *Singers*, but in the Form of *Assertions* or *Prophecies* indited by the fore-seeing SPIRIT of Inspiration.

V. Instead of the diminutive Terms of *Hills, Floods, Lands* and *Skies*, commonly us'd by our brightest Poets, I use wherever I can, the more grand and noble Words —*Mountains, Seas, Earth* and *Heavens*; where these greater Ideas are express'd in the *Original.*

As the *Psalmist* paints the Works of GOD in *Nature* in perfect Purity, I try to keep *as near as possible to Nature.* For *grand Ideas*, I seek the *most majestick Words; for tender Sentiments,* the *softest Words;* for
affecting

The PREFACE.

affecting, the most *moving*; for *wondrous*, the most *striking*: and in all aiming at the *clearest Simplicity* of Style; wherein the *Sentiments* are more easily seen, more directly reach the Heart, and touch it with a stronger Energy. I use no *Words, Ellipses,* or *Terminations,* but what are us'd by the best Poets of the present Age: and as for *Epithets* and *Words* of *Explication*, I rarely use them but where I think they are plainly implied in the exceeding full *Original*.

Some *Notes* I add for the Satisfaction of the *Learned :* the *Rest*, for the Instruction of *others ;* that they may not sing in Uncertainty or meer Amusement, but with Understanding. A *Star** signifies—*It is so in* HEBREW *according to all the* LEXICONS. In such *Marks* as these [ ] are *brief Explications* I tho't convenient to be inserted for the clearer View of the Sense : as in some *Titles*, &c.

If any would compare *This* with *any other Versions ;* I only beg, that they would seriously, either *First* read the Place in *Hebrew*, or at least in the *English Bible* with the *Margin*.

Having begun this Work on *April* 29, 1755, and being encouraged to proceed by the *Respectable Brethren* of the *Congregation* I belong to, I desire to praise the MOST HIGH for carrying me on, through Multitudes of Avocations, Interruptions and Infirmities, to the *End* of the *Psalms* by the *Last* of *August* 1756, and to the *End* of the *other Scripture-Songs* by the 20th of *March* 1757 : And to HIS Glory and Blessing, and the Edification of *his People*, I humbly resign it. Rendering my hearty Thanks to the ingenious Gentlemen, who generously helped me with their acute Corrections; I close with my earnest Prayers in the Terms of the *Final Clause* of the Authors of the *ancient Preface* to the *New-England Version*, expressed in their usual beautiful Simplicity of Language; " That we may sing
" in *Zion* the LORD's Songs of Praise according to his
" own Will, until he take us hence, and wipe away all
" our Tears, and bid us enter into our MASTER's Joy,
" to sing eternal HALLELUJAHS !"

Boston in *N. E.*
May 26. 1758.   T. PRINCE.

PSALM I.

[*The Happiness of the Godly, & Misery of the Ungodly*]

1 O Blessed Man who walks not in
the council of ill † men,
Nor stands within the sinners way;
nor scoffers * seat sits in.

2 But on JEHOVAH's written law
he places his delight;
And in his law he meditates,
with pleasure day and night.

3 For he is like a goodly tree
by rivers planted near;
Which timely yields its fruit, whose leaf
shall ever green appear:
And all he does shall prosper still. ‡

4 Th' ungodly are not so;
But like the chaff which by the wind
is driven to and fro.

5 Therefore in Judgment shall not stand
such as ungodly are;
Nor in th' assembly of the just
shall sinners then appear.

6 Because the way of righteous men
the LORD approves and knows;
Whereas the way of evil men
to sure destruction goes.

B [*Long*

† *Ill*, rather than *Wicked*, seems more suitable for the *lowest Step* of the treble and beautiful *Gradation* here observed by the Learned.

* The *Hebrew* signifies *Scoffers*; and so the *Chaldee, Syriack* and *Arabick*: i. e. such as *scoff* at the Religion inspir'd by God, or at those who practice it.

‡ i. e. *Continually*—as is plainly implied; to comport with the Sense of the preceeding Part of the Verse.

PSALM I. II.

[*Long Metre.*]

1 O Blessed man who walks not in
  The counsel of ungodly men,
  Nor stands within the sinners way,
  Nor will the scoffers seat sit in.
2 But in JEHOVAH's written law
  He takes exceeding great delight;
  And in his law he meditates
  With pious pleasure day and night.
3 For he is like a goodly tree
  To streams * of waters * planted near;
  Which in due season yields its fruit,
  Whose leaf shall ever green appear;
  And all he does shall prosper still.
4 But the ungodly are not so:
  For they are like the chaff which by
  The wind is driven to and fro.
5 Therefore in judgment shall not stand,
  Such as ungodly are, as clear;
  Nor in th' assembly of the just
  Shall sinners in that day appear.
6 Because the way of righteous men
  The LORD with approbation knows;
  Whereas the way of evil men
  To their entire destruction goes.

PSALM II.

[*The Exaltation and universal Reign of* CHRIST.]

1 WHY do the tribes and nations ‖ rage
  and form a vain design?
2 Kings of the earth do set themselves
  and princes plotting join,
  Against JEHOVAH and his CHRIST, ‡
  with one consent, and say,
3 " Let us asunder break their bands
  " and cast their cords away!"

4 But

* So it is exactly, and most properly, in the *Hebrew.*
‖ So the *Hebrew* and *all the ancient Versions.*
‡ In *Hebrew* 'tis MESSIAH; i. e. CHRIST in *Greek, Latin* and *English*; and so all the *ancient Versions.*

PSALM II.

4 But He who sits in heav'n will laugh,
   the *Lord* will them deride;
5 In anger then to them He'll speak,
   in wrath to vex their pride.
6 " See I have set my king upon
   " Zion my holy hill,
7 " And the immutable decree
   " proclaim abroad I will."

8 The LORD said, " Thou my Son, this day,
   " have I begotten thee ! †
   " Ask, and the nations * I will give
   " thine heritage to be.
9 " And of the earth thou shalt possess
   " the utmost coasts abroad;
   " Thy foes shalt break as potters ware,
   " and crush with iron rod."

10 And now ye kings, be wise ; be learn'd
   ye who earth's judges are ;
11 Serve ye the Lord with reverence,
   rejoice with trembling fear.
12 Kiss ye the Son, lest by his wrath
   ye perish in your way :
When once his wrath a little burns,
   bless'd all that on him stay.

[*Long Metre.*]

1 WHY do the nations move and rage,
     And people form a vain design?
2 Kings of the earth do set themselves
   And princes in deep plots combine,
With one consent against the LORD,
   And his Messiah, * and dare say,
3 " Let us asunder break their bands,
   " And cast their cords of rule away ?"

† Applied to Christ, *Acts* xiii. 33. *Heb.* iii. 5.
* So the *Hebrew, Septuagint, Syriack* and *ancient Latin.*

PSALM III.

4 But He who sits in heav'n will laugh,
   The *Lord* at first will them deride ;
5 In anger then to them He'll speak,
   In wrath to vex them in their pride;
6 " See I have set my king upon
   " Zion my mount of sanctity,*
7 " And the immutable decree
   " Proclaim abroad to all will I."

8 The LORD to me said, " Thou my Son,
   " This day have I begotten thee ;
   " Ask, and the nations I will give
   " For thine inheritance to be :
9 " And of the earth Thou shalt possess
   " The utmost coasts and lands abroad ;
   " Thy foes shalt break as potters ware,
   " And crush as with an iron rod."

10 Now therefore, O ye kings, be wise ;
   Be learn'd, ye who earth's judges are ;
11 Serve ye the LORD with reverence ;
   Rejoice, but yet with trembling fear :
12 Kiss ‖ ye the Son, lest He be wroth,
   And ye should perish in your way ;
   When once his wrath a little burns,
   Blessed are all that on him stay.

PSALM III. A Psalm of David :
When he fled from the Face of Absalom *his Son.*

1 LORD, how my troubles multiply ?
   How many up against me rise ?
2 Of my sad soul, how many say,
   " His GOD to him no help supplies."
3 Yet Thou, O LORD, my glory art,
   My shield, and raisest up my head.
4 I to JEHOVAH cry'd, who from
   His holy hill me answered. *(Selah.)*

‖ i. e. Kneel and kiss his Hand in token of cordial and intire submission.

PSALM IV.

5 I lay down, slept, and then awak'd ;
   For up JEHOVAH did me bear :
6 Tho' people round against me set,
   Ten thousands of them I'll not fear.
7 O LORD my God, to save me rise ;
   For all my foes have felt thy stroke
   Upon their faces, and the teeth
   Of the ungodly Thou hast broke.

8 Salvation wholly to the LORD,
   Does and shall ever appertain ;
   And on thy people evermore
   Thy blessing does and shall remain.

PSALM IV. *A Psalm of* David.

1 GOD of my righteousness to me,
   while calling, * bend thine ear :
   Thou hast enlarg'd me when distress'd ;
   me pity ; hear my pray'r.
2 Ye sons of men, how long will ye
   my glory villify ?
   How long love vanity will ye ?
   and how long seek a lie. *(Selah.)*
3 But know, the LORD hath set apart
   the pious for his own :
   The Lord will hear me when to him
   I make my humble moan.
4 Stand ye in awe, and sin no more ;
   consider seriously,
   Within your hearts with silence deep,
   as on your beds ye lie.
5 The sacrifice of righteousness
   let freely off'red be ;
   And therewith place your confidence
   upon the LORD do ye.
6 While multitudes enquiring are,
   who'll cause us good to see ?
   The light, LORD, of thy countenance
   let on us lifted be.

B 3   7 Thou

7 Thou giv'ſt * more gladneſs in my heart
   than their's in times wherein
Their harveſt-corn and their new wine,
   have much increaſed been.
8 In *peace with Him I will lie down,
   and I my ſleep will take;
For me in confidence to dwell,
   Thou, LORD, alone doſt make.

PSALM V. *A Pſalm of* David.

1 JEHOVAH, to my words give ear;
  *My ſolemn meditation weigh:
2 O hear my cry, my king, my God,
   For I to Thee alone, will pray.
3 In early morning Thou my voice
   Wilt, O JEHOVAH kindly hear;
For in the morning I'll look up,
   And will to thee direct my pray'r.

4 For Thou art not a God who doſt
   Allow the leaſt iniquity;
Neither ſhall evil dwell with Thee;
   Nor fools ſhall ſtand before thine eye.
5 Thou all ill doers doſt abhor;
   Wilt them deſtroy who utter lies:
6 JEHOVAH loaths the bloody man,
   And thoſe who fraudful arts deviſe.

7 But in thy many mercies now
   Enter into thy houſe will I,
And in thy fear will bow my ſelf
   Before thy houſe of ſanctity.
8 Becauſe of my obſerving foes,
   LORD lead me in thy righteouſneſs;
Direct me in thy perfect way,
   And make it plain before my face.

9 For in their mouth there is no truth;
   Their heart full of iniquities;
An open ſepulchre their throat;
   Their tongue is mov'd with flatteries.

PSALM VI.

10 O GOD, Thou wilt them quite deftroy,
  By their own counfels make them fall,
  And in their many * Sins caft out;
  For they to thee are rebels all.

11 But let all thofe who truft in Thee,
  For ever fhout with joyful noife,
  For thou defendeft them; and thofe
  Who love thy name, in Thee rejoice.

12 For to the righteous, Thou, O LORD,
  Wilt caufe thy bleffing to extend;
  As with a fhield, thy favour, them
  Wilt crown and round about defend.

PSALM VI. *A Pfalm of* David.

1 O LORD, rebuke me not in wrath,
  Nor in thine anger chaften me:
2 LORD, pity; I am weak: Lord heal;
  My bones are vex'd exceedingly.
3 My foul is alfo in diftrefs:
  How long delay, LORD, wilt Thou make?
4 Return, O LORD; my foul relieve;
  O fave me for thy mercies fake.

5 Shall the dead praife Thee in the grave?
  Of Thee no mem'ry there have they.
6 I'm tir'd with groans: by night my bed
  With tears fwims, and my couch by day.
7 Mine eye confum'd with grief grows old,
  Becaufe of all mine enemies:
8 But now depart away from me,
  All ye who work iniquities;

  Becaufe JEHOVAH now hath heard
  The voice of my lamenting tears:
9 The LORD hath heard my humble fuit,
  JEHOVAH will accept my pray'rs.
10 Let all my foes be put to fhame,
  And greatly troubled let them be.
  Yea let them be returned back,
  And made afhamed fpeedily.

PSALM VII.

PSALM VII. A Pfalm † of David, which he fang to the LORD *concerning* Cufh *the* Benjamite.

1 O LORD my God, I wholly place
    my confidence in Thee :
From all my perfecuting foes,
    fave and deliver me.
2 Left like to rending lions they
    my foul in pieces tear ;
And when they tear, to refcue me
    there fhould not one appear.

3 O thou JEHOVAH, O my God,
    if this thing done have I ;
If in thefe hands of mine there be
    wrongful iniquity ;
4 If I have rendred ill to him
    who was at peace with me ;
(Yea rather I releafed have
    my caufelefs enemy ;)
5 Then let the foe purfue my foul,
    and feize it as a prey ;
Let him my life tread to the earth,
    in duft my honour lay. *(Selah.)*
6 LORD, rife in wrath ; lift up thy felf ;
    my raging foes withftand ;
Wake for me to the judgment thou
    doft rightfully command.

7 So the great congregation fhall
    encompafs thee with joy ;
O therefore for their fake return,
    to thy bright feat on high.
8 The LORD will all the people judge :
    JEHOVAH judge thou me
According to my righteoufnefs, ‖
    and mine integrity.
                                             [2 *Part.*]

† So the *Septuagint.*
‖ i. e. The Righteoufnefs of his *Caufe* and *Conduct*, with refpect to his Neighbour.

PSALM VIII.

[2 Part.]

9 Let end the wicked's wickedness,
   but the just ratify,
Because O thou the righteous GOD,
   the hearts and reins dost try.
10 In GOD is my defence, who saves
   the right in heart and way:
11 But GOD the righteous judge is wroth,
   with sinners ev'ry day.
12 Unless that turning they repent,
   his sword he sharp will whet:
Yea has already bent his bow,
   and has it ready set.
13 Against the persecutors made
   his arrows ready hath;
He ready has prepar'd for them
   the instruments of death.
14 Behold they travail as in birth
   with vain iniquity:
Behold how mischief they conceive,
   and then bring forth a lie.
15 He dig'd a pit, and dig'd it deep,
   the innocent to take;
But he is fall'n into the pit,
   which he himself did make.
16 Return on his mischievous head
   his mischief surely shall;
And on his crown, his violence
   in righteousness shall fall.
17 According to his righteousness,
   JEHOVAH praise will I;
And to his name a psalm I'll sing,
   who is the LORD most high.

PSALM VIII. *A Psalm of* David.

1 O LORD, our *Lord*, in all the earth
   how does thy name excel!
Who high above the heav'ns hast set
   thy majesty † to dwell.

† The *Hebrew* signifies both *Majesty, Magnificence* and *Glory*.

2 From mouths of babes and fucklings thou
   doſt pow'r and praiſe ordain;
  That thou may'ſt ſtill thine enemies,
   and ſpiteful foes reſtrain.

3 When I thy glorious heav'ns behold,
   thy fingers work divine,
  The moon and ſtars which thou haſt ſet
   in order as they ſhine;

4 O what is wretched man * that thou
   ſhould'ſt have him in thy mind,
  And *Adam*'s ſon, * that thou ſhould'ſt be
   to viſit him ſo kind?

5 For than the Angels thou haſt him
   but little lower made;
  With glory and with majeſty
   thou crowned haſt his head.

6 To Him dominion Thou haſt giv'n
   over thy works below;
  Under his feet haſt put them all,
   to him haſt made them bow.

7 Both all the tamer flocks and herds,
   wild beaſts that range more free,
8 Swift in the air the fowls that fly,
   and fiſhes of the ſea.
9 Yea thoſe that make great paths along
   the ſea, and paſs the ſame. ‡
  O LORD, our *Lord*, in all the earth,
   how excellent thy name!

PSALM IX. *A Pſalm of* David.

1 LORD I'll Thee praiſe with all my heart,
   thy wonders all proclaim.
2 O Thou moſt high, in Thee I'll joy,
   exult, and ſing thy name.

3 My

‡ In the *Chaldee* it is with great Beauty and Propriety explained Thus—*And the Leviathans*, i. e. *Whales* and *Crocodiles*; who *paſſing thro' the Seas*, make great *Paths*, paſs thro' them, and leave them ſhining along behind them; alluding to thoſe fine and noble Paſſages in *Job* xli. 31, 32.

PSALM IX.

3 My foes in turning backward fall,
   and perish at thy sight;
For thou maintainest my just cause,
   enthron'd thou judgest right.
4 The heathen thou rebuked hast,
   the wicked overthrown;
5 Thou blottest out their name, that they
   may never more be known.
6 Thy desolations, O thou foe,
   are ended utterly;
Who many cities hast destroy'd,
   and made their mem'ry die.
7 But now JEHOVAH ever shall
   endure and ever reign;
His throne He hath established,
   just judgment to maintain.
8 Yea, he the universal world
   shall judge in righteousness;
And to all people † judgment give
   in perfect ‡ uprightness.
9 A refuge high * for the oppress'd
   JEHOVAH will become;
He is to them a refuge safe
   in seasons troublesome.
10 And they who duly know thy name,
   in Thee their trust will place;
Because Thou, LORD, hast never left
   the seekers of thy face.
11 O sing ye praises to the LORD,
   who does in Zion dwell;
His wondrous doings all abroad
   among his people tell.
12 For when he after blood enquires,
   he minds them carefully:
Of those who meek and humble are
   he ne'r forgets the cry.

[2 *Part.*]

† Heb.—*People*—in the *Plural Number*: i. e. *all People.*
‡ Heb.—*Uprightnesses* in the *Plural Number,* i. e. *Perfect Uprightness.*

PSALM IX.

[2 *Part.*]

13 LORD, pity me, and weigh my grief,
  which I from foes suſtain;
And from the op'ning gates of death
  O raiſe me up again.
14 That I in Zion's daughter's gates
  may ſhew forth all thy praiſe:
And my triumphant ſhouts of joy
  in thy ſalvation, raiſe.

15 The heathen people are ſunk down
  into the pit they made;
Their foot is taken in the net
  which ſecretly they laid.
16 By judgments which He executes
  more known JEHOVAH is;
Ill men are caught in their own ſnares;
  deeply conſider this. ‖ *(Selah.)*

17 Thoſe who continue wicked, ſhall
  be turned down to hell;
Where all the nations of the earth
  who GOD forget, ſhall dwell.
18 Thy needy, tho' diſtreſs'd a while,
  ſhall never be forgot;
The expectations of thy poor,
  defer'd, yet periſh not.

19 O let not wretched man * prevail;
  but O JEHOVAH riſe;
The heathen people in thy ſight
  let judged be likewiſe.
20 O thou JEHOVAH, ſtrike them all
  with trembling fear; and then
Thou wilt the nations make to know,
  thay are but wretched men. * *(Selah.)*

PSALM

‖ This Line is the Meaning of the Word—*Higgaion*,

PSALM X.

1 WHerefore JEHOVAH standest thou
 away from us so far?
And wherefore hidest thou thy self
 when times so troublous are?
2 Because the wicked in their pride
 the needy make a prey;
They shall be taken in the plots
 which they for others lay.

3 The wicked in their heart's desire
 do glory; and they praise
The worldly man as blest; but they
 JEHOVAH's anger raise.
4 The wicked thro' their lofty pride
 on God refuse to call;
And in their multitude of thoughts
 there is no GOD at all.

5 Their ways at all times grievous are:
 thy judgments are on high
Above their sight: at all their foes
 they blow disdainfully.
6 Within their heart they vainly say,
 " we mov'd shall never be,
" Nor yet in any time to come
 " adversity shall see."

7 His mouth with cursing filled is,
 with wiles*, deceit and wrong;
And mischief and iniquity
 lie hid beneath his tongue.
8 In coverts near the villages
 they sit; the harmless slay;
And for the poor who pass along
 with hidden eyes they lay.

9 As lions in their coverts watch,
 the feeble to surprise;
As fowlers draw them in their net,
 and on a sudden seize.

10 A

PSALM X.

10 As maim'd* and crouching they will seem;
: that numbers of the poor
At unawares may fall into
their paws of cruel power.

11 In heart they say, " God has forgot
" these things eternally;
" He wholly hides his face away,
" and them will never see."

[2 *Part.*]

12 JEHOVAH rise thou up; O God,
lift up thine hand on high;
Cast not the meek afflicted ones
out of thy memory.
13 O why do wicked men provoke
the mighty GOD, and say
Presumptuously within their heart,
' Thou never wilt repay.'

14 But spite and mischief thou dost see;
thy hand will them reward:
The poor commits himself to Thee;
Thou art the orphan's guard.
15 The wicked's arm wilt wholly break,
and of the evil one;
And search out his impieties
until thou findest none;

16 JEHOVAH King of ages* is
and of eternity :.*
Out of his land the heathen tribes
are perish'd utterly.
17 The meek, afflicted ones desire
JEHOVAH thou dost hear;
Thou dost prepare their heart, and then
give thine attentive ear.

18 To

PSALM XI.

18 To judge and help the fatherlefs,
  the feeble and the poor;
That earthly men may not deftroy ‡
  nor vex them any more.

PSALM XI.

1 I In JEHOVAH place my truft:
    why therefore fay do ye
  To my poor foul, " like frighted birds
  " to your high mountain flee."
2 For lo, the wicked bend their bows,
    and on the ftring prepare,
  Their arrows in the dark to fhoot
    at thofe who upright are.
3 But if the great foundations of
    our ftate they overthrow;
  [Which are thy facred laws and truths;]
  what fhall the righteous do?
4 JEHOVAH's in his holy place, †
    and in the heav'ns* on high
  JEHOVAH's throne: his eyes obferve,
    men's fons his eye-lids try.
5 The men who truly righteous are
    JEHOVAH does approve:
  His foul the wicked hates, and them
    who violence do love.
6 Snares, fire and brimftone, dreadful ftorms,
    on finners He will rain:
  This is the portion of the cup
    He does for them ordain.
7 Becaufe the LORD, who righteous is,
    all right'oufnefs does love;
  His countenance the upright one,
    beholding does approve.   _ PSALM

‡ So the *Syriack* renders it; the *Chaldee—break*; the Englifh
—*oppress*; Buxtorf—*violently use*: and the *Hebrew* may
comprehend them all.
† Heb. *Palace*; as in *Pfal.* xlv. 9. cxliv. 12. *Prov.* xxx. 28,
and by a Figure—*Temple*, both on *Earth* and in *Heaven*.
* Heb.—*not Sky*, but *Heavens*.

PSALM XII. *A Psalm of* David.

1 HELP, O JEHOVAH now, because
  the godly man doth cease,
And from among the sons of men
  the faithful men decrease.

2 The most, now, to their neighbours speak
  deceitful vanities;
With flatt'ring lips they smoothly speak,
  with double hearts and lies.

3 But every flatt'ring lip the LORD
  will cut off certainly;
And all proud tongues that utter forth
  words boasting, great and high:

4 Who thus declare, 'We with our tongues
  'prevailing pow'r will gain:
'Are not our lips our own? and who
  'Lord † over us shall reign?'

5 For poor oppress'd and needy sighs,
  the LORD says, now I'll rise,
And them in safety I will set
  from those who them despise.

6 JEHOVAH's words are words most pure;
  they are as silver try'd
In earthen furnaces o'er fire,
  and sev'n times purify'd.

7 JEHOVAH, thou wilt safely keep
  the upright-hearted poor,
And from this generation them
  preserve for evermore;

8 Tho' wicked walk on every side,
  grow bold and multiply;
And vile ones by the sons of men
  exalted be on high.

PSALM XIII.

1 HOW long wilt thou forget me, LORD?
  shall it for ever be?
How long wilt thou so sadly hide
  thy face away from me?

2 How long within my foul confult,
    and grieve in heart fhall I?
  How long exalted over me
    fhall be my enemy?
3 O LORD my God, confider me
    and anfwer to me make;
  Mine eyes enlighten, left the fleep
    of death me overtake.
4 Left my proud foes in boafting fay,
    againft him we prevail;
  Left thofe who trouble me rejoice,
    to fee me wholly fail.
5 But as I fet my confidence
    upon thy bounteous grace;
  My heart in thy falvation fhall
    rejoice with thankful praife.
6 Yea to JEHOVAH fongs of praife
    I'll fing melodioufly;
  Who in his kindnefs deals with me
    exceeding bounteoufly.

PSALM XIV. *A Pfalm of* David.

1 FOOLS in their hearts fay, there's no GOD,
    and fo corrupt they grow,
  Abominable fins commit,
    and nothing good they do.
2 From heav'n JEHOVAH looked down
    on fons of men, to fee
  If any who do underftand,
    or feek to GOD there be.
3 They altogether filthy are;
    they all are backward* gone;
  There are not any that do good,
    no verily, not one.
4 The workers of iniquity,
    do they not know at all?
  That they my people eat as bread,
    nor on the LORD will call.

5 Yet

* *Hebrew* and *Chaldee.*

PSALM XV.

5 Yet they shall with a grievous fear
   appalled greatly be,
When GOD among the righteous race
   they once shall come to see.
6 The counsel of the poor oppress'd,
   ye mock'd and try'd to shame;
Because the LORD their refuge ‖ is,
   and they hope ‖ in his name.
7 Who will from Zion' Isr'el save?*
   when back the LORD shall bring
His captives; Jacob will rejoice,
   and Isr'el gladly sing.

PSALM XV. A Psalm of David.

1 LORD, in thy tabernacle, who
   a sojourner shall be?
And who is he inhabit shall
   thy mount* of sanctity*?
2 Who walks in his integrity,
   who acts in righteousness;
And who the truth within his heart
   does uprightly express.

3 Who with his tongue will not backbite,
   nor do his neighbour hurt;
Nor yet against his neighbour will
   take up an ill report.
4 Whose eyes the vile, tho' great, contemn;
   but all the LORD who fear,
He honours; and he changes not,
   tho' to his hurt he swear.

5 Who to oppressing usury,
   his money hath not lent;
Who takes not a reward or bribe
   against the innocent.

6 Who

‖ *Cocceius, Gejer*, and the *English*, translate it REFUGE; the *Syriack* with *Piscator* and *Castalio*—TRUST; all the other ancient *Versions*, with *Montanus* and *Muis*—HOPE: and the *Hebrew* seems to comprehend them all.

PSALM XV. XVI.

6 Who conſtantly obſerves theſe things,
   is gracioufly approv'd,
He's ſurely in a happy ſtate,
   and never ſhall be mov'd.

[*Long Metre*] ‡

1 LORD, in thy tabernacle who
    Wilt thou with welcome entertain?
Who on thy mount of ſanctity,*
A conſtant dweller ſhall remain?
2 Who walks in his integrity,
Who always acts in righteouſneſs,
And what is in his honeſt heart
Does truly with his mouth expreſs.

3 Who with his tongue will not backbite,
Nor do his neighbour any wrong,
Nor takes up a reproach to hurt
His neighbour from another's tongue.
4 Whoſe eyes the vile, tho' great, contemn,
But honours all who fear the LORD:
Who ſwears the truth, tho' to his hurt;
And changes not, but keeps his word.

5 Who to oppreſſing uſury
Hath not for gain his money lent;
Who takes not a reward or bribe
To wrong a perſon innocent.
6 Who conſtantly obſerves theſe things,
And does all in ſincerity;
Is ſurely in a happy ſtate,
And he ſhall never moved be.

PSALM XVI.

Mictam, *or a golden Pſalm of* David.

1 O Mighty God, preſerve thou me;
    for upon thee I reſt.
2 "Thou art my *Lord*," thou O my ſoul,
   haſt to the LORD profeſs'd.

3 My

‡ Chiefly from Dr. *Ford*: but nearer the Original.

PSALM XVI.

3 My goodnefs reaches not to thee;
  but to the faints, th' upright
  On earth who are the excellent,
  in whom is my delight.

4 Who haft'n a ftrange one* to adore,
  their forrows fhall abound;
  Their blood-drink-off'rings I'll not pour,
  nor names my lips fhall found.

5 The LORD the only portion is
  of mine inheritance;
  And of my cup; and of my lot
  fecures the maintenance.

6 The lines that fallen are to me,
  in pleafant places are;
  And goodly is the heritage
  allotted to my fhare.

7 I will JEHOVAH humbly blefs,
  who counfels me aright,
  So that my reins do me inftruct
  in feafons of the night.

8 Before me I the LORD have fet
  as prefent evermore:
  Becaufe he is at my right hand,
  I fhall not flide therefore.

9 Therefore my heart rejoices much,
  my glory's glad withal;
  Moreover alfo dwell in hope ‖
  my flefh fecurely ‖ fhall:

10 Becaufe thou wilt not leave my foul
  in death's eftate to be;
  Nor fuffer wilt THINE HOLY ONE ‡
  corrupting there to fee.

11 Thou wilt me fhew the path of life,
  which to thy prefence goes;
  Where joy in fulnefs is, and where
  pure pleafure ever flows.

* i. e. a ftrange *Lord*. ‖ The *Hebrew* feems to fignify *Both*.
‡ i. e. CHRIST: as the Apoftles *Peter* and *Paul* explain it, *Acts* ii. 31. xiii. 35—37.

PSALM XVII.

PSALM XVII. *A Psalm of* David.

1 JEHOVAH hearken to the right,
    attend to my loud cry;
And hear my pray'r that cometh forth
    from lips that do not lie.
2 O from thy presence let there come
    a just decree to me:
And let thy just and holy eyes,
    things that are equal see.

3 My HEART thou searched hast by day,
    and visited by night:
Thou hast me in a furnace try'd,
    and found my heart is right.
As for my MOUTH; as I resolv'd
    my words should not transgress,
Thy righteous laws which guide the tongue;
    I kept my purposes.

4 And as for WORKS of men; thy word
    hath me directed so,
That I observ'd and shun'd the paths
    wherein destroyers go.
5 My goings in thy beaten paths
    do thou uphold and guide;
That so my footsteps thus secur'd
    may never turn aside.

6 On Thee I called have, O God,
    because Thou wilt me hear;
O now incline thine ear to me,
    and hear my humble pray'r.

[2 *Part.*]

7 O shew thy wondrous grace to them
    whose trust on thee relies;
Who sav'st by thy right hand from those
    who up against them rise.

PSALM XVII.

8 O keep me now as thou would'ft keep
   the apple of thine eye;
Under the fhadow of thy wings
   hide me continually.

9 From all the threat'ning faces of
   the wicked who me wafte,
And from my deadly enemies,
   who me around inveft.
10 In their grofs fat they are enclos'd,
    boaft with their mouths likewife;
11 In all our. fteps they compafs us;
   to earth they bow their eyes.

12 They like a roaring lion are,
   who greedy is for prey;
Like a young lion watching in
   his fecret place, are they.
13 But LORD arife, his face prevent;
   O make him down to bow;
And from the wicked one, thy fword,
   my foul deliver thou.

14 From mortal ‡ men, thy hand, O LORD,
   from mortal men ‡ me fave,
Who in this tranfient time of life
   their only portion have.
15 Thy hidden ftores their bellies fill,
   and filled are their fons;
And all the reft they fave and leave
   to their young little ones.

16 But I in righteoufnefs thy face
   with joy fhall clearly fee;
And waking with thine image, I
   fhall fatisfied be.

PSALM

---

‡ The *Hebrew* Word being derived from another which fignifies *Death*, I apprehend it may imply Men who are not only *mortal themfelves*, but alfo *bring Death* on *others*.

PSALM XVIII.

PSALM XVIII.

A Pſalm of David, *the Servant of the* LORD; *who ſpake to the* LORD *the Words of this Song in the Day that the* LORD *delivered him from all his Enemies, and from the Hand of* Saul: *and he ſaid;*

1 LORD thee my ſtrength I'll dearly love:
2 The LORD's my rock † and refuge ſure,
 My fortreſs, ſaviour, God and ſhield,
 My rock, ‡ on whom I reſt ſecure;
 My horn of ſafety, ‖ my high tow'r:
3 JEHOVAH I will call on Thee
 Who worthy to be praiſed art;
 So from my foes ſav'd I ſhall be.

4 Amazing ſorrows ſeiz'd my ſoul,
 While death its cords* around me laid;
 As when impetuous torrents roll
 Ungodly men my ſoul diſmay'd.
5 The cords of hell encompaſs'd me,
 And death it's ſnares around me drew,
 They ſeiz'd and caught me unawares,
 E'er I th' approaching danger knew.*

6 Diſtreſs'd, I called on the LORD,
 Cry'd to my God, and He did hear;
 He from his temple heard my voice,
 My cry receiv'd into his ear.
7 And then the earth affrighted ſhook,
 The utmoſt trembling on it ſeiz'd:
 The mountains their foundations mov'd,
 Becauſe they ſaw him high diſpleas'd.

8 Smoke from his noſtrils there aroſe;
 And fire devouring dreadfully
 Forth from his mouth there iſſued;
 Bright coals enkindled were thereby.
9 The heav'ns aloft He made to bow,
 Deſcending in a martial form;
 And all beneath his feet appear'd
 Thick darkneſs, and a gath'ring ſtorm.

† i. e. my *High* Rock. ‡ i. e. my *Great* and *Firm* Rock.
‖ The *Hebrew* ſignifies both *Safety* and *Salvation.*

PSALM XVIII.

10 He on a flying cherub rode,
   In his exalted majesty:
   And on the wings of swiftest winds,
   He irresistably did fly.
11 He darkness made his secret place:
   His awful covert round him were
   Darkness of waters and thick clouds,
   Which overspread the gloomy air.
12 But at the brightness flashing forth
   Before him, his thick clouds conspire
   To pass along, and cast abroad
   Hail-stones, and burning coals of fire.

[2 *Part.*]

13 From heav'n JEHOVAH thundred loud;
   The highest gave his mighty voice;
   Hail-stones, and glowing coals of fire
   He cast with dreadful pow'r and noise.
14 His arrows forth he sent abroad,
   Which made my foes disperse and fly;
   His light'nings shot and multiply'd,*
   Which them defeated utterly.
15 Then were the waters channels seen,
   The world's foundations op'ned were,
   At thy rebuke LORD, at the blast
   Of thy displeasure's breath, laid bare.
16 From heav'n he sent and on me seiz'd,
   And from the mighty waters drew;
17 He sav'd me from my mighty foes,
   Whose pow'r too mighty for me grew.
18 In my dark day they me surpriz'd;
   Yet was the LORD a stay to me.
19 Because in me He took delight,
   He hath enlarg'd and set me free.
20 The LORD rewarded my pure hands,
   And recompenc'd my upright heart:
21 For I did keep JEHOVAH's ways,
   Nor wickedly my God desert.

PSALM XVIII.

22 For all his laws before me were,
   His statutes from me put not I:
23 Yea I before him was upright,
   And kept from mine iniquity.
24 According to my uprightnefs
   Therefore the Lord rewarded me ;
   And to the purenefs of my hands,
   Which his all-viewing eye did fee.

[3 *Part.*]

25 Thou gracious to the gracious art,
   To upright ones wilt upright be ;
26 Pure to the pure ; but ftrive with them
   Who froward are, and ftrive with thee.
27 For thou wilt the afflicted fave,
   And high looks thou wilt bring down low :
28 But thou wilt light my lamp; the LORD
   My God, my darknefs fhine into.
29 By thee with dauntlefs courage fir'd,
   Embattled troops I pierced thro' :
   And by my God affifting me,
   I fcal'd the ramparts of my foe.
30 The way of God moft perfect is ;
   JEHOVAH's word is throughly try'd ;
   He is their fhield, their fure defence,
   Who ftedfaftly in him confide.

31 For who is God except the LORD ?
   Or who a rock our God befide ?
32 It's God who girdeth me with ftrength,
   And in a perfect way does guide :
33 He makes my feet fwift as the roe ;
   On my high places makes me ftand ;
34 Mine arms can break the brazen bow, †
   So well for war he taught my hand.

35 The fhield of thy falvation Thou
   Beftowed likewife haft on me ;
   And thy right hand hath me upheld ;
   Thy favour made me great to be.

C   [4 *Part.*]

† *Heb. Septuagint, Syriack, Arabick, Montanus, Ainfworth,* &c.

PSALM XVIII.

[4 Part.]

36 My steps Thou mad'st both large and sure,
   As I my flying foes pursu'd:
37 I overtook them: nor did turn,
   Till I had wholly them subdu'd.
38 So fatally I wounded them,
   In vain they try'd their heads to rear;
   And all bereav'd of strength they fell,
   Beneath my feet, and grovel'd there.

39 Thou girdest me with fortitude
   To battle with my mighty foes;
   And hast subdued them to me
   Who fiercely up against me rose.
40 The necks of all mine enemies,
   By Thee to me subjected are;
   That I might justly cut them off *
   Who to me mortal hatred bear.

41 They cry'd and call'd out earnestly;
   But there was none appear'd to save:
   Yea even to the LORD himself;
   But He to them no answer gave.
42 Then like the dust driv'n all abroad,
   When boist'rous winds arise and blow,
   I beat them small; and as the dirt
   Into the street, I them did throw.

43 From all the people's strivings Thou
   Hast me deliv'red this glad day,
   And of the nations made me head:
   People unknown shall me obey.
44 At the first hearing they'll submit:
   Strangers shall bow themselves to me:
45 The strangers sons shall fade away,
   And from their coverts frighted be.

[5 Part.]

46 Live LORD, and let my rock be bless'd;
   My Saviour God † exalted be;
47 God who avenges me and who
   Brings down the people under me.   48 My

† *Hebrew*, God of my Salvation,

PSALM XIX.

48 My faviour* from mine enemies:
Yea me thou haft advanc'd indeed
Above them that. againft me rofe,
And from the vi'lent man me freed.

49 Therefore among the nations, LORD,
To Thee my thanks I will proclaim;
To Thee, victorious loudly will
Sing forth the praifes of thy name.

50 He great deliv'rance gives his king,
And boundlefs favour has in ftore,
For his MESSIAH, ‡ DAVID fure,
And for HIS SEED ‖ for evermore.

PSALM XIX.

1 THE heav'ns on high abroad declare
the majefty of God;
And forth the firmament doth fhow,
his handy work abroad.

2 Day fpeaks to day, and night to night,
the knowledge hath declar'd.

3 There neither fpeech nor language is
where their voice is not heard.

4 Their line thro' all the earth is gone;
and to the utmoft end
Of all the world, their founding words
their clear inftruction fend.

5 In them a vaft pavilion he
hath fpread around the fun;
A bridegroom from his chamber goes,
ftrong, his glad race to run.

6 From the eaft end of heav'n he moves,
afcends, and round he flies,
To the weft end; and from his heart
there nothing hidden lies.

C 2   [2 *Part.*]

‡ *Hebrew, Septuagint, Syriack, Arabick,* &c.
‖ *David* was the *Typical* MESSIAH, and CHRIST *his promifed Seed* the *Real.*

PSALM XIX.

[2 Part.]

7 JEHOVAH's law moſt perfect is,
  and does the ſoul convert:
  JEHOVAH's teſtimony ſure ‖
  makes wiſe the ſimple heart;
8 The ſtatutes of the LORD are right,
  and they rejoice the heart;
  The LORD's commands are clear; and they
  light to the eyes impart.

9 Both pure and everlaſting is
  JEHOVAH's ſacred fear:
  JEHOVAH's judgments are the truth,
  and wholly righteous are.
10 Than gold, than much refined gold,
   more to be prized far;
   Sweeter than honey, or the juice
   in honey-combs they are.

11 By them thy ſervant warned is,
   [*his heart and life to guard :*]
   In carefully obſerving them,
   there is a great reward.
12 Who can his errors fully know?
   from ſecret faults cleanſe me;
   And from preſumptuous ſins do Thou,
   keep me thy ſervant free.

13 O never ſuffer them to have
   dominion over me;
   Then I ſhall rightly walk, and from
   great ſin preſerved be.
14 LORD let the ſpeeches of my mouth,
   and thoughts within my heart,
   To Thee be pleaſing; who my rock
   and my redeemer art.

‖ Or *faithful*: ſo the *Hebrew, Greek, Chaldee, Syriack, Arabick, Montanus, Ainſworth,* &c.

PSALM XX.

PSALM XX. *A Pſalm of* David.

1 JEHOVAH hear thee in the day
 of thy calamity;
 The name of Jacob's mighty God
 defend ‖ and ſet thee high:
2 Help ſend thee from his holy place,
 and ſtrength from Zion give.
3 Remember all thy offerings,
 and ſacrifice receive. *(Selah.)*

4 Grant thee according to thy heart;
 thy counſel all fulfil:
5 In thy ſalvation granted, we
 rejoice with ſhouting will.
 And in the name of our own God
 our banners we will rear:
 Moſt kindly hear thee may the LORD
 and anſwer all thy pray'r.

6 Now know I that JEHOVAH will
 ſave his MESSIAH * dear,
 With his right hand of ſtrength; and from
 his holy heav'n he'll hear.
7 In chariots ſome their confidence,
 and ſome in horſes ſet;
 But of the LORD our God the name
 we never will forget.

8 So we ſhall riſe and ſtand upright,
 while they bow down and fall.
 Save LORD, and hear us let the king,
 ſwhen we to him do call.

C 3 *PSALM*

‖ The *Hebrew* ſeems to comprehend them both. See *Pool's Synopſis*, *Ainſworth*, the *Engliſh Margin*, &c.

* In *Hebrew*, *Chaldee* and *Arabick*, 'tis—*his* MESSIAH; and in the *Septuagint* and *ancient Latin*—*his* CHRIST: i. e. *David* his *Typical*, and CHRIST his *Real* MESSIAH.

PSALM XXI.

PSALM XXI. *A Psalm of* David.

1 JEHOVAH in thy strength
  the king † shall joyful be:
In thy salvation, how exult
  exceedingly shall he!
2 Thou granted hast to him
  that which his heart would have;
Yea thou from him hast not with-held
  all that his lips did crave. *(Selah.)*
3 With blessings very great
  thou hast prevented him;
Of finest gold, thou on his head,
  hast set a diadem.
4 Of Thee he asked life;
  to him Thou didst it give,
Yea such a length of days, that he
  for evermore should live.
5 In thy salvation is
  his glory very great,
Honour and majesty thou hast
  distinguish'd on him set.
6 For thou for evermore
  hast him most blessed made;
Thou mak'st him with thy countenance,
  to be exceeding glad.
7 Because the King relies
  upon JEHOVAH; He
Thro' mercy of the highest One,
  shall never moved be.
8 Thy hand shall find out all
  who foes to thee still are;
And thy right hand shall find out them
  who hatred to thee bear.
9 Like as a fi'ry ov'n,
  thine anger make them shall:
The LORD in wrath will them devour,
  and fire consume them all.   10 Thou

† The *Chaldee* says—*The King* MESSIAH: i. e. *David* the *Typical*, and CHRIST the *Real* MESSIAH. See *v.* 4.

PSALM XXII.

10 Thou wilt deſtroy their fruit,
　　from off the earth, their race ;
So that among the ſons of men
　　their ſeed ſhall have no place :

11 Becauſe againſt thee they
　　a miſchief did intend ;
A wicked plot did they deviſe ;
　　but cannot reach their end.

12 For thou wilt make them fly,
　　whenever thou ſhalt place
Thine arrows ready on the ſtring,
　　and point them at their face.

13 Exalt thy ſelf, O LORD !
　　thy ſtrength in glory raiſe ;
So joyful pſalms we'll ſing to Thee,
　　thy mighty pow'r we'll praiſe.

PSALM XXII. *A Pſalm of* David.

[*The Sufferings, Prayers, and Praiſes of* CHRIST.]

1 MY God, my God, wherefore haſt thou
　　forſaken me ? ‖ and why
Art thou ſo far from helping me,
　　and from my earneſt cry ?

2 My God, I in the day-time cry,
　　but me thou doſt not hear ;
And in the night-time, but to me
　　no quiet reſt is there.

3 Nevertheleſs, thou holy art,
　　who conſtantly doſt dwell,
Among the thankful praiſes of
　　thy people Iſrael.

4 Our fathers heretofore in Thee
　　did put their confidence ;
They truſted Thee, and Thou to them
　　didſt give deliverance.

‖ So JESUS cried out on the Croſs, *Mat.* xxvii. 46.

PSALM XXII.

5 To Thee they cry'd out earneſtly,
 and then ſalvation came ;
They plac'd their truſt in Thee alone,
 and were not put to ſhame.
6 But as a worm, and not a man,
 I'm us'd as one forlorn ;
I'm the reproach among the high,
 among the low the ſcorn.
7 With laughter all the gazing crowd
 my agonies ſurvey ;
They ſhoot the lip, they ſhake the head,
 and thus deriding ſay ;
8 ' You on JEHOVAH caſt your ſelf,
 ' that He might you redeem ;
' Let him now come and reſcue you,
 ' ſince you delight in him.'
9 But thou art He who from the womb
 didſt tenderly me take :
When I was on my mother's breaſts
 to hope Thou didſt me make.
10 I even from the womb have been
 entirely caſt on Thee ;
And from my mother's bowels Thou
 haſt been a God to me.

[2 *Part.*]

11 Be not Thou far away from me,
 now trouble is ſo near ;
For there is none to give me help,
 unleſs Thou wilt appear.
12 My foes, as bulls on ev'ry ſide
 have me encompaſſed ;
Like mighty bulls of Baſhan have
 me round environed.
13 Their mouth they open upon me,
 yea open wide do they ;
Like lions ravenous who roar,
 when ſeizing on their prey.

PSALM XXII.

14 Like water I am poured out;
　my bones disjointed are;
　My heart amidſt my bowels melts,
　like wax amidſt the fire.

15 My ſtrength is like a potſherd dry'd,
　my parched tongue cleaves faſt
　To my dry mouth, and to the duſt
　of death, me brought Thou haſt.

16 Like furious dogs they me ſurround;
　in crouds the wicked meet;
　Their rude aſſembly me encloſe,
　and pierce my hands and feet.

17 Ev'n I may number all my bones;
　on me they look and ſtare:

18 For my whole veſture, lots they caſt,
　and they my garments ſhare.

19 But be not far, O LORD, my ſtrength;
　haſte Thou to ſuccour me.

20 My precious ſoul, both from the ſword,
　and pow'r of dogs ſet free.

21 O ſave me from the lion's mouth;
　as thou haſt anſwer'd me,
　When on the horns of unicorns
　I cry'd aloud to Thee.

22 Then to my brethren I'll declare
　the glories of thy name;
　Amidſt the congregation I
　thy praiſes will proclaim.

[3 Part.]

23 All ye who fear the LORD, Him praiſe;
　all Jacob's ſeed who are;
　Him glorify; all Iſrael's ſeed,
　do ye Him greatly fear.

24 For He th' affliction of the poor,
　nor loaths, nor does deſpiſe;
　Nor hides his face from him, but hears
　when loud to Him he cries.

25 Ev'n in the congregation great,
   my praise is of Thee still:
 Before them who Him reverence
   perform my vows I will.
26 The meek shall feed, and be suffic'd:
   and praise the LORD shall ye
 Who seek his face; your heart shall live
   ev'n to eternity.

27 All ends of th' earth remember shall,
   and turn all to the LORD:
 Thee all the heathen families
   to worship shall accord:
28 Because to our JEHOVAH does
   the kingdom appertain;
 And He among the nations is
   the ruler sovereign.

29 Earth's rich ones eat, and worship shall,
   all who to dust descend
 (For none can keep alive their souls)
   before his face shall bend.
30 A seed for ever shall Him serve,
   which to the *Lord* alone
 A generation shall be call'd,
   which He will ever own.

31 They shall come forth, and shall declare
   his glorious righteousness;
 To generations yet unborn,
   that he hath done all this.

PSALM XXIII. *A Psalm of* David.
1 THE LORD himself my shepherd is,
   want therefore shall not I:
2 He in the folds † of tender grass
   soft makes me down to lie:
 He leads me to the waters still:
   3 Restore my soul does He:
 In paths of righteousness He will
   for his name sake lead me.
                                4 Tho'

† i. e, *Enclosures* for **Flocks** of **Sheep.**

PSALM XXIV.

4 Tho' in death's gloomy vale I walk,
   yet I will fear no ill;
   For Thou art with me; and thy rod
   and ſtaff me comfort will.
5 Thou haſt for me a table ſpread
   in preſence of my foes:
   Thou doſt my head with oil anoint,
   and my cup overflows.
6 Goodneſs and mercy all my days
   ſhall ſurely follow me;
   And in the LORD's houſe I ſhall dwell
   as long as days * ſhall be.

PSALM XXIV. *A Pſalm of* David.

1 THE earth is all the LORD's,
     it's fulneſs all is his;
   The world and all who dwell therein
   his own poſſeſſion is.
2 For its foundation He
   upon the ſeas hath laid;
   And it on the unſtable floods
   hath firm eſtabliſhed.
3 But who JEHOVAH's hill
   ſhall happily aſcend?
   And in his place of ſanctity,
   who ſhall on Him attend?
4 The man whoſe hands are clean,
   whoſe heart is pure; and he
   Who hath not lift his ſoul to lies,
   nor ſworn deceitfully.
5 The benediction he
   ſhall from the LORD receive,
   And righteouſneſs ſhall from the God
   of his ſalvation have.
6 Of thoſe who ſeek for Him,
   this is the bleſſed race;
   And they are Jacob's genuine ſeed,
   who chiefly ſeek thy face. *(Selah.)*
                                    [2 Part.]

* So the *Hebrew,* and *all* the *ancient Verſions.*

PSALM XXV.

[2 *Part.*] ||
7 Ye gates lift up your heads,
    eternal doors give way ;
    Lift up on high, that enter in
    the king of glory may.
8 Who is this glorious king?
    we beg you now declare !
    He is JEHOVAH great in pow'r,
    the mighty LORD of war.

9 Ye gates lift up your heads,
    eternal doors give way ;
    Lift up on high, that enter in
    the king of glory may.
10 Who is this glorious king ?
    reveal and let us see !
    He's the triumphant LORD of hosts :
    this glorious king is He. (*Selah.*)

PSALM XXV. *A Pfalm of* David.

1 TO Thee, O LORD, I lift my foul :
    2 My God, I truft in Thee :
    Let me not be afham'd ; nor let
    my foes joy over me.
3 Yea, let not any be afham'd,
    who hope and wait on Thee :
    But all who are unjuft † and vain, ‡
    let them afhamed be.

4 Thy ways, JEHOVAH, to me fhow,
    thy paths make me difcern ;
5 O make me in thy truth to go,
    and caufe Thou me to learn.
    For of my health Thou art the God,
    on Thee I wait all day :
6 Thy bowels, LORD, and mercies mind ;
    for, evermore are they.   7 Re-

¶ The following Verfes feem to reprefent both the victorious Entrance of CHRIST by his Word and Spirit into the *Hearts* of the Children of Men on Earth, and his triumphant Entrance into *Heaven*.

† *Septuagint, Syriack, Arabick,* ‡ *Chaldee ;* and the *Hebrew* may include both.

PSALM XXV.

7 Remember not my faults of youth,
nor later fins record :
In mercy, for thy goodnefs fake
remember me, O LORD.
8 The LORD is good and juft ; therefore
the way He'll finners fhow :
9 The meek He will in judgment guide,
and make his way to know.
10 JEHOVAH's paths all mercy are,
and truth all of them too,
To them who keep his covenant
and teftimonies do.
11 JEHOVAH, for thy own name fake,
I humbly Thee intreat
To pardon mine iniquity,
for it is very great.

[2 *Part.*]

12 Who fear the LORD, them He will teach,
the way that they fhould chufe ;
13 Their fouls fhall dwell at eafe ; their feed
as heirs the earth fhall ufe.
14 With them who humbly fear the LORD;
his fecret love doth dwell ;
And his moft gracious covenant
to them He will reveal.

15 Mine earneft eyes continually
rais'd to JEHOVAH are ;
For He it is that can fet free
my feet out of the fnare.
16 O turn Thou now to me thy face,
and on me mercy fhow ;
For I am in a lonely cafe,
afflicted, poor, and low.
17 The troubles of my heart are great ;
bring me from my diftrefs,
18 My pain and my affliction fee,
and all my fins releafe.

19 Confider

19 Confider Thou mine enemies ;
   for multiply'd they are,
   And it a cruel hatred is
   which they againft me bear.
20 O do Thou fafely keep my foul,
   do Thou deliver me ;
   And let me never be afham'd,
   becaufe I truft in Thee.
21 Let foundnefs and let uprightnefs*
   keep me who wait* on Thee :
22 From all his troubles Ifrael,
   O GOD, do thou fet free.

PSALM XXVI. *A Pfalm of* David.

1 JUDGE me, O LORD, as I have walk'd
   in mine integrity :
   And as I on JEHOVAH truft,
   flide therefore fhall not I.
2 O fearch and prove me LORD ; and try
   my reins, my heart likewife :
3 For in thy truth I walk, and fix
   thy grace † before mine eyes.
4 With perfons vain I have not fat,
   nor with diffemblers gone :
5 All evil company I hate,
   and all the wicked fhun:
6 In purenefs, LORD, I'll wafh my hands ;
   thine altar then furround,
7 With thankful voice that I may tell,
   and all thy wonders found.
8 The dwelling of thy houfe, O LORD,
   moft dearly love do I ;
   The place and tabernacle where
   refides thy majefty.
9 With bloody or with wicked men,
   O gather not my foul ;
10 Whofe hands with fraud, and whofe right hands
   with bribery are full.

11 But

† *Hebrew*—Loving-kindnefs or Benignity.

11 But I in my integrity
  will walk, secur'd by Thee:
  O me redeem, and of thy grace
  be merciful to me.
12 Upon an even place my foot
  stands firm in uprightness:
  In the assemblies* therefore I
  the LORD will ever bless.

PSALM XXVII. *A Psalm of David.*

1 THE LORD my light and SAFETY‡ is:
  who shall make me dismay'd?
  The LORD is of my life the strength:
  who shall make me afraid?
2 For when my spiteful enemies
  me to devour drew near;
  To stumble and fall down at once,
  by Him they forced were.
3 Against me tho' an host encamp,
  my heart undaunted is:
  If war against me should arise,
  I am secure in this.
4 One thing I asked of the LORD,
  which still I will request;
  That in the LORD's house all my days
  I happily may rest;
  That I the beauty of the LORD
  may view, and there admire;
  And in his holy temple may
  continually enquire.
5 For He in his pavilion will
  me hide in evil days;
  In secret of his tent me hide,
  and on a rock me raise:
6 Moreover at this time my head
  on high shall lifted be,
  Above my num'rous enemies,
  who round encompass me. There-

‡ SAFETY or SALVATION, *Hebrew;* or SAVIOUR, *Arabick;*
It comprehends them all.

PSALM XXVII.

Therefore a sacrifice of joy,
  and shouting* I will bring
Into his tent; and sing aloud,
  praise to JEHOVAH sing.

[2 *Part.*]

7 While with my earnest voice I cry,
  me O JEHOVAH hear;
O have Thou mercy upon me,
  and to me give thine ear.
8 When Thou to seek thy blessed face,
  me kindly dost advise;
" Thy blessed face, LORD, I will seek,"
  my grateful heart replies.

9 O hide not Thou thy countenance,
  away from me therefore;
Thy servant put thou not away
  in thy displeasure sore.
My helper Thou hast ever been,
  do not from me depart;
Nor me forsake, for Thou the God
  of my salvation art.

10 My father and my mother both,
  tho' they from me remove;
Yet then the LORD will take me up,
  and a kind father prove.
11 JEHOVAH teach thou me thy way,
  and be a guide to me,
In righteous paths, because of those
  who watch my faults to see.

12 O give me not up to their will,
  who are mine enemies:
Against me rise false witnesses,
  who breath out cruelties.
13 I should have fainted, had not I
  believ'd that I should see,
Ev'n in the land of living ones
  the LORD's benignity.

14 Wait

14 Wait on the LORD, couragious be;
and He will ſtrength afford
To thy faint heart: I ſay again,
wait ſtill upon the LORD.

PSALM XXVIII. *A Pſalm of* David.

1 O LORD, my rock, to Thee I cry;
Be not thou ſilent then to me;
Leſt by thy ſilence I like them
Deſcending to the pit ſhould be.

2 Of my intreaties hear the voice,
While to Thee loud for help I cry;
While I lift up my hands towards
Thine oracle of ſanctity.

3 With ill men draw me not away,
With workers of unrighteouſneſs;
Who peace to all their neighbours ſpeak,
But in their heart is wickedneſs.

4 Thou wilt reward them for their deeds,
According to their ill intents;
According to their handy-works,
Thou wilt them juſtly recompence.

5 Since they JEHOVAH's, wonders ſlight,
And working of his hand diſdain;
He will them righteouſly deſtroy,
And will not build them up again.

6 The LORD be bleſs'd; for He hath heard
The voice of my imploring cry:
The LORD my ſtrength, my ſhield; on Him
My heart rely'd, and help'd was I.

Therefore my heart exults with joy,
And with my ſong I'll Him confeſs.

7 JEHOVAH is his people's ſtrength,
The ſtrength of his MESSIAH * is.

8 Salvation

---

* Of his MESSIAH; *Hebrew, Chaldee, Syriack, Arabick*: of his CHRIST; the *Septuagint* and *ancient Latin*: i. e. both of *David* his *Typical*, and of the *Man* CHRIST JESUS his *Promiſed* and *Real* MESSIAH.

8 Salvation to thy people give;
And bleſs Thou thine inheritance;
Yea even to eternity
Do Thou them feed and them advance.
[*This Verſe in Common Metre.*]
8 Salvation to thy people give;
  bleſs thine inheritance;
And even to eternity
  them feed and them advance.

PSALM XXIX. *A Pſalm of* David.

1 O Ye the ſons of mighty ones, †   (†*Elim.*)
   give to the LORD on high!
All glory to JEHOVAH give,
  and boundleſs potency.
2 O to the LORD the glory give
  which to his name is due:
In beauty of his holineſs,
  down to JEHOVAH bow.
3 The LORD's voice on the waters ſounds,
  the God of glory, hear,
Thunders aloud: JEHOVAH ſits,
  on many waters there.
4 The voice is full of pow'r, which ſounds
  forth from the LORD on high:
JEHOVAH's mighty voice is full
  of glorious majeſty.
5 See how JEHOVAH's voice at once
  the ſhiv'ring cedars tears:
See how the LORD the cedars breaks
  which Lebanon high rears.
6 Like calves He makes the mountains leap,
  ev'n That great Lebanon;
And like a youthful unicorn,
  that mountain Syrion.
7 JEHOVAH's voice ſtrikes flames of fire,
  and ſcatters them around:
8 JEHOVAH's voice the deſart makes
  to tremble with the ſound.

JEHOVAH makes the wilderness
of Kadesh shake with fear:
9 The LORD's voice makes the frighted Hinds
to cast their young ones there.
With glares of lightning thro' the dark
He makes the forests bare.
But his full * glory He within
his temple does declare.
10 The LORD sits on the flood as king;
the LORD's reign ne'er shall cease:
11 The LORD will give his people strength;
the LORD them bless with peace.

PSALM XXX.
A Psalm and Song at the Dedication of the House of David.

1 LORD, I will thee extol on high;
for Thou hast made me rise;
And joyful hast not made to be
o'er me mine enemies.
2 O LORD my God, I cry'd to thee,
and Thou hast made me whole.
3 JEHOVAH, Thou ev'n from the grave
hast raised up my soul:

Thou from the pit hast quick'ned me:
4 O sing ye to the LORD,
Ye saints of his, give thanks when ye
his holiness record.
5 For but a moment * is his wrath;
life in his love doth stay:
Tho' weeping last thro' all the night,
joy comes at break of day.
6 For in my prosp'rous state I said,
" I ne'er shall moved be;
7 " Since, LORD, my mountain by thy grace
" is made so strong by Thee."
8 But quickly thou thy face didst hide;
I greatly was dismay'd:
LORD then I call'd aloud on Thee,
and to the LORD thus pray'd;   9 " What

PSALM XXXI.

9 " What gain is in my blood when I
   " into the pit go down?
   " Shall dust give glory then to Thee?
   " Shall it thy truth make known?
10 " Do thou me, O JEHOVAH, hear;
   " and on me, mercy have:
   " To me, JEHOVAH, be Thou near,
   " an helper me to save!"

11 My mourning then into a dance
   for me Thou turned hast;
With gladness Thou hast girded me,
   and off my sackcloth cast.
12 So shall my glory sing thy praise,
   and never silent be:
O LORD my God, I will give thanks
   for evermore to Thee.

PSALM XXXI. *A Psalm of* David.

1 IN Thee, O LORD, I put my trust;
   asham'd ne'er let me be:
According to thy righteousness,
   do Thou deliver me.
2 Bow down thine ear to me: with speed
   give me deliverance.
To save me, be my rock of strength,
   and house of my defence.

3 Because Thou art my rock and fort,
   in whom I will confide,
Therefore for thy name sake do Thou
   me safely, lead ‖ and guide.‖
4 O pull me from the net which they,
   for me in secret laid;
Because Thou only art my strength,
   in whom I trust for aid.

‖ i. e. either, *Lead me by thy Hand*, and *guide me by thine Eye*; or—*Lead, yea lead me along continually*.

PSALM XXXI.

5 Into thy hands I safe commit
   my soul; for Thou art He,
O Thou JEHOVAH, God of truth,
   who hast redeemed me.*
6 The men who lying vanities
   regard, I have abhor'd:
But I have plac'd my confidence
   alone upon the LORD.

7 I in thy mercy will exult
   and will rejoice; for Thou
Did'st my affliction see and weigh,
   my soul in trouble know;
8 And didst not let my foe keep me,
   enclosed in his hand;
But in the place of liberty
   hast made my feet to stand.

[2 Part.]

9 O LORD, because I am distress'd,
   in mercy send relief:
My soul, my bowels, and mine eye,
   consumed are with grief.
10 Because my life with trouble fails;
   with groans my years decay;
And for my sins my strength is spent,
   my bones consume away.

11 To all my foes I am a scorn,
   neighbours especially;
A fear to friends; and those abroad
   who see me from me fly.
12 Ev'n like a dead man, out of mind,
   I quite forgotten lie;
And as a potter's vessel broke, ||
   so much despis'd am I.

---

* *Hebrew, Septuagint, ancient Latin, Chaldee, Syriack, Arabick.*
|| *Hebrew, Septuagint* and *ancient Latin*—a Vessel destroyed;
  Arab. a Vessel broken; *Chaldee*, a Potter's Vessel broken
  to Pieces.

PSALM XXXI.

13 For slanders I of many heard,
   and fears around me lay,
While they consulted and devis'd
   to take my life * away.
14 But all this while on Thee, O LORD,
   I trusted still for aid;
" For Thou art my almighty God,"
   my soul within me said;
15 My times are wholly in thy hand;
   now therefore set me free
Far from the hand of all my foes,
   and those who trouble me.

[3 *Part.*]

16 The brightness of thy face to shine
   on me thy servant make;
And thy salvation to me grant,
   for thy free mercy sake
17 LORD, let me not ashamed be;
   for call'd on Thee I have;
But wicked men shall be asham'd,
   till silent in the grave.
18 The lying lips shall silenc'd be,
   which grievous things have said;
And hard reports in pride and scorn
   against the righteous spread.
19 How great thy goodness in thy store,
   for those who fear Thee, then!
Yea wrought for them who trust in Thee,
   before the sons of men!
20 In secret of thy presence Thou
   wilt screen them from man's pride;
And safely wilt from strife of tongues
   in thy pavilion hide.
21 O let JEHOVAH blessed be,
   for wondrous kindness shown,
When threatning dangers me enclos'd
   within a fenced town. || 22 For

* No doubt alluding to his being in *Keilah*; 1 Sam. xxii. 5—12.

PSALM XXXII.

22 For in my haste I thought and said;
 "I'm cut off from thine eyes,"
 Yet when I cry'd to Thee, then Thou
  didst kindly hear my cries.
23 O love the LORD, all ye his saints!
  the LORD the faithful guards;
 But those who live and act in pride,
  He dreadfully rewards.
24 Encourage then your selves in him,
  and he'll more strength afford
 To your enfeebled hearts, all ye
  whose hope is in the LORD.

PSALM XXXII. *A Psalm of* David.

1 O Blessed is the man to whom
   trespass is pardoned;
 And he whose faults of ev'ry kind
  are wholly covered!
2 O blessed is the man, to whom
  the LORD imputes not sin;
 And he who such a spirit hath,
  that guile is not therein.
3 For while I no confession made,
  but silent kept my tongue,
 My bones, as if with age, decay'd
  with groaning all day long.
4 For heavily thy hand did lie
  upon me day and night;
 That into summer's scorching drought
  my moisture turned quite. *(Selah.)*
5 At length my sin I did confess,
  with humble shame to Thee;
 And hid not from Thee any part
  of mine iniquity.
6 Against my self, I said, "my sins
 "I'll to the LORD confess;"
 And then of mine iniquity
  Thou didst the guilt release. *(Selah.)*

7 For

7 For this each godly one to Thee
   in finding time shall pray :
Surely in floods of waters great,
   reach to * him shall not they.
Thou art my hiding place : thou wilt
   from trouble keep ‡ me free ;
With songs of glad deliverance ;
   thou wilt encompass me. *(Selah.)*

8 To me thou sayst, " I'll thee instruct,
   " thee teach the way will I,
   " Wherein 'tis best for thee to go,
   " and guide thee with mine eye."
9 " Be neither like a horse or mule,
   " who never understand ;
   " Whose mouths with bits and reins are held,
   " to keep them in command.
10 " To ev'ry one who wicked is,
   " shall many griefs abound :
   " But him who on the LORD relies,
   " shall mercy compass round."
11 Be glad, ye righteous, in the LORD,
   greatly in Him rejoice ;
And all who upright are in heart,
   shout with a joyful voice.

PSALM XXXIII.

1 YE righteous, in the *Lord*,
   exceedingly rejoice ;
For it is comely for th' upright,
   with praise to lift their voice.
2 With psaltries, harps and lutes,
   sing praises to the LORD ;
3 A new song loudly sing to Him,
   with skill and sweet accord ;

4 Because

---

* *Hebrew, Munster, Montanus,* &c. i. e. being plac'd as on the Top of a high Rock above the Waves ; *Gejer.*
‡ *Hebrew, Chaldee, Montanus.*

PSALM XXXIII.

4 Becaufe JEHOVAH's word
  is altogether right;
And all his work is done in truth,
  and brings his truth to light.
5 He loves all righteoufnefs,
  judgment and equity:
And all the earth is filled with
  the LORD's benignity.
6 For by JEHOVAH's word
  the heav'ns had all their frame;
And by the fpirit of his mouth,
  all armies of the fame.
7 The waters of the fea
  he gathers as an heap;
In channels as in treafuries
  he lays up all the deep.
8 Let all throughout the earth,
  the great JEHOVAH fear,
Let all the dwellers of the world
  to Him deep rev'rence bear:
9 Becaufe he did but fpeak
  the word; and it was made;
He did but his commandment give,
  and it was firmly ftaid.
10 JEHOVAH brings to nought
  the fchemes of nations wife;
He renders all in vain the plots
  the fubt'left men devife.
11 The counfel of the LORD
  abide for ever fhall;
The cogitations of his heart,
  to generations all.

[2 *Part.*]

12 O bleffed nation they,
  whofe God JEHOVAH is;
That people, for an heritage
  He chofen hath as his.

PSALM XXXIV.

13 The LORD from heav'n looks down,
   on all the human race:
14 He all who dwell around the earth
   views from his dwelling place.
15 He fashions at his will
   the hearts of all mankind;
And all their operations he
   attentively does mind.
16 By multitudes of hosts
   no king himself can save;
The mighty by their greatest strength,
   can not deliv'rance have.
17 A horse a vain thing is
   to save one in the fight;
Neither can he deliv'rance give
   by greatness of his might.
18 But lo, who fear the LORD,
   on them He sets his eye; ‖
On them who place their lively hope
   in his benignity.
19 To save our souls from death
   by war and famine, free;
20 Our souls will for JEHOVAH wait;
   our help and shield is he.
21 We trust his holy name;
   so our hearts in Him joy.
22 LORD, let thy mercy be on us,
   as we on Thee rely.

PSALM XXXIV. *A Psalm of David, when he changed his Behaviour before Abimelech; who drove him away.*

1 IN all the seasons of my life
   JEHOVAH bless will I,
And in my mouth his praises shall
   abide continually.
2 My soul shall glory in the LORD,
   and praise him with my voice;
And when the humble hear of this,
   they greatly will rejoice.

3 With

‖ i. e, with a fatherly Care and Watchfulness.

PSALM XXXIV.

3 With me together, O do ye
   JEHOVAH magnify;
  And let us all herein agree,
   to lift his name on high.
4 In my diſtreſs I ſought the LORD;
   and He to me gave ear,
  And graciouſly deliver'd me
   from all that was my fear.
5 They look'd to him; enlighten'd were;
   no ſhame did them appall:
6 This poor man cry'd; the LORD did hear,
   and ſave from troubles all.
7 The angels of the LORD encamp
   and round about them ſtand,
  Who fear Him, to preſerve them from
   all evil near at hand.
8 How bountiful JEHOVAH is,
   O taſte and ſee likewiſe!
  O great is that man's bleſſedneſs
   who firm on him relies!
9 O ye JEHOVAH's holy ones,
   ſee that ye Him revere;
  For there ſhall be no want to them
   who Him ſincerely fear.
10 Young lions often ſuffer want,
   and hungry pine for food;
  But they who truly fear the LORD,
   ſhall want no real good.

[2 Part.]

11 O come ye children now to me,
   give ye attentive ear;
  And I will you inſtruct how ye
   the LORD aright ſhall fear.
12 Who is the man that would have ‡ life,
   and many days deſires,
  That he may long enjoy the good
   to which his heart aſpires.

‡ So the *Hebrew* and *all the ancient Verſions*.

13 Thy tongue from evil keep, thy lips
   from speaking guile keep thou:
14 Depart from evil and do good;
   seek peace and it pursue.
15 Upon the men who righteous are
   the LORD doth set his eye;
   And bows down his attentive ear,
   when e'er to Him they cry.

16 Against those who do wickedly
   JEHOVAH sets his face;
   That he may quite from off the earth
   their hateful mem'ry raze.
17 But when the righteous cry to Him,
   JEHOVAH hears their call;
   And will deliv'rance give to them
   out of their troubles all.

18 To those who broken are in heart,
   the LORD is ever near;
   And He will surely save such as
   in spirit contrite are.
19 Tho' the just man has many griefs,
   the LORD from all will free:
20 And all his bones He keeps secure,
   that none shall broken be.

21 Evil shall slay the wicked man;
   and all whoever hate
   The righteous man, and ne'er repent,
   shall sure be desolate.
22 But who JEHOVAH serve, their souls
   He freely will redeem:
   Nor utterly shall any fail,
   who put their trust in Him.

PSALM XXXV. *A Psalm of* David.

1 LORD strive with them who with me strive;
     Against them fight who fight with me:
2 Of shield and buckler take thou hold;
   And O arise my help to be.

3 Draw

PSALM XXXV.

3 Draw forth the spear and stop the course
Of my pursuers speedily;
And to my soul O do thou say,
" I will a saviour be to Thee."

4 With shame shall they confounded be,
Who seek my harmless soul to seize;
And with disgrace be turned back,
Who plot to do me injuries.

5 JEHOVAH's angel shall them chase
As chaff before the driving wind:

6 Their way shall dark and slipp'ry be,
JEHOVAH's angel drive behind!

7 For causelesly within a pit
They hid a net me to ensnare;
A pit which they without a cause
Did dig, and for my soul prepare.

8 But ruin on them unawares
Shall come; and in their hidden net
They shall be caught, and ruin'd by
The snare their hand for me had set.

9 My soul shall in the LORD rejoice,
In his salvation joyful be;

10 And all my bones with joy shall sing
" JEHOVAH, who is like to Thee!"
" Who sav'st the poor and weak from those
" Who for him are too great and strong;
" The poor and needy one from those
" Who him oppress with spoil and wrong!"

[2 *Part.*]

11 False witnesses arose; and things
I never knew, to me they laid:

12 To spoil my soul, ungratefully
they evil for my good repaid.

13 But as for me, when they were sick;
I put on sackcloth, and I mourn'd;
My soul with fasting griev'd; my pray'r
Within my bosom oft return'd.

PSALM XXXV.

14 As for my friend or brother dear;
So tenderly behave did I;
As for a dying mother wept,
And I bow'd downward heavily.
15 Yet they in my diftrefs rejoice,
And they againft me gathered are;
The bafeft meet unknown to me,
And never ceafe my name to tear.*

16 With fcoffing hypocrites at feafts,
Who get their bread with flatteries;
They gnafh againft me with their teeth,
And fland'rous jefts on me devife.
17 O *Lord* how long wilt thou look on?
From their deftruction refcue me!
My precious foul make hafte to fave,
My deareft from young lions free;

18 So I to thee will render thanks
Within the congregation great;
And I will celebrate thy praife,
Where multitudes to worfhip meet.

[3 *Part.*]

19 O let them not o'er me rejoice,
Who are my wrongful enemies;
Nor thofe who hate me caufelefly,
Deride me with their fcornful eyes.
20 For they, nor fpeak, nor aim for peace;
But they the words of fraud contrive,
Againft thofe people in the land
Who love in quietnefs to live.

21 Yea they with open mouths on me
Laugh out and fay, " Our eye it faw!"
22 LORD, Thou haft feen: hold not thy peace:
Lord do not far from me withdraw.
23 O to my judgment and my caufe
My God, my *Lord*, awake and rife:
24 LORD judge me in thy righteoufnefs,
My God, left they o'er me rejoice.

25 O never let their hearts exult,
 "Ha! ha! our souls desire have we!"
 Nor ever suffer them to boast,
 That they have wholly swallow'd me.
26 Confounded and asham'd shall be
 All those who at my hurt are glad;
 And those who now against me boast,
 With shame and with disgrace be clad.

27 Let those who love my righteous cause,
 Rejoice and shout; and never cease
 To say, "The LORD be magnify'd,
 "Who loves to see his servants peace."
28 And so, to shout thy righteousness,
 Shall be th' employment of my tongue;
 And thy high praises to set forth,
 From day to day, and all day long. ‡

PSALM XXXVI. A Psalm of David, the Servant of the LORD.

1 THE trespass of the wicked man
 so plain and open lies;
 My heart concludes, the fear of GOD
 is not before his eyes.
2 For in his own deceitful view
 self-flatteries abound;
 Till his iniquity breaks out,
 and odious is found.

3 The words that issue from his mouth,
 are vain and guileful too;
 He quite hath ceased to be wise,
 and any good to do.
4 Yea, when he lies upon his bed,
 he mischief meditates;
 He sets himself in no good way,
 nor any evil hates.

[2 Part.]

‡ The *Hebrew* comprehends all this line.

[2 *Part.*]

5 Thy mercy, O JEHOVAH is
   within * the heav'ns on high;
   Thy faithfulness does also reach
   above the cloudy sky.
6 Like mountains great † thy righteousness !
   thy judgments a great deep !
   Both man and beast, Thou kindly LORD
   dost condescend to keep. ‡

7 O God, thy loving-kindness is
   of wondrous excellence :
   Therefore in shadow of thy wings,
   men's sons put confidence.
8 Ev'n of the fatness of thy house,
   they to the full shall take ;
   And of the stream of thy delights,
   to drink Thou wilt them make.

9 Because the flowing spring of life,
   ever abides in thee ;
   And in thy light, the light of grace
   and glory we shall see.
10 O stretch thy loving-kindness forth
   to all who Thee do know;
   And to all those of upright heart
   thy righteousness still show.

11 O suffer not the foot of pride
   to make approach to me ;
   Nor by the hand of wicked men
   let me removed be.
12 Lo, There they all are fallen down,
   who work iniquities ;
   Down are they cast, and never shall
   be able to arise.

PSALM

† The *Hebrew* may be render'd either *the Mountains of God*,
   or, *the great Mountains*.
‡ The *Hebrew* signifies—*preserve and keep*.

PSALM XXXVII.

PSALM XXXVII. *A Psalm of* David.

1 FRET not thy self at wicked men,
for their prosperity;
Nor be thou envious at the men
who work iniquity.
2 For like the grass that flourished,
cut quickly down are they;
And like the green and tender herb,
shall wither soon away.

3 Upon JEHOVAH put thy trust,
and be thou doing good;
So shalt thou dwell within the land,
and truth ‖ shall be thy food.
4 See that thou set thy heart's delight
chiefly upon the LORD;
Then the just wishes of thy heart
to thee He will afford.

5 Upon the LORD devolve * thy way,
by faith on Him depend;
And He will bring thy good designs
to a most happy end.
6 Yea, like the shining light will he
thy righteousness display;
And He thy judgment will bring forth
clear-shining as noon-day.

7 Rest on the LORD, and patiently
wait for Him; fret not thou
At him who prospers in his way
in ill devices now.
8 All wrath relinquish * utterly;
cease from rash anger too:
In no wise fret thy self, to move
thee any ill to do.

D 5   9 For

‖ In the *Hebrew* 'tis—*Feed on Truth*, i.e. *not thy own*, nor
the *Truth of Men*, but of GOD. *Deut.* viii. 3. *Mat.* iv. 4.
See *Montanus, Avenarius, Buxtorf, Schindler, Bythner,.*
* So the *Hebrew, Septuagint* and *ancient Latin*.

PSALM XXXVII.

9 For, those who evil doers are
   shall be cut off and fall;
But those who on JEHOVAH wait
   the earth inherit shall.
10 For, yet a little while, and here
   the wicked shall not be;
Yea thou shalt look and view his place,
   but him thou shalt not see.
11 Whereas the meek and humble shall
   the earth as heirs possess;
And thankfully delight themselves
   in plenteousness of peace.

[2 *Part*.]

12 The wicked plot against the just:
   they gnash their teeth and foam;
13 But them the *Lord* derides, and sees
   their fatal day will come.
14 The wicked forth their sword have drawn,
   and bent their bow have they;
To cast the poor and needy down,
   and upright men to slay.
15 But their own swords into their hearts
   shall enter suddenly;
Their bows which they have bent shall all
   in pieces broken be.
16 The little that a righteous man
   enjoys, is better far,
Than when to many wicked join'd
   their stores of riches are.

17 For of ungodly men the arms
   shall wholly broken be;
But those who righteous are, the LORD
   will hold up carefully.
18 The LORD, the days of upright men
   exactly knows; and sure
Their promised inheritance
   for ever shall endure.

19 In

PSALM XXXVII.

19 In dangerous and evil times,
    from shame they shall be free;
   And when the days of famine come,
    they satisfy'd shall be.
20 But wicked men shall perish soon;
    and who the LORD provoke,
   Shall like the fat of lambs consume,
    and vanish into smoke.

[3 *Part.*]

21 The man ungodly borrows much,
    and takes no care to pay;
   Whereas the just man mercy shews,
    and freely gives away.
22 For such as blessed are by Him, ‖
    the earth inherit shall:
   But those who by him cursed are,
    shall be cut off and fall.

23 The steps of good men by the LORD
    are ordered aright;
   And in their good and righteous way,
    He takes a great delight.
24 Altho' they fall, yet shall they not
    be cast down utterly;
   Because JEHOVAH with his hand
    upholds them carefully.

25 Nor in my youth, nor in my age,
    ev'n to my hoary head;
   Nor have I seen the just forsook,
    nor their seed begging bread. §
26 He shews his mercy ev'ry day,
    and lends to those who need;
   And blessings he behind him leaves,
    to all his godly seed.

27 Wherefore

‖ i. e. by the LORD, *ver.* 18—20.
§ i. e. It was *Then* so rare in *Israel*, that *David* in all his Time
  had never seen it.

PSALM XXXVII.

27 Wherefore from evil far depart;
   do good; and then besure,
Thou shalt have such a dwelling place
   as ever shall endure.
28 Because the LORD doth judgment love,
   his saints forsakes not He;
Kept ever are they; but cut off
   the sinner's race shall be.

29 The just inherit shall the land,
   and ever therein dwell.
30 The just man's mouth does wisdom speak;
   his tongue right judgment tell.
31 His God's pure law is in his heart;
   none of his steps shall stray.
32 The wicked watches for the just,
   and seeks for him, to slay.

33 But yet JEHOVAH will not leave
   the just man in his hands;
Nor will the righteous man condemn,
   when He in judgment stands.

[4 *Part.*]

34 Wait on the LORD, and keep his way;
   and Thee exalt will He,
Th' earth ‖ to inherit, when cut off
   the wicked thou shalt see.
35 The wicked man I have beheld
   in dreadful pow'r and pride;
Ev'n like a laurel * flourishing,
   and spreading far and wide.

36 Nevertheless he pass'd away,
   and, lo he quite was gone;
I searched for him, but could find
   no glimpse of such a one.

37 But

‖ By *Earth* may possibly here be meant *the new Earth* after the Conflagration of *This*; *Isai.* lxv, lxvi. *Mal.* iv. 2 *Pet.* iii. &c. when *this Psalm* and *many others* may be ultimately and gloriously fulfilled.

PSALM XXXVIII.

37 But mark the perfect, and obſerve
the man of uprightneſs;
And thou ſhalt ſee, that of this man
the latter end is peace.

38 Whereas thoſe who tranſgreſſors are,
together periſh ſhall;
To be cut off ſhall be the end
of men ungodly all.

39 But the ſalvation of the juſt
does from JEHOVAH come;
And he's their ſtrength to whom they look
in times moſt troubleſome.

40 Yea help and free them will the LORD;
he will defend the juſt
From wicked men; He will them ſave,
becauſe in Him they truſt.

PSALM XXXVIII.

A Pſalm of David, *to bring to Remembrance.*

1 LORD in thy wrath rebuke me not,
Nor in thine anger me chaſtiſe:
2 For fix'd in me thine arrows are,
And ſore thine hand upon me lies.
3 No ſoundneſs is there in my fleſh,
Becauſe thy wrath on me doth lie;
Nor in my bones is any reſt,
Becauſe of mine iniquity.
4 Becauſe my many treſpaſſes
Paſs'd o'er my head and paſſing are;
And as a mighty burden, they
Too heavy preſs for me to bear.
5 My wounds are noiſome and corrupt;
My fooliſhneſs has made them ſo:
6 I'm bent and greatly bowed down,
I all day long a mourning go.
7 Fill'd are my loins with loathſome ſores,
And in my fleſh is no ſound part:
8 I weak and ſorely broken am,
I roar in anguiſh of my heart. [2. *Part*]

PSALM XXXVIII.

[2 *Part.*]

9 *Lord*, with Thee is my whole defire,
My groaning is not hid from Thee:
10 My heart pants hard, my ftrength all fails,
And mine eye fight is gone from me.
11 My lover and familiar friends
Stand far off from my noifome fore:
My neighbours and my kindred dear
Aloof ftand, nor come near me more.

12 Yea they who feek my life, lay fnares;
And they who wifh to do me wrong,
Speak mifchief, and their hearts devife
Deceits againft me all day long.
13 But I, as deaf, feem'd not to hear;
And filent, as one dumb was I;
14 Was like a man * that did not hear,
And in whofe mouth is no reply.

15 For LORD, my hope againft my foes,
Is fixed wholly upon Thee;
And Thou, O *Lord* my God, I truft
Wilt kindly hear and anfwer me.
16 O hear Thou me faid I, leaft they
Should triumph over me with pride;
Themfelves againft me magnify,
When they fhall fee my feet to flide.

17 For I am ready now to halt,
Thro' grief continually with me;
18 Wherefore my faults I will declare,
And for my fins will grieved
19 But lively are mine enemies,
Their pow'r moft formidably grows;
They multiply with great encreafe,
Who are without a caufe my foes.

20 Yea thofe who ill for good return,
Are to me deadly enemies;
And thus malicious are, becaufe
I what is good purfue and prize.

21 JEHOVAH,

PSALM XXXIX.

21 JEHOVAH, O forsake me not!
 My God, be not far off from me!
22 O *Lord*, who my salvation art,
 Make haste to help and set me free!

PSALM XXXIX. *A Psalm of* David.

1 I Said, I to my ways will look,
 lest I sin with my tongue;
 With curb I'll keep my mouth while I
 the wicked am among.
2 With silence I as dumb abode,
 my mouth did I refrain
 From speaking good; but then the more
 excited was my pain.
3 My heart within me waxed hot,
 while I was musing long;
 Until the fire enkindled was;
 then spake I with my tongue.
4 O LORD, teach me to know mine end,
 and measure of my days;
 How short it is, how frail I am,
 how swift my time decays.
5 Lo, Thou my days hast made a span,
 mine age is nought to Thee:
 At his best state sure ev'ry man
 is wholly vanity. *(Selah.)*
6 Sure man walks in an empty show,
 and stirs himself in vain;
 Who heaps up wealth, but knows not who
 shall gather all his gain.

[2 Part.]

7 And now, O *Lord*, what wait I for?
 my hope is set on Thee:
8 Free me from all my trespasses:
 the fools scoff make not me.
9 I silent was, and shut my mouth,
 this done because Thou hast:
10 Remove thy stroke away from me;
 by thy hands-blow I waste. 11 When

PSALM XL.

11 When with rebukes Thou chaſtneſt man
    for his iniquity;
His beauty, like a moth, conſumes:
    ſure each man's vanity. *(Selah.)*
12 LORD hear my pray'r, regard my tears,
    give ear to my loud cry:
For as my fathers all, with Thee,
    a ſojourner am I.

13 O ſpare me for a little ſpace,
    and ſtrength to me reſtore
Before, by death, from hence I go,
    and ſhall be here no more.

PSALM XL. *A Pſalm of David.*

1 WITH expectation from the LORD,
    I waited patiently;
And He inclin'd to pity me,
    and heard my humble cry.
2 He brought me from the dreadful pit,
    and from the miry clay;
And on a rock he ſet my feet;
    eſtabliſhed my way:
3 A new ſong put He in my mouth,
    to praiſe our God on high;
Which many ſhall behold, and fear,
    and on the LORD rely.
4 O greatly bleſſed are the men,
    who in the LORD confide;
Who value not the proud, nor ſuch,
    as turn to lies aſide.*

[2 *Part.*]

5 O LORD my God, how many are
    the wonders thou haſt wrought;
What multitudes of kindneſſes,
    towards us haſt thou thought.
6 Their ſum, in order, never can
    be reckon'd up to thee:
If I would count them, they are more
    than e'er can number'd be.

7 Thou

PSALM XL.

7 Thou doſt no ſacrifice of beaſts
   nor off'ring now deſire;
   Sin off'rings thou requireſt not,
   nor off'rings made by fire:
8 But mine ear pierceſt: * then ſaid I,
   ' Lo now I come to Thee;
   ' As in the volume of thy book
   ' 'tis written thus of me;'
   " To do thy will, is my delight,
   " O Thou my God who art!
   " Yea thy whole law is fixed in
   " the centre of my heart." ||
9 " I in the congregation great,
   " thy righteouſneſs did ſhow:
   " Lo, I have not refrain'd my lips,
   " JEHOVAH thou doſt know.
10 " I have not in my heart conceal'd,
   " thy perfect righteouſneſs;
   " But thy ſalvation have declar'd,
   " and ſhown thy faithfulneſs.
   " Neither thy great benignity
   " have I at all conceal'd;
   " Nor from the congregation great
   " have I thy truth with-held."

11 And now thy tender mercies, LORD,
   with-hold thou not from me:
   But let thy mercy and thy truth
   keep me continually.
12 For evils more than can be told,
   encompaſs me around;
   My ſins ſo ſeize and hold me faſt,
   that they my ſight confound.

They're more than hairs upon my head,
   my heart is quite diſmay'd:
13 O LORD, be pleas'd to reſcue me,
   LORD, haſten to my aid.   [3 *Part.*]

|| Theſe Paſſages in ver. 7, 8, are expreſly applied to *the Man* CHRIST JESUS, in *Heb.* x.

[3 *Part.*]

14 With shame be they confounded, who
    my soul to ruin aim;
Yea, all who evil wish to me,
    be driven back with shame.
15 With shame their spite shall be repaid,
    who mock my hope in Thee;
Who sport of me in trouble make,
    they desolate shall be.

16 Let all who seek Thee, joy in Thee,
    who firm in Thee confide;
Who thy salvation love, cry out,
    " the LORD be magnify'd."
17 I poor and needy am; and yet
    the *Lord* does think on me:
For thou my help and saviour art:
    my God me quickly free.

PSALM XLI. *A Psalm of* David.

1 O Bless'd is he who does the poor
    consider and relieve! ‖
The LORD deliv'rance will to him
    in time of trouble give.
2 The Lord will keep and make him live;
    on earth he bless'd shall be;
Thou wilt not give him to the will
    of any enemy.

3 Upon his bed of languishing,
    the LORD will him sustain;
Yea thou wilt easy make his bed,
    when sick or seiz'd with pain.
4 I said, " JEHOVAH now to me
    " thy tender grace I crave;
" Heal Thou my wounded soul, because,
    " I sinn'd against Thee have."

5 Those

‖ No doubt the *Original* intends so, to *consider* as to *relieve*.

PSALM XLI.

5 Thofe men who are mine enemies,
   with evil me defame:
   Their fpeeches are---" when will he die,
   " and perifh fhall his name?"
6 And when they come to vifit me,
   they wholly fpeak in fraud;
   But gather evil in their hearts,
   and fpread it then abroad.

[2 Part.]

7 My foes againft me all confpire
   and whifper fecretly,
   Concerning me; to work my hurt,
   they plot malicioufly.
8 With joy they fay, " There cleaves to him
   " fome bad difeafe or fore;
   " Which mortifies and cafts him down,
   " that he fhall rife no more."

9 Yea, ev'n my own familiar friend,
   on whom I did rely;
   Who eat my bread, yet hath his heel
   againft me lifted high.
10 But Thou, O LORD, be merciful
   to me, I humbly pray;
   And raife me up, that I their crimes
   may properly repay.

11 By this I know affuredly,
   I favour'd am by Thee;
   That thou alloweft not my foes
   to triumph over me.
12 But Thou, in mine integrity,
   doft always me fuftain;
   And fetteft me before thy face
   for ever to remain.

13 The LORD, the God of Ifrael,
   hath from eternity
   Been blefs'd, and fhall be evermore:
   AMEN, AMEN, fay we.

PSALM

PSALM XLII.

1 AS the chas'd hart with vehemence
   pants for the cooling brooks;
So pants my soul for Thee, O GOD,
   for Thee so longing looks.
2 My soul for GOD, the living God,
   does thirst exceedingly:
Oh, when before the face of GOD,
   come and appear shall I!
3 My flowing tears have been to me,
   as food by night and day;
While, taunting, constantly 'to me,'
   " where is thy God?" they say.
4 My soul is poured out in me,
   as this I think upon;
How to GOD's house with multitudes
   I in times past have gone;

With them, I with the voice of joy
   and praise in triumph sung;
With multitudes, who as we went,
   with joy did leap along. †
5 O why art thou cast down my soul?
   and why in such distress?
Hope thou in GOD: Him praise I shall:
   for health ‡ is from his face.
   [2 Part.]
6 My God, my soul is quite cast down;
   Thee therefore mind I will,
From Jordan-land, and Hermon-mount,
   and from the Mizar-hill. *
7 At sounding of thy water-spouts,
   deep loud to deep does call; ||
Thy dashing waves pass over me,
   thy rolling billows all.   8 His

† In the *Hebrew* 'tis—*the Multitudes leaping with the Voice of Ovation* [i. e. triumphing Joy] *and Praise:* the *Hebrew* signifying—*Leaping with Joy,* as in 1 Sam. xxx. 16. So *Montanus, Ainsworth,* and *Gejer.*
‡ The *Hebrew* signifies both *Health, Safety* and *Salvation.*
|| i. e. One mounting Wave of the great Deeps roars and calls out to another to follow.

PSALM XLIII.

8 His loving-kindnefs yet the LORD,
   command will in the day;
And in the night his fongs with me;
   to God my life I'll pray.
9 To God my rock, I'll fay, " O why
   " doft Thou forget me fo?
" Why go I mourning grievioufly,
   " oppreffed by my foe?"
10 As with a fword within my bones,
   fo me my foes upbraid;
While ev'ry day they fay to me,
   " where is thy God, thy aid?"
11 My foul, O wherefore doft thou bow
   thy felf down heavily?
And wherefore fo difquieted,
   and troubled art in me?

Hope thou in GOD, becaufe I fhall
   with praife Him yet advance;
Who is my God; He alfo is
   health ‡ of my countenance.

PSALM XLIII.

1 JUDGE me, O GOD, and plead my caufe
   with nations mercilefs:
And from the men of guile and wrong,
   O fend thou me redrefs.
2 For of my ftrength Thou art the God:
   reject me why doft Thou?
Why go I mourning grievoufly,
   oppreffed by the foe?
3 O fend thou forth thy light and truth,
   let them conduct me near,
And bring me to thy holy hill,
   and to thy dwellings there.
4 Then will I to GOD's altar go,
   to God, my higheft joy:
Yea Thee to praife, O GOD, my God,
   I will my harp employ.

5 My foul, O wherefore doſt thou bow
   thy ſelf down heavily?
  And wherefore ſo diſquieted,
   and troubled art in me?
6 Hope thou in GOD; becauſe I ſhall
   with praiſe Him yet advance;
  Who is my God; He alſo is
   health ‡ of my countenance.

PSALM XLIV.

1 O GOD, our fathers oft have told
      in our attentive ears,
  Thy wondrous works wrought in their days,
   and elder time than theirs.
2 Thy hand did drive the heathen out
   but plant them in their place:
  Thou didſt the heathen people waſte,
   but thine thou didſt increaſe.
3 For 'twas not their own ſword, to them
   the land's poſſeſſion gave;
  Nor was the ſtrength of their own arm
   the pow'r that did them ſave:
  But Thy right hand, thine arm, the light
   that ſhined from thy face;
  Becauſe on them thou pleaſed waſt
   thy favour free to place.
4 Thou art my king, O mighty God;
   deliverances * command
  For Jacob in his deep diſtreſs,
   who needs thy mighty hand.
5 Thro' Thee, as with an horn, we will
   puſh down our enemies:
  We thro' thy name will tread down thoſe
   who up againſt us riſe.
6 Becauſe it is not in my bow
   that I affiance have;
  Nor is it any ſword of mine
   that ever can me ſave.   7 But

‡ The *Hebrew* Word is the *ſame* as in the *foregoing* Pſalm,
  ver. 5 and 11.

PSALM XLIV.

7 But thou haſt ſav'd us from our foes,
   and haters put to ſhame.
8 In GOD we all the day triumph,
   and ever praiſe thy name

[2 Part.]

9 But now thou ſeem'ſt to caſt us off;
   thou ſhameſt us alſo;
   And with our military troops
   to battle doſt not go.
10 Thou mak'ſt us from our enemies
   baſely to turn our back;
   And they who hate us, for themſelves
   our ſpoils deſerted, take.
11 As ſheep, for meat and ſlaughter doom'd,
   thou giv'ſt us to their hands;
   And ſcatt'reſt our poor captives through
   their barb'rous, heathen lands.
12 Thy people Thou haſt ſold for nought;
   no wealthier art thou found:
13 Thou mak'ſt us a reproach and ſcoff
   to all our neighbours round.
14 Yea ev'n among the heathen Thou
   a proverb doſt us make;
   And people round us in contempt
   at us their heads to ſhake.
15 Before our eyes continually
   appears our great diſgrace;
   And wholly with confounding ſhame
   o'er-covered is our face;
16 By reaſon of the voice of him
   who taunts and vilifies;
   By reaſon of the faces * of
   our ſpiteful enemies.

[3 Part.]

17 But tho' all this be come on us;
   yet we forget not thee,
   Nor falſly to thy covenant
   behave our ſelves do we.

18 Nor have our hearts returned back,
    nor feet from thy way stray'd;
19 Tho' us Thou break'st in dragons dens,
    and cov'rest in death's shade.
20 If our God's name forget, or hands
    to a strange God we raise;
21 Would not GOD find it out? who sees
    the heart's most hidden ways.
22 Yet we're as sheep to slaughter doom'd,
    kill'd for thy sake all day:
23 Wake *Lord!* why sleep'st Thou? rise! nor us
    for ever cast away.
24 Thy countenance away from us,
    O wherefore dost Thou hide?
    Why dost Thou mindless of our grief,
    and great distress, abide?
25 For down to dust our soul is bow'd,
    to earth our bellies cleave;
26 O rise our mighty help, and us
    in thy great mercy save.

PSALM XLV. *A Song of Loves.*

[*The Glories of* CHRIST *in his Royal Character, represented by King* Solomon; *with the Beauty and Happiness of his Spouse the* CHURCH, *represented by King* Pharoah's *Daughter.*]

[1 Part, *Address to* CHRIST.]

1 GOOD matter springs up (1) in my heart;
    my words respect the King; (2)
    And ready as a writer's pen
    my tongue his praise to sing.
2 O fairer than the sons of men; (3)
    what wondrous grace we see
    Pour'd on thy lips; (4) GOD therefore hath
    for ever blessed Thee.

3 Thy

(1) The *Hebrew* seems to signify *Boiling up* as a living Spring of clear, sweet and overflowing Water.
(2) The *Chaldee* renders it—*O King* MESSIAH! i. e. not so much King *Solomon* the *Typical* MESSIAH, as CHRIST the *Real,* inexpressibly surpassing.
(3) i. e. on Account of thy most amiable Excellencies.
(4) i. e. the most gracious Words of thy Lips in Scripture.; *Luke* iv. 16—22. *Joh.* vii. 46.

2 Thy conqu'ring fword, (5) O mighty one,
   gird Thou upon thy thigh ; (6)
   With glorious magnificence
   and comely majefty :
4 Ride profp'rous on the word of truth,
   meeknefs and righteoufnefs ;
   And thy right hand fhall wonders fhow
   of terror and of grace. (7)

5 Within the hearts of the King's foes, (8)
   thine arrows fharp fhall be ; (9)
   Whereby the people overcome,
   fhall fall down under Thee.
6 Thy univerfal throne, O GOD,
   ever and ever is ;
   The fcepter of thy kingdom fway'd
   in perfect righteoufnefs.

7 Thou loveft right, and hateft ill ;
   fo GOD thy God in love
   Anointed Thee with oil of joy
   thy fellow-kings above. (10)
8 Thy fragrant robes with aloes, myrrh,
   and caffia, which Thee clad,
   Brought from the iv'ry palaces, (11)
   confpire to make Thee glad.

E   9 In

(5) i. e. Thine all-conquering Power, Authority and Spirit.
(6) i. e. in Readinefs to conquer all before Thee.
(7) See thefe two Verfes, 3 and 4, glorioufly exemplified in CHRIST, *Rev.* xix. 11—16.
(8) i. e. Thine own Foes ; who are rebellious Sinners.
(9) Thine Arrows of powerful Conviction and Illumination.
(10) i. e. above all the Kings, Conquerors, and Rulers in the World ; yea *far above* all Principalities and Powers, and every Creature named both in Earth and Heaven.*Rev.*xix.16. *Eph.* i. 21. And *thefe two Verfes* 6, 7, are exprefly applied to CHRIST in *Heb.* i. 7, 8.
(11) i. e. *Thy Robes of Righteoufnefs, Beneficence* and *Holinefs* ; inexpreffibly more fragrant than thofe in the fpicy Chambers of the Ivory Palaces of *Solomon.*

9 In thy bright circles (12) round thy view
   kings daughters happy ſtand;
   And the fair Queen (13) in ophir-gold
   appears at thy right hand.

[2 *Part, Addreſs to the* CHURCH.]

10 O daughter, hearken and behold,
   do thou incline thine ear:
   See thine own people thou forget
   and father's houſe ſo dear.
11 Then will thy beauty to the King,
   ſtill more delightful be:
   Yet muſt thou humbly worſhip Him,
   becauſe thy *Lord* is He.
12 The daughter of rich Tyre ſhall ſoon
   her preſents bring to thee;
   And richeſt people ſeek that they
   may in thy favour be.
13 But the King's Daughter is within
   all glorious to behold; (14)
   And all her robes are bright'ned with
   embroideries of gold. (15)
14 Thus to the King in royal robes,
   with needles richly wrought,
   And fellow-virgins (16) in her train,
   ſhe ſhall to Thee be brought.

15 With

(12) Interpreters are greatly divided about the Meaning of this *Hebrew* Word; but conſidering the *Circles* of *Noble Perſons* about *Kings* and *Queens* in their *Royal Palaces*, This ſeems to be the real Idea hinted.
(13) As King *Pharoah's Daughter* is called the *Wife* of *Solomon*, for whom he built a diſtinguiſh'd Palace, 2 *Chron.* viii. 11; ſhe ſeems to be the *Queen* Here and in the following Part of the Pſalm deſcribed, as a ſplendid Emblem of the CHURCH of CHRIST.
(14) i. e. as to her internal Graces, Endowments, Ideas and Joys.
(15) i. e. her ſhining Robes of external Righteouſneſs, Benignity and Holineſs.
(16) *Virgins of Honour*, choſen *Companions* for *Queens*: and may mean thoſe diſtinguiſhingly Fair and Pure Souls who have the Honour of being aſſociated to the *Church* of CHRIST.

15 With gladness and increasing joy,
    they'r brought along in state,
  Till all exulting enter in
    the royal palace gate.
16 In their stead who thy fathers are
    thy lovely sons shall be;
  Whom thou may'st place in all the earth
    in princely dignity.
17 By this my song in ages all,
    I will transmit thy name,
  And make the world with one consent
    thy endless praise proclaim.

PSALM XLVI.

1 GOD is our refuge, strength and shield,
    When num'rous evils us surround;
  In troubles great a present help, *
  And always ready to be found. *
2 Therefore we will not be afraid,
  Altho' the earth removed be,
  Altho' the mountains should be hurl'd
  Into the center of the sea.
3 Nor tho' the seas tempestuous waves
  Should all disturb'd a roaring make,
  Nor tho' her waters swelling rage
  Should make the lofty mountains quake. (*Selah.*)
4 There is a river whose pure streams
  The city of our GOD make glad;
  The holy place which the most high
  Hath happily his dwelling made.
5 For GOD is in the midst of her;
  Therefore be moved shall not she;
  As early morning doth appear
  GOD will her mighty helper be.
6 The nations make tumultuous noise,
  The kingdoms greatly moved are;
  He utters forth his thund'ring voice,
  And all the earth dissolves with fear.

7 The

7 The LORD of armies is with us,
  Who firmly upon Him rely;
  The God of Jacob is for us
  A refuge safe and sure on high. * *(Selah.)*
8 O come, behold what wondrous works
  The mighty LORD around hath wrought;
  What fearful desolations He
  Upon the earth hath justly brought.

9 But yet throughout the wearied earth
  Wars into peace he kindly turns,
  The spear he cuts, the bow he breaks,
  In fire the martial chariot burns.
10 Be still and know that I am GOD!
  I will o'er all exalted be;
  The nations shall exalt my name,
  The earth supreamly honour me.

11 The LORD of armies is with us,
  Who firmly upon Him rely;
  The God of Jacob is for us
  A refuge safe and sure on high. * *(Selah.)*

PSALM XLVII.

1 O All ye people clap your hands,
    To GOD with shouts of triumph sing:
2 For dreadful is the LORD most high,
  O'er all the earth a mighty King.
3 To us the people he subdues;
  Lays nations at our feet in fear:
4 For us an heritage he chose,
  The glory of his Jacob dear. *(Selah.)*

5 GOD is gone up in shouts of joy,
  The LORD with noise the trumpets raise:
6 Sing praise to GOD, sing praise aloud;
  Sing praises to our King, sing praise.
7 For GOD of all the earth is King;
  With all your skill his praise be shown:
8 GOD over all the nations reigns;
  GOD sits upon his holy throne.

PSALM XLVII.

9 To people own'd by Abr'ham's God
  The princes of the nations fly:
  The shields of th' earth to GOD belong;
  O how is He exalted high!

[*Hallelujah-Metre.*]

1 YE people all abroad!
     clap hands and voices raise
  In honour to our GOD,
     and loudly sing his praise.
2   The LORD most high
     a dreadful King,
     rules ev'ry thing
  With majesty.

3 Whole nations of our foes
     beneath our feet has thrown:
4 A fair possession chose
     for us who are his own:
     The dignity
     of Israel
     belov'd so well
  By the most High.   *(Selah.)*

5 GOD is gone up on high,
     the LORD with trumpets sound,
  With shouts triumphantly:
6   O praise our GOD renown'd:
     His praises sing,
     yea loudly raise
     your voice to praise
  Our sov'reign king.

7 For GOD is sov'reign King
     of all the spacious earth:
  With understanding sing
     his praise with sacred mirth:
8   GOD reigns alone,
     the nations stills;
     GOD sits, and fills
  His holy throne.

9 The princes gath'red are,
    the princes of all lands,
 And people far and near
    whom Abr'ham's God commands:
 The shields of all
    the earth abroad
    belong to GOD;
 Him high extol!

PSALM XLVIII.

1 GREAT is JEHOVAH! greatly He
    is to be prais'd on high,
 Within the city of our God,
    his mount of sanctity.
2 How beauteously mount Zion stands?
    her northern sides how fair?
 She is the joy of all the earth;
    the great King's city there!
3 GOD in her palaces is known
    to be a refuge high.
4 For lo, the kings assembled were,
    but pass'd together by.
5 They saw her, and so marvelled,
    they dare not near her stay;
 But troubled and affrighted were,
    and hast'ned fast away.
6 Yea then such terror seiz'd on them,
    such painful agonies,
 As on a lab'ring woman when
    her pangs upon her seize.
7 As when Thou raisest eastern storms
    on the tumultuous sea,
 Thou didst the ships of Tarshish break,
    and drive our foes away.

[2 Part.]

8 In city of the LORD of hosts,
    we see, as we were told
 In our God's city, that our GOD
    will ever her uphold. (Selah.)

PSALM XLIX.

9 O GOD, our thoughts are oft employ'd
   on thy benignity;
But most of all when we are in
   thy house of sanctity.
10 For as thy name, O GOD, so through
   the earth extends thy praise;
And thy right hand we know is full
   of righteousness always.
11 O let mount Zion joyful be,
   and Judah's daughters glad;
Because of all thy judgments now,
   so wondrously display'd.
12 Walk forth and compass Zion round,
   and all about her go;
Her stately tow'rs distinctly count,
   and all their numbers know.
13 Attentively her bulwarks mark,
   her palaces view well;
That to the age to come ye may
   her strength and beauty tell.
14 Because this GOD is our's; our God
   for evermore is he;
Therefore our never-failing guide,
   He ev'n to death will be.

PSALM XLIX.

1 HEAR this all people, and give ear,
   all in the world who dwell;
2 Both low and high, both rich and poor,
   together listen well.
3 I with my mouth variety
   of wisdom will impart,
And prudent knowledge rising from
   the musing of my heart.
4 To an instructive parable
   I'll first incline mine ear;
And then will with my song and harp,
   my mystery declare.

PSALM XLIX.

5 Why should I fear in evil days,
   when the iniquities
Of my stray feet surround me with
   hosts of calamities?

[2 *Part.*]

6 Those men who make their great estates *
   their stay whereon to trust,
Or in th' abundance of their wealth
   who confidently boast;
7 Yet none of them his brother can
   by any means redeem,
Neither to GOD can ever pay
   a ransom meet for him.

8 So dear his life's redemption is,
   that bought it cannot be;
9 That he should still for ever live,
   and not corruption see.
10 For they must see that wise men die,
   the fool, the brutish too,
All perish, and their great estates ||
   to others leave they do.

11 They think their houses ever stand,
   and dwelling places shall
Last to all ages; and their lands
   by their own names they call:
12 But such men in their honour set
   continue but a night;
And like the beasts are soon cut off,
   and quickly perish quite.

13 This way of theirs, their folly is:
   and yet their mouth ‡ and way
Their sons approve, and will pursue;
   like foolish sheep are they.

|| The *same Word* in *Hebrew* with That mark'd thus * in the 6th verse, and therefore signifies the *same Thing*.
‡ *Heb.* i. e. Their stupid Speeches and Advices.

PSALM XLIX.

14 They in the fepulchre * are laid,
    and death fhall them devour;
But in the morning over them
    the juft fhall have the pow'r.

And from the houfes where they dwell,
    the beauty now they have,
Shall utterly confume away
    in the corrupting grave.
15 But GOD my foul will from the pow'r
    ev'n of the grave redeem;
And he will furely me receive
    to live in blifs with him. *(Selah.)*

[3 *Part.*]

16 Be not difturb'd when thou doft fee
    riches to any flow,
Nor when the glory of his houfe
    abundantly does grow.
17 For he fhall carry nothing hence,
    when death his days fhall end;
Nor fhall his glory after him
    into the grave defcend.

18 Tho' he his foul doth greatly blefs,
    while he on earth does live;
And when thou to thy felf doft well,
    men will thee praifes give;
19 Yet in their fathers fteps they tread;
    and when like them they die,
Their wretched anceftors and they
    in utter darknefs lie.

20 For man how great foever here,
    unlefs he's truly wife;
As like a fenfual beaft he lives,
    fo like a beaft he dies.

PSALM L.

PSALM L. A Pfalm of Afaph.

3   THE God ‡ of GODS, ‡ the LORD doth fpeak,
    and to ● earth proclaim;
Ev'n from the rifing of the fun
    to fetting of the fame.

2 From out of Zion's facred hill,
    which, by his dwelling there,
Of beauty the perfection is,
    GOD fhining doth appear.

3 Behold our God in glory comes,
    nor filent in the fkies;
Before him goes devouring fire,
    great † ftorms around him rife.

4 To heav'n He calls out from on high,
    and to the earth below,
That all his equal judgment may
    on his own people know.

5 Gather to me, fays he, my faints,
    bring them before mine eyes;
Who have a covenant confirm'd
    with me by facrifice.

6 And now the heav'ns moft clearly fhall
    his righteoufnefs make known;
Becaufe the mighty GOD Himfelf,
    is fov'reign judge alone. *(Selah.)*

[2 *Part*]

7 Hear O my people Ifrael!
    and I will fpeak on high;
Yea I will teftify to thee,
    that GOD, thy God, am I.

8 For want of facrifices I
    will find no fault with thee,
Or that burnt off'rings have not been,
    continually with me.

‡ In *Hebrew* the Words are ÆL ÆLOHIM, which fignify—*The God of GODS*: and fo the *Septuagint, Syriack* and *Arabick*.
† The *Hebrew* fignifies *a Storm exceeding great, mighty, vehement and terrible*.

9 I'll take no bullocks from thy stalls,
    nor goats from folds of thine :
10 For forrest-beasts and cattle on
    a thousand hills are mine.
11 The fowls that on the mountains fly,
    are all to me well known ;
And all wild beasts which range the fields,
    are with me as my own.

12 If hunger ever could me seize,
    I would not tell it thee ;
For the whole world and fulness of
    the whole belong to me.
13 Or eat the flesh of beeves, or drink
    the blood of goats shall I ?
14 Thanks offer thou to GOD, and pay
    thy vows to the most high.
15 And in the day of thy distress,
    confiding, to me cry ;
And I'll deliver thee, and then
    thou shalt me glorify.

[3 *Part.*]

16 But to the wicked GOD doth say;
    " how dar'st thou to proclaim
My statutes ? or with thy vile mouth
    my covenant to name ?
17 Whereas thou hatest discipline,
    nor wilt instructed be ;
And all my words, as nothing worth,
    thou castest off from thee.
18 When thou dost see a thief, with him
    thou joinest with thy heart;
Yea with unclean adulterers
    thou a partaker art.
19 Thy mouth to evil thou dost give,
    thy tongue deceit to frame,
20 Against thy brother sit and speak,
    thy mother's son defame.

21 These

21 Thefe things thou didſt: I ſilent was:
  and thou didſt me ſurmiſe
Quite like thy ſelf; I'll thee reprove,
  and rank them in thine eyes.
22 O now conſider this, all ye
  who God forgotten have;
Leſt I ſhould you in pieces tear,
  and there be none to ſave.

23 But he whoſe ſacrifice is praiſe,
  great glory yields to me;
And he who orders right his way
  ſhall GOD's ſalvation ſee.

PSALM LI.

A Pſalm of David, *when* Nathan *the Prophet came to him, after he had gone in to* Bathſheba.

1 O GOD, have mercy upon me,
    according to thy grace;
  According to thy mercies great,
    my treſpaſſes efface.
2 O 'waſh me throughly from my guilt,
    and from my ſin me clear;
3 For I my treſpaſs own; my ſins
    before me ſtill appear.

4 Againſt Thee, Thee alone, I ſinn'd;
    the crime was in thy ſight:
  So when Thou ſpeakeſt Thou art juſt;
    and thy whole judgment right.
5 Behold, how in iniquity
    I did my ſhape receive;
  And that my mother ſtain'd with ſin,
    in ſin did me conceive.

6 Behold, thou doſt deſire the truth
    within the inward part:
  O do Thou make me wiſdom know
    in ſecret of my heart.

7 With

PSALM LI.

7 With sprinkling hyssop cleanse Thou me,
and I shall spotless grow:
O wash thou me, and then shall I
be whiter than the snow.

[2 *Part.*]

8 Of joy and gladness make Thou me
to hear again the voice;
That so the bones which Thou hast broke
may yet again rejoice.

9 From the beholding of my sins
O turn away thy face;
And all my vile iniquities
O do Thou quite efface.

10 Clean heart O GOD, in me create;
renew a spirit right
In me: (11) and cast me not away
out of thy happy sight:
Nor thy pure Spirit from me take.

12 Restore the joy to me,
Of thy salvation, and uphold
me with thy spirit free.

13 Then will I teach thy ways to those
who work iniquity;
And happily shall sinners then,
converted be to Thee.

[3 *Part.*]

14 O GOD! of my salvation God! *
free me from guilt of blood;
And of thy saving righteousness
my tongue shall sing aloud.

15 *Lord*, open Thou my lips, and forth
my mouth thy praise shall sing:

16 For Thou desir'st not sacrifice;
or I the same would bring:

Burnt off'rings Thou delight'st not in.

17 Of GOD the sacrifice
A spirit broke: a contrite heart,
GOD, Thou wilt not despise.

18 In

PSALM LI.

18 In thy good pleasure, O do good
    to Zion bounteously:
    The walls of thy Jerusalem,
    O build Thou up on high.

19 The sacrifice of righteousness
    shall please Thee then; and they
    Burnt off'rings, whole burnt off'rings, calves,
    will on thine altar lay.

[*Long Metre.*]

1 O GOD! have mercy upon me,
    According to thy bounteous grace;
    And in thy mercies multitude *
    My many trespasses efface.

2 O wash me throughly from my guilt,
    And from my sin me purify:

3 For all my sins I freely own;
    My sin is always in mine eye.

4 Against Thee, Thee alone, I sinn'd,
    This crime committed in thy sight;
    So when Thou speakest, Thou art just,
    Thy judgment stands intirely right.

5 Behold, I with abasement own,
    I shap'd was in iniquity;
    And that my mother stain'd with sin,
    She ev'n in sin conceived me.

6 Behold, it is the truth that Thou
    Desirest in the inward part:
    O do thou make me wisdom know
    Within the secret of my heart.

7 With sprinkling hyssop cleanse Thou me,
    And I shall pure and spotless grow:
    O wash and make me wholly clean;
    And I shall whiter be than snow.

[2 *Part.*]

8 Of joy and gladness make Thou me,
    To hear again the welcome voice;
    That so the bones which Thou hast broke
    May happily again rejoice.

9 From

PSALM LI.

9 From the beholding of my sins
For ever turn away thine eyes;
And do Thou utterly efface
All my abhorr'd iniquities.

10 O GOD, create in me an heart
Both clean and holy in thy sight,
And in me, O do thou renew
A spirit steady ‡ and upright. ‡
11 Cast me not from thy face; nor take
Thy Holy Spirit now from me:
12 Restore me thy salvation's joy:
Uphold me with thy spirit free.

13 Then from a bless'd experience I
Will sinners teach thy happy ways;
And sinners shall converted be,
To Thee, to love, obey and praise.

[3 *Part.*]

14 O GOD! of my salvation God! *
Deliver me from guilt of blood;
And of thy saving righteousness
My joyful tongue will sing aloud.
15 *Lord*, open Thou these lips of mine,
Which by my sin fast closed are:
And then will my enlarged mouth
Thy praises publickly declare.

16 For Thou desir'st not sacrifice
Of beasts, that I might bring to Thee;
Nor in burnt off'rings dost delight,
That Thou should'st them accept of me.
17 But 'tis a spirit broke for sin,
Is GOD's approved sacrifice:
A broken and a contrite heart,
O GOD, Thou never wilt despise.

18 And

‡ The *Hebrew* seems to comprehend both these Ideas.

18 And now to Zion O do good
In thy good pleasure bounteously;
And of our dear Jerusalem
Do Thou build up the walls on high.
19 Then Thou shalt with the sacrifice
Of righteousness well pleased be;
Burnt off'rings, whole burnt off'rings, calves,
They'll at thine altar offer Thee.

PSALM LII.

A Psalm of David, *when* Doeg *the* Edomite *came and told* Saul, *and said unto him,* 'David is 'come to the House of Ahimelech.'

1 WHY gloriest thou in injury,
  O mighty man of pow'r?
  The goodness of almighty God
  for ever does endure.
2 Thy tongue vents mischief which thy heart
  devises wickedly;
  And like a sharp'ned razor works
  and wounds deceitfully.

3 Thou lovest Evil more than good;
  more to speak wrong than right:
4 And in devouring words dost thou,
  deceitful tongue, delight. ‖
5 God will for ever thee destroy,
  will pull and pluck thee out
  From thine own house; and from the land
  of life, he will thee root. *(Selah.)*

6 The righteous this shall also see,
  with trembling in that day;
  And yet with holy triumph then,
  pointing at thee, shall say;
7 'Lo! this the man that made not GOD
  'his strength; but trusted in
  'His store of riches, and himself,
  'ev'n strength'ned in his sin.' 8 But

‖ Mr. *Baxter* goes no further in *this Psalm,* on Account of the *Curses.* But we turn them into the Form of *Prophesies.*

8 But in the house of GOD am I,
   as a green olive tree;
   And in the grace of GOD my trust
   for evermore shall be.
9 Because thou this hast justly done,
   I'll praise thee evermore;
   And on thy name will wait; for this
   is good thy saints before.

P S A L M LIII. *A Psalm of* David.

1 FOOLS in their heart say, there's no GOD;
   and so corrupt they grow,
   Abominable sins commit,
   and nothing good they do.
2 GOD from the heav'ns hath looked down
   the sons of men to see,
   If any that does understand,
   that seeks to GOD there be.
3 They altogether filthy are,
   they all are backward gone;
   There is not any that does good,
   no not so much as one.
4 The workers of iniquity,
   do they not know at all?
   That they my people eat as bread,
   on GOD they never call.
5 There they shall fear where no fear is:
   for GOD will scatter them
   Who thee beset: them He disdains,
   and thou shalt put to shame.
6 O when will He salvation give
   to his poor Israel,
   From out of his own Zion, where
   He graciously does dwell?

   When GOD his people shall return,
   who have been captive led;
   Then Jacob will be mov'd with joy,
   and Isr'el greatly glad.

P S A L M

PSALM LIV.

A Pſalm of David, *when the* Ziphims *came, and ſaid to* Saul, ' *Doth not* David *hide himſelf with us?*'

1 O Save me in thy name, O GOD,
  and judge me by thy pow'r :
2 O GOD, now to my pray'r give ear,
  and hear in this ſad hour.
3 For ſtrangers whom I never wrong'd,
  yet up againſt me riſe :
 My ſoul, oppreſſors ſeek, who GOD
  ſet not before their eyes. *(Selah.)*

4 Lo GOD my help ; the *Lord* with thoſe
  who my poor ſoul ſuſtain :
5 My foes he'll juſtly recompence,
  and in his truth reſtrain.
6 Then I to Thee ſhall ſacrifice
  with 'grateful willingneſs :
 Yea LORD, becauſe 'tis good, I will
  with praiſe thy name confeſs.

7 For thou haſt me delivered
  from all adverſities ;
 And made mine eye ſee my deſire
  upon mine enemies.

PSALM LV. *A Pſalm of* David.

1 O GOD, thine ear give to my pray'r ;
  and hide not Thou thy face
 From me now ſupplicating Thee,
  and ſuing for thy grace.
2 O be attentive now to me,
  and hear my doleful voice :
 I in my meditation mourn,
  and make a troubled noiſe ;
3 Thro' my foes voice, and face * of thoſe
  who wickedly oppreſs ;
 Who charge iniquities * on me,
  and hate with ſpitefulneſs.

PSALM LV.

4 My heart in me is rack'd with pain;
   death's terrors me furprize;
5 Great fear and trembling on me come,
   and horrors on me feize.

6 O that I like a dove had wings,
   then I away would flee;
   That I might find a fecret place,
   where I at reft could be.
7 Lo, I would wander then afar,
   and in fome defart ftay; *(Selah.)*
8 From ftorms and tempefts here would I
   make hafte to get away.

[2 *Part.*]

9 Confound their pow'r, O *Lord*, and let,
   their tongues divided be:
   For rapine, violence and ftrife,
   I in the city fee.
10 Upon her walls both day and night
    they go their conftant rounds;
    And in the midft all mifchief reigns,
    and grievoufnefs abounds.

11 Yea in the midft, all wickednefs
    at ev'ry corner meets;
    And fraud and circumventing guile
    are ever in her ftreets.
12 'Twas no known foe that flander'd me,
    for that I could abide;
    Nor one who op'nly hated me,
    for I from him could hide.

13 But thou the man, mine equal, who
    haft done me this defpight;
    My guide and my familiar friend,
    in whom I took delight.
14 We oft together counfel took
    in fweet fociety;
    And walk'd on to the houfe of GOD,
    in pleafant company.

15 But

PSALM LV.

15 But death shall seize them; and they shall
   go down alive to hell:
   For wickednesses * in their hearts *
   and in their houses * dwell.

[3 *Part.*]

16 On GOD I'll call; and then the LORD
   to save me will appear:
17 At ev'ning, morning, noon I'll cry;
   and He my voice will hear.
18 For from the war against me rais'd
   He did my soul set free;
   He brought me to a state of peace;
   and many join with me.

19 God will me hear, and humble them:
   He rule did ever bear: *(Selah.)*
   Because they with no changes meet,
   ev'n GOD they do not fear.
20 On him, who was at peace with them,
   they stretched forth their hand;
   Their sacred covenant with him
   by breaking they prophan'd.

21 Smoother than butter were their words,
   while in their heart was war?
   Their speeches softer were than oil,
   but now drawn swords they are.
22 O cast thy burthen on the LORD;
   and He will thee sustain:
   He will not let the just be mov'd,
   but ever them maintain.

23 But Thou, O GOD, wilt send to hell
   the men of blood and guile;
   Who shall not live out half their days:
   but trust in thee I will.

PSALM

PSALM LVI.

PSALM LVI.

Michtam *of* David, *when the* Philiſtines *took him in* Gath.

1 O GOD, have mercy upon me;
 for men would me devour;
 They fighting with me conſtantly,
  oppreſs me with their pow'r.
2 Mine enemies continually,
  to ſwallow me, deviſe;
 And they are many, O moſt high,
  who up againſt me riſe.

3 But whenſoever I'm afraid,
  or terror ſeizes me;
 Then I repair to Thee my ſtrength,
  and reſt my ſelf on Thee.
4 In GOD his faithful word I'll praiſe:
  O GOD, I'll truſt in Thee;
 And then I will not be afraid
  what fleſh * can do to me.

5 They daily wreſt my words to ſpeak
  a ſenſe I never meant;
 And to bring injuries on me,
  their thoughts are wholly bent.
6 In cloſe aſſemblies they combine,
  and wicked projects lay:
 They watch my ſteps, and lie in wait,
  to make my ſoul their prey.

7 Shall they by all their wickedneſs
  eſcape thy dreadful frown?
 O GOD, Thou wilt in anger caſt
  thoſe wicked people down.

[2 *Part.*]

8 Of all my wand'rings to and fro,
  Thou haſt the reck'ning took;
 Into thy bottle put my tears:
  are they not in thy book?

9 Then

9 Then turned back shall be my foes;
   when I cry out to Thee:
   For this I know assuredly,
   that GOD will be for me.
10 In GOD I'll praise his faithful word,
   which He fulfils always;
   His word which He to me performs,
   I in the LORD will praise.
11 In GOD I trust, and will not fear
   what flesh can do to me.
12 Thy vows upon me are, O GOD:
   I'll render praise to Thee.
13 For Thou hast sav'd my soul from death,
   when it was near to me:
   And wilt Thou not uphold my feet,
   and keep from falling * free?
   That I before the face * of GOD
   may walk * in uprightness!
   And in the light of those who live
   continually Thee bless.

PSALM LVII.

Mictam of David, when he fled before Saul in the Cave.

1 O GOD, to me be merciful,
     be merciful to me;
  Because my soul for shelter safe
     betakes it self to Thee.
  Yea in the shadow of thy wings
     my refuge I have plac'd,
  Until these great calamities
     be wholly overpast.
2 I'll cry aloud to GOD most high,
     till heard my cry shall be;
  Ev'n to the God who still performs
     all things most fit for me.
3 From heav'n will He send down, and me
     from their reproach defend,
  Who wou'd devour me: † GOD will forth (†Selah.)
     His truth and mercy send.

4 My

PSALM LVIII.

4 My foul amidſt fierce lions is,
   I fire-brands lie among;
   Men's ſons whoſe teeth are darts and ſpears,
   and like ſharp ſwords their tongue.
5 Above the lofty heav'ns do Thou
   exalt thy ſelf, O GOD:
   O let thy glory be advanc'd
   o'er all the earth abroad.

[2 Part.]

6 They for my ſteps prepar'd a net,
   my foul was bowed down: *
   They dig'd a pit for me; but they
   in midſt thereof are thrown. (Selah.)
7 My heart is fix'd, my heart is fix'd;
   O GOD, I'll ſing and praiſe:
8 Awake my glory, pſalt'ry, harp,
   my ſelf I'll early raiſe.

9 Thy praiſe, O. Lord, will I proclaim
   among the people round:
   Among the nations I with ſongs
   thy praiſes will reſound.
10 For great thy riſing mercy ſpreads,
   ev'n to the heav'ns on high;
   And equally thy truth extends
   up to the cloudy ſky.
11 Above the lofty heav'ns do thou
   exalt thyſelf, O GOD!
   And let thy glory be advanc'd
   o'er all the earth abroad.

PSALM LVIII. Mictam of David.

1 O Ye aſſembly, do ye now,
     ſpeak righteouſneſs indeed?
   In judgment do ye ſons of men
   with uprightneſs proceed?
2 Or do ye miſchief in your hearts
   deviſe; and with your hand
   Then weigh, * and deal out violence
   throughout the injur'd land?

3 The

3 The wicked from the womb estrang'd
   from ev'ry holy way;
  And from the birth their practice is
   to lie and go astray.
4 Ev'n like a serpent's poison is
   the poison that they bear;
  And they are like the adder deaf
   that stops up close her ear.
5 Who will not hear the charmer's voice,
   but deaf will still remain;
  And tho' he charms with utmost skill,
   can no attention gain.
6 Break Thou their teeth within their mouths,
   O GOD of mighty pow'r;
  The great teeth, LORD, of lions young,
   prepared to devour.
7 They shall as waters melt away,
   which run continually;
  And all their arrows ready bent
   shall cut in pieces be.
8 As melting snails shall they dissolve,
   and all shall pass away;
  And even like untimely births,
   that never see the day.
9 E're pots perceive * the blaze of thorns, †
   He'll seize on them alive;
  And bear them in his wrath away,
   as whirlwinds stubble drive.
10 The righteous shall rejoice when they
   this righteous vengeance see;
  And in the blood of impious men
   their feet shall washed be.
11 So men shall say; sure for the just
   there is a recompence;
  Sure there's a GOD, a Judge on earth,
   who justice will dispense,

PSALM

† i. e. So *suddenly*, as before the kindling Blaze of Thorns
  can reach the Pots it flashes under.

PSALM LIX.

PSALM LIX.

Michtam *of* David ; *when* Saul *sent, and they watched the House to kill him.*

1 O Thou my God, deliver me
  from all mine enemies ;
And raise me up above all those
  who up against me rise.
2 Do thou deliver me from them
  who work iniquity ;
And do thou save me from the men
  of blood and cruelty.

3 For lo, they for my soul lay wait :
  the mighty men combine
Against me, LORD, not for my sin,
  nor any fault of mine.
4 They run and ready make themselves,
  for no offence in me :
But O do thou behold, and rise,
  and meet me speedily.

5 Awake therefore, LORD GOD of hosts,
  Thou God of Israel,
To judge the nations : favour none
  who impiously rebel. *(Selah.)*
6 At ev'ry ev'ning they return,
  and like the rav'nous hound,
They make a noise on ev'ry side,
  and range the city round.

7 Behold they belch out of their mouths ;
  within their lips are swords :
' For who is he that hears us speak ?'
  are their disdainful words.
8 Yet Thou, O LORD, wilt laugh at them,
  the heathen all deride.
9 But GOD my strength is, and my tow'r,*
  and in Thee I confide.

F [2 *Part.*]

PSALM LIX.

[2 *Part.*]

10 The God of all my mercies * will
 prevent and succour me;
 And GOD will give me on my foes
 my just desire to see.
11 Them slay not, lest thy people should
 forget thy favour soon:
 But by thy pow'r, O *Lord*, our shield,
 disperse and bring them down.

12 Because their mouths and lips abound
 with sins; thou wilt surprize,
 And take them in their pride, who speak
 such curses and such lies.
13 Thou wilt consume them in thy wrath,
 and make them understand,
 That GOD rules over all the earth,
 who rules in Jacob's land. *(Selah.)*

14 When ev'ning comes shall they return;
 and like a rav'nous hound,
 A discontented noise shall make,
 and range the city round.
15 With hunger they shall roam about,
 in seeking food to eat;
 And murmur as their hunger grows,
 and howl for want of meat.

16 But ev'ry morn I'll sing thy pow'r
 thy mercy loud confess;
 Who art my refuge, and my tow'r, ‡
 in days of my distress.
17 Therefore to Thee, O Thou my strength,
 I praise will ever sing;
 For GOD is my high tow'r, ‡ the God,
 whence all my mercies spring.

PSALM

‡ *Heb.*—My Elevation.

PSALM LX.

Michtam of David, *to teach ; when he strove with* Aram Naharaim, *and with* Aram Zobath ; *when* Joab *returned, and smote of* Edom *in the Valley of Salt,* Twelve Thousand. [2 *Sam.* viii.]

1 O GOD, Thou hast deserted us,
 and scatter'd in disdain !
 Thou hast been awfully displeas'd !
 O turn to us again.
2 The land to tremble thou hast caus'd ;
 didst it asunder break !
 O now the breaches of it heal ;
 for it doth greatly shake !

3 Thou hast thy people made to see
 things that are hard to bear !
 And thou hast caused us to drink
 the wine of trembling fear !
4 But thou a banner hast bestow'd
 on those who Thee revere,
 That it on high before the truth ‖
 displayed may appear. *(Selah.)*

5 That thy beloved people may
 a full deliv'rance have ;
 O hear the fervent pray'rs I make,
 and let thy right hand save !
6 GOD in his holiness * hath spoke ;
 my joy therein is high ;
 Shechem divide, and Succoth's vale,
 measure for mine will I ;

7 Gilead is mine, Manasseh mine,
 who both espouse my cause :
 Ephraim is of my strength the head,
 and Judah gives my laws.

8 Moab

‖ i. e. before the army marching in the Cause of the true Religion.

8 Moab my wafhpot † I will make,
  o'er Edom caſt my ſhoe; ‡
And ye Philiſtia's haughty tribes,
  I'll triumph over you. ‖
9 Who will me to the city lead
  ſo ſtrongly fortify'd?
And who is he that to the land
  of Edom will me guide?
10 Didſt thou not caſt us off, O GOD?
  yet ſtill we look to thee:
Wilt thou not with our armies go?
  and God our leader be?

11 O then to us in our diſtreſs
  thy ſpeedy ſuccour ſend!
For vain it is on human aid
  for ſafety to depend.
12 But by the helping pow'r of GOD
  we ſhall do valiantly;
And He'll our foes tread down, and make
  beneath our feet to lie.

P S A L M LXI. *A Pſalm of* David.

1 GIVE ear, O GOD, to my loud cry,
    and to my pray'r attend;
As from the corners of the earth,
  my cries to Thee aſcend.
2 And now my heart is overwhelm'd,
  ready to fail and die,
O lead me up into the rock,
  that higher is than I.
3 For in my danger Thou haſt been,
  a ſhelter ſafe to me;
A tow'r of ſtrength and ſure defence
  againſt my enemy.

4 Within

† i. e. will uſe as ſuch a Veſſel in mean Services.
‡ To caſt a Shoe over a Perſon, ſeems to have been, among the ancient *Hebrews*, a Sign of Subjection and Servitude.
‖ So it is explain'd in *Pſalm* cviii. 9.

PSALM LXII.

4 Within 'thy tabernacle I,
  for ever will abide;
And in the covert of thy wings
  will truſt and ſafely hide. *(-Selah.)*
5 For Thou, O GOD, haſt heard my vows,
  as They before Thee came;
And gav'it me an inheritance,
  with thoſe who fear thy name.
6 O wilt Thou give this to the King,
  yet many days to ſee;
To many generations let
  his years prolonged be.
7 Let him before the face of GOD,
  for evermore remain;
And let benignity and truth,
  ſecure his happy reign.
8 So will I ever to thy name
  ſing grateful ſongs of praiſe;
And chearfully perform my vows
  thro' all my future days.

PSALM LXII. A Pſalm of David.

1 TRULY my waiting ſoul on GOD,
    in ſilent hope relies:
For my ſalvation wholly does
  from Him alone ariſe.
2 He only my ſalvation is,
  my rock of ſtrength is He;
My only ſure defence and tow'r,
  mov'd much I ſhall not be.

3 How long againſt a man will ye
  plot miſchief? ye ſhall fall;
For as a tott'ring fence ye are,
  and like a bowing wall.
4 To caſt him from his dignity,
  conſpiring they deviſe;
Bleſs with their mouth, but curſe in heart,
  and take delight in lies.

5 My soul wait thou on GOD alone:
    my only hope is He;
6 My rock, my saviour, my high tow'r,
    I shall not moved be.
7 In GOD alone my glory is,
    and my salvation sure:
  In GOD the rock of all my strength
    my refuge most secure.
8 Ye people, place your confidence
    on Him continually:
  Pour out your hearts before his face:*
    GOD is our refuge high.
9 Sure mean men's sons are vanity,
    and high men's sons a lie;
  When all are in a balance laid,
    they rise * like vanity.
10 Then trust not in oppressive ways,
    by rapine grow not vain;
  Nor let your hearts, if wealth increase,
    be set on earthly gain.
11 Once spoken hath the mighty GOD,
    yea, twice I heard Him loud;
  That sov'reign and almighty pow'r
    belongs alone to GOD.
12 Yea boundless mercy appertains
    to Thee, O *Lord,* alone;
  And Thou according to his work
    rewardest ev'ry one.

P S A L M LXIII. *A Psalm of* David,
when he was in the Wilderness of Judah.

1 O GOD, Thou art my God, I will
      betimes for Thee enquire.
  My soul does thirst and long for Thee;
    my flesh for Thee desire.
2 As in a dry and weary * land,
    wherein no waters are;
  To see, as in thy house I've seen
    Thy pow'r and glory there.

3 Because

PSALM LXIII.

3 Becaufe thy loving-kindnefs more
    in goodnefs doth excel,
  Than life it felf, therefore my lips
    thy praifes forth fhall tell.
4 Thus I'll Thee blefs continually,
    while yet alive I am;
  And I thefe hands of mine on high
    will lift up in thy name.
5 With marrow and with fatnefs fill'd
    my longing foul fhall be;
  And then my mouth with joyful lips
    will render praife to Thee.
6 When Thee I to remembrance call,
    as on my bed I lie,
  In watches of the filent night;
    then on Thee mufe do I.
7 Calling to mind, how thou haft been
    a conftant help to me;
  I'll in the fhadow of thy wings
    rejoice exceedingly.
8 My longing foul yet follows hard, †
    and clofely cleaves ‡ to Thee;
  And Thou with thy right hand of pow'r
    in love upholdeft me.
9 But who my foul feek to deftroy,
    go down the pit fhall they:
10 Some flain by fwords, their carcaffes
    fhall be the foxes prey.
11 Yet fhall the King in GOD rejoice:
    and all that by HIM ‖ fwear §
  In HIM ‖ fhall glory: but their mouths
    be ftop'd that liars are.

F 4   *PSALM*

† So *Septuagint, Syriack, Arabick.*
‡ So *Chaldee*, ancient *Latin* and *Montanus*: The *Hebrew* comprizing *both Ideas.*
‖ i. e. GOD.   § i. e. who reverently fwear by HIM, as the only true and adorable GOD.

PSALM LXIV.
A Psalm or Song of DAVID.

1 O Mighty GOD, hear Thou the voice,
   I utter in my pray'r;
 Preserve my life from cruel foes,
   and free me from their fear.
2 From secret plots of wicked men
   O hide me carefully;
 From insurrections of all those
   who work iniquity.
3 Who their ill tongues in malice whet
   and sharpen them like swords,
 And set as arrows in their bows
   to shoot out bitter words.
4 That they in secrecy may shoot
   at those who upright are;
 Yea suddenly against them shoot
   and strike them without fear.
5 In ill designs excite themselves,
   consulting how to lay
 Their snares in utmost secrecy;
   " and who shall see," they say.
6 Injurious evils they search out,
   and search with utmost art:
 Most inward is their plotting thought,
   and deep their subtil heart.
7 But GOD will arrows shoot at them,
   and wound them suddenly.
8 Yea their own tongue shall them confound,
   and all who see them, fly.
9 Yea all around shall fear, and shall
   the work of GOD declare;
 For wisely they shall understand,
   that these his doings are.
10 The just shall in the LORD rejoice,
   and safe on Him rely;
 Yea all of upright heart shall sure
   exult in Him on high.

PSALM

PSALM LXV.

PSALM LXV.
A Pſalm or Song of David.

1 SILENCE ! For Thee, the praiſe O GOD,
doth wait in Zion-hill ;
And all the vows we made to Thee
we chearfully fulfil.
2 O Thou who heareſt humble pray'rs,
which to Thee off'red are,
To Thee all ſons of men ſhall come,
and to Thee we repair.
3 Works of iniquity prevail
againſt us at this day ;
Yet as for our tranſgreſſions, Thou
wilt cleanſe them clear away.
4 O bleſſed is the man of whom
Thou thy free choice doſt make ;
And that he in thy courts may dwell
him near to Thee doſt take.

For there we ſhall be ſatisfy'd,
with thine abundant grace,
With all the good things of thy houſe,
thy choſen holy·place.
5 By dreadful things in righteouſneſs
by Thee wrought wondrouſly,
O God of our ſalvation, Thou
wilt anſwer to our cry :

Who of the ends of all the earth
art the firm hope and ſtay ;
And of all thoſe who far abroad,
are toſs'd upon the ſea.
6 Girded with ſtrength, He fixes faſt
the mountains and high hills ;
7 And all the noiſe of ſeas and waves,
and rage of nations ‡ ſtills.

F 5 [2 *Part.*]

‡ *Heb.—Lamim* ; i. e. *Nations :* and ſo the *Septuagint, Chaldee, Arabick,* ancient *Latin,* and *Montanus,*

[2 *Part.*]
8 All in the utmoſt parts who dwell
 are at thy ſigns afraid;
Yet Thou the goings forth of morn
 and ev'ning makeſt glad.
9 Thou viſiteſt the thirſty earth,
 and mak'ſt it rich with rain:
GOD's river full of water is;
 and Thou prepareſt grain.
10 Her ridges richly wat'reſt Thou,
 her furrows Thou ſet'ſt faſt;
With ſhow'rs Thou mak'ſt her ſoft to be,
 her ſpringing bleſt Thou haſt.
11 Thou with thy goodneſs doſt the year
 adorn as with a crown;
And thy full paths along the clouds,
 drop their rich fatneſs down.
12 On paſtures of the wilderneſs,
 refreſhing they diſtill:
And girt with joy on ev'ry ſide,
 is ev'ry little hill.
13 With flocks the paſtures cloathed are,
 with corn the vallies ſpring;
All over cover'd, all adorn'd,
 they ſhout for joy and ſing.

P S A L M LXVI. *A Song or Pſalm.*

1 O All ye lands, with ſhouts of joy,
  to GOD your voices raiſe:
2 Sing forth the honour of his name,
 and glorious make his praiſe.
3 Say ye to GOD; 'In thy great works
 ' how terrible art thou;
' Thro' thy almighty pow'r thy foes
 ' to Thee are made to bow:
4 ' Yea all the nations of the earth
 ' ſhall bow and ſing to Thee;
' To thine exalted Name ſhall ſing
 ' with joy and melody.' *(Selah.)*

5 Come,

PSALM LXVI.

5 Come, and the mighty works of GOD
   with admiration fee;
   In doings to the fons of men,
   how terrible is He?
6 He turn'd the channels of the fea
   to dry and folid ways.;
   Our fathers pafs'd the flood on foot;
   and there we fang his praife.
7 He by his pow'r for ever rules;
   his eyes the nations fpy;
   Let none who are rebellious dare
   to lift themfelves on high. (*Selah.*)

[2 *Part.*]

8 O all ye people, blefs our God,
   and found aloud his praife;
9 Who puts and holds our fouls in life,
   and feet from fliding ftays.
10 For Thou, O GOD, haft proved us,
   and try'd as filver try'd;
11 Into a net haft wound us faft,
   our loins haft ftraitly ty'd.
12 Men o'er our heads Thou mad'ft to ride,
   thro' fire and floods we paft;
   Yet Thou into a happy place,
   of freedom brought us haft.
13 With off'rings I'll go to thy houfe,
   my vows I'll pay to Thee;
14 Which my lips utter'd and mouth fpake,
   when trouble was on me.
15 Burnt off'rings I will offer Thee,
   that full of fatnefs are;
   The beft of all my flocks and herds,
   with incenfe I'll prepare. *(Selah.)*
16 O come and hearken now to me
   all ye who GOD revere;
   And what He for my foul hath done,
   I'll gratefully declare.

17 My

17 My mouth to Him in my diftrefs
   fent forth my earneft cry:
He heard me, and my joyful tongue
   extolled Him on high.
18 If in my heart I fin allow'd,
   the *Lord* would not give ear:
19 But furely GOD gave ear to me,
   and kindly heard my pray'r.
20 O let this kind and mighty GOD,
   for ever bleffed be;
Who turned not my pray'r from Him,
   nor mercy held from me.

PSALM LXVII. *A Pfalm or Song.*

1 LET GOD be merciful to us,
      and with his favour blefs,
And let Him on us caufe to fhine
   the brightnefs of his face.
2 That fo thy way reveal'd to us
   all the glad earth may know;
And that thy great falvation Thou
   may'ft to all nations fhow.
3 O GOD, let all the people round,
   give praifes to thy name;
Let all the people thro' the world
   thy higheft praife proclaim.
4 O let the nations fing for joy,
   and be exceeding glad;
Thou wilt the people rightly judge,
   and all the nations lead. * *(Selah.)*
5 O GOD, let all the people round
   give praifes to thy name;
Let all the people through the world
   thy higheft praife proclaim.
6 And then the fruitful earth around,
   fhall yield her great increafe;
And GOD, the God who is our own,
   fhall us with plenty blefs.

7 Our

PSALM LXVII. LXVIII.

7 Our GOD will greatly bless us all,
    who his own people are;
  And all the regions of the earth,
    shall Him supremely fear.

[*Hallelujah Metre.*]

1 LET GOD show'r down his grace,
    enrich with gifts divine;
  Let his illustrious face
    on us his people shine:
2   That all below
        the arched sky,
      may Thee and thy
        Salvation know.

3 Let all to GOD give praise,
    with one consent agree:
4 Their voice the nations raise,
    and gladly sing to Thee;
  Thy pow'r obey,
    whose justice shall
  dispose of all,
    All sceptres sway.

5 O GOD, let people praise,
    Thee praise, both great and small:
6 Earth yield shall her increase;
    GOD, our God bless us all.
  GOD will us bless;
    and every where
  all men his fear
    Thro' earth profess.

PSALM LXVIII. A Psalm or Song of David.

1 LET GOD arise, and all his foes
    abroad dispersed be:
  Let all who haters of Him are,
    away before Him flee.
2 As smoke, the wicked Thou wilt drive
    and quite disperse abroad:
  As wax by fire, so shall they melt
    before the face of GOD.

3 But

PSALM LXVIII.

3 But let the righteous all be glad;
   O let them joyful be
Before GOD's face; yea let them all
   rejoice exceedingly.
4 Sing ye to GOD, O sing his praise;
   with joy extol his name:
His name is JAH, and high he rides
   on heav'ns exalted frame.

5 For He a tender father is
   to children fatherless;
And GOD the widow's judge is in
   his place of holiness.
6 GOD sets the single * in an house; *
   frees captives from their bands;
But those who rebels are to Him,
   inhabit thirsty lands.

[2 *Part.*]

7 O GOD, when once Thou didst go forth
   before thy people's face,
And thro' the hideous wilderness
   didst as their leader pass; (*Selah.*)
8 The earth did at GOD's presence shake:
   the heav'ns then drop'd and fell:
Sinai shook at the sight of GOD,
   the God of Israel.

9 O·GOD, Thou on thy heritage,
   didst pour a plenteous rain;
Whereby, Thou, when it weary was,
   didst it revive again.
10 Thy congregation then did make
   their habitation there;
And of thy goodness for the poor,
   O GOD, Thou didst prepare.

11 The *Lord* gave forth his word on high,
   abroad it quickly came;
And great the army was of those
   who published the same.

PSALM LXVIII.

12 The kings of mighty armies fled,
in haste they fled away :
And she that safely stay'd at home,
help'd to divide the prey.

13 Tho' slaves among the pots ye lay;
you soon we did behold,
Like a fair dove with silver wings
and feathers bright with gold.

14 When the Almighty scatter'd kings,
so glorious then ye were ;
Like glitt'ring snow on Salmon-hill,
ye did as bright appear.

[3 *Part.*]

15 Like to the mount of Bashan is
the mountain of our GOD :
More choice than Bashan is the mount
of his design'd abode.

16 Why leap ye so, ye lofty hills?
for this, this is the hill,
Where GOD desires to dwell, and where
the LORD will ever dwell.

17 The chariot † of the mighty GOD
millions of ‡ angels are ;
And still among them is the *Lord*,
as on mount Sinai, there.

18 Thou hast ascended up on high
as our victorious head :
Thou num'rous hosts of captives hast
thy happy captives led.

Thou hast rich gifts receiv'd for men,
for such as did rebel ;
That GOD, whose name is JAH,* with them
might condescend to dwell. ‖

19 O

† *Heb.* in the singular Number.
‡ *Heb.—Twenty Thousand Thousand doubled* ; which is at least *Forty Millions* ; or rather a great Number, for a Number vastly greater and exceeding our Imagination.
‖ Expressly applied to CHRIST's *Ascension*, in *Eph.* iv. 7—13.

PSALM LXVIII.

19 O bleſſed be this gracious *Lord*,
    who daily doth us load
  With many benefits, and is
    of our ſalvation God. (*Selah*.)
20 He of ſalvation is the God,
    who is our God moſt ſtrong;
  And to the *Lord* JEHOVAH do
    iſſues from death belong.
21 But GOD will deeply wound their heads,
    who are his ſtubborn foes;
  The hairy crown of him who ſtill
    on in his treſpaſs goes.

[4 *Part.*]

22 The *Lord* ſaid, I'll bring back again,
    again from Baſhan-land,
  My people thro' the depth of ſeas,
    by my almighty hand.
23 That Thou may'ſt vanquiſh thy proud foes,
    ſo mercileſs and ſtrong;
  And in the chaſe may'ſt dip in blood
    thy foot, and dogs their tongue.
24 Thy goings to thy holy place,
    O GOD, they all have ſeen:
  Thy goings O my God, my king,
    how glorious have they been!
25 Sweet ſingers marching in the van,
    muſicians in the rear;
  And in the midſt a virgin train,
    with timbrels charm the ear.
26 Bleſs GOD thro' all your companies,
    and forth his praiſes tell:
  The ſov'reign *Lord*, O bleſs all ye,
    who ſpring from Iſrael.
27 Princes of Benjamin's ſmall tribe,
    and Judah's heads combine;
  And Zebulon's and Naphtali's
    he glad proceſſion join.

PSALM LXVIII.

28 Thy God commanded all thy strength,
  and thus hath strengthned thee:
  Confirm, O GOD, what Thou for us
  hast wrought so wondrously.

[5 Part.]

29 Ev'n for thy sacred temple sake
  built at Jerusalem,
  The kings around shall come and bring
  their costly gifts with them.

30 Rebuke the spearmen's companies,
  and all the multitude
  Of people fierce as mighty bulls,
  and fatted calves as rude;
  Till all submit and tribute bring
  of silver from afar;
  O scatter Thou the people who
  delight in spoil and war.

31 Princes shall then bow down to Thee
  and come from Egypt lands;
  And Ethiopia shall to GOD,
  stretch out in haste her hands.

32 O sing aloud to GOD with joy,
  ye kingdoms of the earth,
  And to the sov'reign *Lord* O sing
  with psalms in sacred mirth. (*Selah.*)

33 To Him who rides on heav'ns of heav'ns,
  which he of old did found;
  Lo how he sends his awful voice,
  a voice of mighty sound.

34 Ascribe ye boundless pow'r to GOD;
  whose glorious dignity
  Is over Isra'l, and his pow'r
  shines in the lofty sky.

35 O GOD, how terrible art Thou
  out of thy holy place!
  God mighty pow'r his people gives:
  to GOD be all the praise.

PSALM

PSALM LXIX. *A Psalm of* David.

1 SAVE me, O GOD : for mighty streams
   break now into my soul :
2 In depths of mire and floods I sink,
   and torrents o'er me roll.
3 I with my crying weary am ;
   my throat is thereby dry :
   And my eyes fail, while for my GOD
   I wait attentively.

4 Those men who for no cause at all,
   to me great hatred bear
   More than the hairs upon my head
   increas'd in number are.
   Yea mighty are my causeless foes,
   who would me hurt and slay ;
   Then I resigned and gave up
   what I ne'er took away.

[2 *Part.*]

5 O GOD, Thou know'st my foolishness,
   Thou dost it fully see ;
   And all my faults of life and heart,
   lie open clear to Thee.
6 Lord, LORD ‡ of hosts, let none who wait
   on Thee have shame for me ;
   Nor those who seek Thee, Isra'el's God,
   for me confounded be.

7 Because 'tis only for thy sake,
   I suffer this disgrace ;
   And for Thy sake alone it is,
   confusion spreads my face.
8 For Thee, to my own brethren I
   a stranger quite became ;
   And to my mother's children I
   an utter alien am.
9 For of thy house the fervent zeal
   hath ev'n consumed me ; ‖
   And on me their reproaches fell,
   who have reproached Thee.

10 My

‡ Hebrew—*Adonai,* JEHOVAH.
‖ Applied to CHRIST, *Joh.* II. 17.

PSALM LXIX.

10 My weeping, fafting, grief of foul,
to my reproach were turn'd ;
11 A proveib to them I became,
when I in fackcloth mourn'd.

12 Who fat in gates of dignity,
on me did cenfures pafs ;
And I the fubject of the fong
of ftupid drunkards was.
13 But, LORD, in an accepted time
I make my pray'r to Thee :
In thy great mercy, O my GOD,
and faving * truth * hear me.

[3 *Part.*]

14 O refcue me out of the mire,
and me from finking keep :
Free me from thofe who hate my foul,
and out of waters deep.
15 Let not the floods me overflow,
nor the deep fwallow me,
Nor mouth of the devouring grave
upon me clofed be.

16 LORD hear me : for exceeding good
is thy benignity ;
And in thy mercies multitude
O turn and look * to me.
17 O do not from thy fervant hide
thy countenance away ;
For I in grievous trouble am :
hear me without delay.

18 O draw Thou near my troubled foul,
redeem and fet it free ;
And from my powerful enemies,
do Thou deliver me.
19 Thou knoweft all my vile reproach,
my fhame, and my difgrace :
Mine adverfaries and their plots
are all before thy face.

20 My

20 My heart is broken with reproach,
    and full of heaviness:
    I look'd, but found no comforter,
    not one to give me ease.
21 But bitter gall was all the food
    they to me offer'd have;
    And in my parching thirst, for drink
    sharp vinegar they gave. ‖

[4 *Part.*]

22 Before them shall their table prove
    a snare: and Thou wilt make
    Their temporal prosperity
    a trap themselves to take.
23 Thick darkness on their eyes shall come,
    that they shall nothing see:
    And thou shalt make their loins to shake
    for fear continually.

24 Thou wilt thine anger on them pour;
    thy wrath shall seize them fast :*
25 Their palace shall be desolate;
    and all their tents be waste : †
26 For, him whom Thou hast smitten down,
    they persecute the more;
    And vex him with malicious words,
    whom Thou didst wound before.

27 Thou wilt them therefore justly leave
    to add more sin to sin;
    And they thy paths of righteousness
    shall never enter in.
28 Out of the book of living ones
    Thou wilt them wholly blot;
    And in the roll of righteous men,
    they never shall be wrote.

[5 *Part.*]

‖ Applied to CHRIST,—Mat. xxvii. Mark xv. John xix.
† Applied to *Judas Iscariot*, Acts i. 20.

[5 *Part.*]

29 I'm poor, diſtreſs'd : ſalvation grant ;
　　raiſe me, O GOD, on high.
30 I'll praiſe the name of GOD with ſongs,
　　with thanks Him magnify.
31 This will be pleaſing to the LORD,
　　and better in his eyes,
　　Than any bullocks fat † and young, ‡
　　mature for ſacrifice. ‖

32 And when the humble this ſhall ſee,
　　it joy to them will give :
　　And ye who ſeek the bleſſed GOD,
　　your heart ſhall ever live.
33 Becauſe JEHOVAH hears the poor,
　　his priſ'ners won't deſpiſe ;
34 Let heav'ns, earth, ſeas, and ev'ry thing
　　that moves therein Him praiſe.
35 For GOD will Judah's cities build,
　　and Zion he will ſave ;
　　That they may dwell therein, and them
　　for their poſſeſſion have.
36 The children of his ſervants too
　　inherit ſhall the ſame ;
　　And thoſe ſhall have their dwelling there
　　who truly love his name.

P S A L M LXX.

A Pſalm of David, *to bring to Remembrance.*

1 O GOD, from my diſtreſs,
　　make haſte to ſet me free :
　　O LORD, with ſpeed do Thou afford
　　thy ſaving help to me.
2 Let them who ſeek my ſoul,
　　be made to bluſh with ſhame ;
　　And with confuſion turned back
　　who make my hurt their aim.

3 They

† So the *Chaldee* and *Syriack.*
‡ So the *Septuagint, ancient Latin* and *Arabick,*
‖ So *Ainſworth* and *Gejer,*

3 They shall be turned back,
   with shame confounded be;
 As a just recompence to them
   for their insulting me.
4 Let all who seek thy face
   be glad and joy in Thee;
 Who thy salvation love, say still,
   " GOD magnified be."

5 But I'm distress'd, O GOD:
   make haste to me, I pray;
 For Thou my help and saviour art,
   O LORD, make no delay.

PSALM LXXI.

1 JEHOVAH, in my great distress
   I place my trust in Thee:
 O let me not be put to shame
   to perpetuity. *
2 But in thy truth and righteousness ‖
   rescue and set me free:
 O bow to me thy gracious ear,
   and save me speedily.
3 Be Thou the rock where I may dwell,
   and constantly resort:
 To save me Thou commanded hast,
   who art my rock and fort.
4 My God, free me from wicked hands,
   hands cruel, as unjust;
5 For *Lord* JEHOVAH ‡ Thou my hope,
   and from my youth my trust;
6 Thou hast upheld me from my birth,
   thro' all my dang'rous days;
 Yea, from my mother's womb me took;
   and I'll Thee ever praise.

[2 Part.]

‖ The *Hebrew* seems to include both *Righteousness* and *Truth*.
‡ Hebrew—*Adonai*, JEHOVAH.

PSALM LXXI.

[2 *Part.*]

7 To many I a wonder am :
   be Thou my refuge ſtrong ;
8 And let my mouth reſound thy praiſe
   and honour, all day long.
9 In time of my declining age
   O caſt me not from Thee :
   And as I find my ſtrength decay
   O now forſake not me.
10 For my malicious enemies
    againſt me falſely ſpeak ;
    And they who for my ſoul lay wait
    together counſel take.
11 For GOD, they ſay, hath him forſook,
    ' Now perſecute ye him,
    And ſeize him Now ; for there is none
    ' to ſave, or him redeem.'
12 O GOD, in this my great diſtreſs,
    be Thou not far from me ;
    But for my help, O Thou my God,
    come to me ſpeedily.

[3 *Part.*]

14 But I with hope and patience ſtill
    on Thee will waiting be ;
    And I will add yet more and more
    to all the praiſe of Thee.
15 My mouth ſhall forth thy righteouſneſs,
    and thy ſalvation ſhow,
    From day to day ; for of the ſame
    no number do I know.
16 I in the ſtrength of God the LORD
    with joy will ſtill go on ;
    I'll celebrate thy righteouſneſs,
    yea mention thine alone.
17 From my youth up, O gracious GOD,
    Thou haſt inſtructed me :
    And hitherto I have declar'd
    the wonders wrought by Thee.   18 And

18 And now forsake me not, O GOD,
   while old and grey I grow ;
 Till to this age, and all to come
   thy mighty pow'r I show.
19 Also thy righteousness, O GOD,
   is high exceedingly,
 Great are the things which Thou hast wrought,
   O GOD, who's like to Thee !

[4 *Part.*]

20 Thou, who hast caused me to see
   afflictions great and sore,
 Wilt turn, revive me, and with joy
   from depths of earth restore.
21 Yea more than this ; Thou wilt ev'n cause
   my greatness to abound ;
 And with exceeding comfort Thou
   wilt wholly me surround.
22 I with the psalt'ry will Thee praise,
   Thy truth, my God, make known ;
 And with the harp I'll sing to thee,
   O Isr'el's HOLY ONE.
23 Now greatly will my lips rejoice,
   while I sing praise to Thee ;
 So shall my soul because thou hast
   redeem'd and set it free.
24 And as Thou those who sought my hurt
   confounded hast with shame :
 My grateful tongue thy righteousness
   shall ev'ry day proclaim.

P S A L M LXXII. *A Psalm for* Solomon.
[*As the* Typical MESSIAH ; *but with a vastly higher
View to the universal happy and eternal Reign
of* CHRIST *the* Real.]

1 O GOD, Thy judgments give the KING,
     Thy righteousness give to his SON :
2 Then he'll thy people rightly judge,
   And to thy poor see justice done.

PSALM LXXII.

3 The mountains shall abundantly
  To all the people bring forth peace;
  And all the little hills abound
  With joyful fruits of righteousness.
4 Poor of the people he will judge,
  And children of the needy save:
  He will to pieces break all those
  Who with their fraud oppressed have.
5 They shall Thee fear while sun and moon
  Endure, thro' generations all:
6 Like rain on mown grass he will come,
  As show'rs on earth distilling fall.
7 The righteous shall lift up their heads,
  Rejoice and flourish in his reign;
  And till the moon to shine shall cease,
  He will abundant peace maintain.
8 His great and bless'd dominion shall
  Abroad from sea to sea extend;
  And from the river ‖ it shall reach
  Quite to the earth's remotest end.
9 They in the wilderness who dwell,
  In homage bow before him must;
  His foes shall, falling at his feet,
  In low prostration lick the dust.

[2 Part.]

10 The kings of Tarshish and the Isles,
   To him shall costly presents bring;
   Sheba's and Seba's kings their gifts
   To him as their superior King.
11 Yea all the kings throughout the earth,
   To him shall bow, and homage pay;
   And all the nations of the world
   Shall Him as the supream obey.
12 Because he will the needy save,
   When they to him for succour call,
   Those who afflicted are, and those
   Who have no human help at all.

G   13 The

‖ i. e. The great River *Euphrates*.

13 The feeble and neceſſitous,
   He will in tender pity ſpare ;
   He will preſerve and ſave the ſouls
   Of thoſe who poor and needy are.
14 Their ſouls from fraud and violence
   His pow'r and mercy will redeem ;
   And in his eyes their blood ſhall be
   Of precious worth and high eſteem.
15 Long ſhall he live ; and they ſhall bring
   To him of Sheba's fineſt gold :
   Pray'rs ſhall be always made for him,
   And daily he ſhall be extoll'd.
16 Of corn an handful in the earth *
   Tho' on the tops of mountains ſown,
   The fruit ſhall riſe, increaſe and wave
   Like the tall trees of Lebanon.
   And they who in the city dwell
   Shall greatly flouriſh and abound,
   In numbers like the fertile graſs,
   Which grows upon the richeſt ground.
17 His name for ever ſhall endure,
   And ſhall continue as the ſun ;
   In him all nations ſhall be bleſt,
   And him proclaim the BLESSED ONE.
18 O let JEHOVAH bleſſed be,
   The GOD, the God of Iſrael :
   For by Himſelf alone he works
   Such things as wondrous are to tell.
19 O let his glorious name be bleſs'd,
   Eternal as his happy reign :
   And let his glory fill the earth :
   Repeat aloud, AMEN, AMEN.

   [*Common Metre.*]
18 O let the LORD GOD bleſſed be,
    the GOD of Iſrael :
   For by Himſelf alone he works,
    things wonderful to tell.

19 O

PSALM LXXIII.

19 O let his glorious Name be bless'd,
    eternal as his reign;
And let his glory fill the earth:
    repeat, AMEN, AMEN.

PSALM LXXIII. *A Psalm of* Asaph.

1 SURE GOD is good to Israel,
    to those in heart sincere.
2 But as for me, my feet had slipt,
    and nigh to falling were.
3 For I was envious and griev'd,
    the foolish ones to see;
And the ungodly, while they liv'd
    in great prosperity.
4 When they seem'd free from bands of death;
    their strength seem'd firm and sure;
5 No plagues had they, nor griefs, nor pains,
    as other men endure.
6 With pride as with a chain of gold
    encompassed they are;
And cloath'd with violence, the same
    as a rich vest they wear.
7 Out of the fulness of their fat
    extended are their eyes:
And they more prosp'rous state enjoy,
    than what their hearts devise.
8 Corrupted are they, and by words
    in malice out they break;
Oppression openly maintain,
    and loftily they speak.
9 Against the heav'ns they set themselves,
    with daring mouths they talk;
And with mischievous, lawless tongues,
    throughout the earth they walk.

[2 *Part.*]

10 From hence his people hither turn;
    to this perplexing doubt;
When waters of full bitter cups
    are to themselves wrung out.

PSALM LXXIII.

11 And in their folly thus they say;
    'How does God all things know?
    'Does the moſt High look down and ſee
    'all things done here below?'

12 'Behold theſe the ungodly are,
    'who live in eaſe and peace;
   'And they who proſper in the world,
    'whoſe riches ſtill increaſe.

13 'Sure I have waſh'd my heart and hands
    'in innocence in vain:

14 'For ev'ry day I plagu'd have been,
    'each morning ſcourg'd with pain.'

15 But if to ſpeak at ſuch a rate
   I raſhly ſhould pretend,
Of thy dear children I the race
   ſhould grievouſly offend.

16 When this I thought to underſtand,
   it was too hard for me;

17 Till to the houſe of God I went,
   where I their end did ſee.

18 For ſure on places ſlippery,
   theſe men diſpos'd Thou haſt;
And down into deſtruction deep,
   Thou doſt them quickly caſt.

19 How in a moment unawares
   to ruin brought are they?
And how with terrors utterly
   ſhall they conſume away?

20 Like a vain dream when one awakes,
   away their glory flies;
And when O *Lord*, Thou riſeſt up,
   Thou wilt their ſhade deſpiſe.

[3 *Part.*]

21 So weak and troubled was my heart,
   my reins were pierc'd in me;

22 So fooliſh I and ignorant,
   ev'n as a beaſt with Thee.

23 Nevertheleſs

PSALM LXXIV.

23 Neverthelefs continually,
 before Thee yet I ftand;
 Thou haft me alfo ftedfaftly
 upheld by my right hand.
24 Thou with thy conftant counfel wilt
 direction to me give;
 Up afterward Thou wilt on high
 to glory me receive.
25 In heav'n above but Thee alone,
 who is it that I have?
 And there is nothing on the earth
 befides Thee that I crave.
26 My flefh and heart intirely fail,
 but Thou wilt me reftore;
 For of my heart GOD is the ftrength,
 my portion evermore.
27 But lo, they that are far from Thee,
 fhall utterly decay;
 And all who faithlefs ftray from Thee,
 Thou wilt confume away.
28 Whereas for me, 'tis good that I
 ftill near to GOD repair;
 I on the *Lord* JEHOVAH truft,
 thy works all to declare.

P S A L M LXXIV. Mafchil *of* Afaph.

1 WHEREFORE, O GOD, for evermore
 haft Thou rejected us?
 Why fmoaks thy wrath againft the fheep
 of thine own pafture thus?
2 O mind thy flock Thou bought'ft of old,
 this heritage of thine,
 By Thee redeem'd, and Zion-hill,
 where Thou didft dwell and fhine.
3 O lift thy feet, and come and view
 the utter ruins wrought;
 And what the foe with wicked rage
 hath on thy temple brought.

4 For where thy congregations met,
   thy foes roar hideously;
  And there for signs of triumph set
   their ensigns up on high.

5 The man who fell'd thick trees to build
   thy temple, had renown;
6 But now thy foes in spite and rage
   beat all the carvings down.
7 They cast thy holy house into
   the fierce devouring flame,
  And throwing to the ground, defile
   the dwelling of thy name.

8 Yea, now said they, we'll break them all
   with our resistless hand;
  And burn up all the synagogues
   of God throughout the land.

[2 *Part.*]

9 We see no more our wonted signs,
   our prophets all are gone;
  To tell us when these things shall end,
   among us there is none.
10 How long shall these insulting foes
    Thee mighty GOD defame?
   Or shall they always be allow'd
    thus to blaspheme thy name?
11 O wherefore thy right hand of pow'r
    dost Thou from us restrain?
   Out of thy bosom now for us,
    draw forth the same again.
12 For GOD the mighty is my king,
    ev'n from the time of old,
   Working in midst of all the earth
    salvations manifold.
13 Thou didst the mighty sea divide
    by thy superiour pow'r;
   And break the dragons dreadful heads,
    who thro' the waters roar.

14 The

14 The heads of the leviathan ‖
    to pieces Thou didst break;
  To those who in the desart dwelt,
    for meat Thou didst him make.

15 Thou clav'st the fountain and the flood,
    Thou bidst the streams to flow;
  Thou dry'st the mighty rivers up,
    to lead thy people through.
16 The cheerful day, the gloomy night,
    Thou mak'st, and they are thine;
  Thou hast prepar'd the beauteous light,
    and made the sun to shine.

17 Thou all the borders of the earth
    hast set by thy decree:
  The summer and the winter both
    are made and rul'd by Thee.

[3ᵈ *Part.*]

18 O LORD, remember how the foe
    does ev'n Thy self defame;
  And how the foolish people dare
    blaspheme thy sacred name.
19 O do not to this multitude
    thy turtle's soul give o'er;
  For ever do not Thou forget
    th' assembly of thy poor.

20 Thy sacred covenant regard:
    for round about we see
  The earth's dark places filled with
    the feats of cruelty.
21 O let not those who are oppress'd,
    ever return with shame;
  But let the destitute and poor,
    for ever praise thy name.

‖ i. e. not only *Pharaoh*, but also *Amalek*, K. *Arad*, *Sihon*, *Ogg* and *Balak*.

22 Arise, O GOD, plead thine own cause:
   and have in memory,
   How day by day the foolish man
   mocks and reproaches Thee.
23 Forget not Thou the voice of those
   who are thine enemies:
   Their noise and tumults daily grow,
   who up against Thee rise.

PSALM LXXV.
A Psalm or Song of Asaph.

1 TO Thee, O GOD, we render thanks,
   to Thee with praise repair;
   For, that thy blessed name is near,
   thy wondrous works declare.
2 When I † th' appointed season ‡ take,
   which shall the fittest be;
   Then judgment done to ev'ry one
   in righteousness I'll see.
3 The earth would quickly all dissolve,
   with all who dwell therein;
   But I the trembling pillars stay,
   and firmly them sustain. *(Selah.)*
4 I to the foolish people said,
   deal not so foolishly;
   And to the wicked and the proud,
   lift not the horn on high.
5 Raise not your horn aloft, as if
   ye dared the most High;
   But bow your stiff'ned neck, and learn
   to speak submissively.
6 For the promotion which ye seek
   comes neither from the east,
   Nor from the mountains * nor the south,
   the desart, * nor the west.

7 But

---

† i. e. not *Asaph*, but *GOD*, ver. 7. &c. and so *Mariana, Grotius, Muis, Hammond.*

‡ So *all* the *ancient Versions, Castalio, Montanus, Pagnine, English Margin, Hammond,* &c.

PSALM LXXVI.

7 But GOD alone is judge fupream,
   and acts with equity;
His pleafure one man puts below,
   and fets another high.
8 For in JEHOVAH's fovereign hand,
   a mixed cup He hath;
The wine above is fparkling red,
   below are dregs of wrath.

From thence He pours to all around,
   to each as He does pleafe;
But all the wicked wring the dregs,
   and drink the bitter lees.
9 But I'll ‖ extol, and ever fing
   the God of Jacob's praife:
10 The wicked's pow'r I will deftroy,
   the juft to pow'r I'll raife.

PSALM LXXVI.
A Pfalm or Song of Afaph.

1 IN Judah GOD is known: his name
   is great in Ifrael:
2 In Salem his pavilion is:
   in Zion He does dwell:
3 There He the burning arrows * brake,
   the bow, fhield, fword and war: *(Selah.)*
4 More glorious Thou than mounts of prey,
   more excellent by far.

5 They that were ftout of heart are fpoil'd,
   in fleep of death they fall:
The mighty could not find their hands
   or pow'r to help at all.
6 O Thou of Jacob mighty God,
   at thy rebuke and blaft
The charioteers and horfe into
   the fleep of death are caft.

‖ i. e. Every one who fang with *Afaph*; comprehending *David*, and all his *Princes* and *Nobles* round him.

7 Thou, even Thou art terrible,
   whom all should greatly fear:
  O who can stand before thy face,
   if once thy wrath appear?
8 When Thou didst from the heav'ns on high
   cause judgment to be heard;
  The earth in awful silence stood,
   exceedingly it fear'd;
9 When GOD his judgment to dispense
   up as a judge arose,
  The meek of all the earth to save
   from all their mighty foes. *(Selah.)*
10 Assuredly the wrath of men
   shall praises to Thee gain;
  And the remainder of their wrath,
   Thou surely wilt restrain.
11 Vow to the LORD your God, and pay,
   all ye that round Him are;
  To Him who is most terrible,
   your presents bring with fear.
12 The spirit that in princes is,
   asunder cut will He;
  And to the kings throughout the earth
   He terrible will be.

PSALM LXXVII. *A Psalm of* Asaph.

1 With my voice to GOD did cry;
   yea with my voice aloud
  I cry'd to GOD; and graciously
   to me his ear He bow'd.
2 In my distress I sought the *Lord,*
   my sore ran in the night,
  And ceased not; my soul refus'd
   all comfort and delight.
3 I thought on GOD and troubled was
   yet more; without relief;
  I meditated * till my soul
   was overwhelm'd with grief. *(Selah.)*

PSALM LXXVII.

4 In ev'ry watch of tedious night,
   Thou kepſt my ſoul awake;
   My trouble ſwell'd to ſuch exceſs,
   I groan'd, but could not ſpeak.

5 I call'd to mind the days of old,
   with ſignal mercies crown'd;
   Thoſe famous years of ancient time,
   for wondrous works renown'd.

6 Yea, to my mem'ry I recall'd
   the ſongs by night I had;
   I commun'd with my thoughtful heart,
   ſtrict ſearch my ſpirit made.

[2 *Part.*]

7 Alaſs! ſaid I, what will the *Lord*,
   caſt off, and not reſtore?
   And from henceforth will He afford
   no favour any more?

8 Is all his mercy ceas'd and gone?
   muſt that no more avail?
   The gracious promiſes He made,
   ſhall they for ever fail?

9 Or is it true, that to be kind,
   my God forgotten hath?
   And that his tender mercies He
   hath ſhut up in his wrath?

10 Then ſaid I, this my weakneſs is,
   who have no pow'r to ſtand;
   But I'll remember the moſt High,
   and years of his right hand.

11 The works of JAH * I'll call to mind,
   his actions manifold;
   I'll ſurely to remembrance call
   thy wondrous works of old.

12 On all thy works I'll meditate,
   and of thy doings talk.

13 Thy way, O GOD, is Holineſs, ‡
   where Thou doſt ever walk.

[3 *Part.*]

‡ *Hebrew, Arabick, Pagnine, Montanus, Tigurine Verſion,*
and *Tremelius.*

PSALM LXXVIII.

[3 *Part.*]

14 What God fo great as our GOD is?
 Thou God, haft wonders done:
 Among the people Thou thy ftrength
 haft openly made known.

15 Thy people Thou from bondage haft
 by thy ftrong arm fet free;
 Of Jofeph and of Ifrael,
 the vaft pofterity. *(Selah.)*

16 Thee did the waters fee, O GOD,
 Thee fee with trembling fear:
 The mighty deeps with all their waves,
 in great commotion were.

17 The clouds their floods of water pour'd,
 the fkies fent forth a found;
 Thine arrows in thy ftorms of hail
 flew terribly around.

18 Thy dreadful voice from heaven above
 in roaring thunders broke:
 Thy light'nings blaz'd throughout the world,
 the earth in horror fhook.

19 Thy way was in the troubled fea,
 a wondrous way was fhown;
 Thy paths thro' mighty waters were,
 thy fteps cannot be known.

20 By Mofes and by Aaron's hand,
 Thou, as thy people's head,
 Thro' the vaft defart, like a flock,
 didft them in fafety lead.

PSALM LXXVIII. Mafchil *of* Afaph.

1 ATTEND my people to my law,
   incline your lift'ning ear;
 And the inftruction of my mouth*
 with ftrict attention hear.

2 My mouth fhall parables explain,
 and fayings dark of old;

3 What we our felves have heard and known,
 and what our fathers told.

4. Them

PSALM LXXVIII.

4 Them from their children we'll not hide,
   but to their race make known,
   JEHOVAH's praises, and his strength,
   and wonders he hath done.
5 This statute He in Jacob set,
   this law in Isr'el made,
   And charg'd our fathers, they should be
   from race to race convey'd:
6 That generations yet to come,
   them happily may know;
   And children to be born and rise,
   the same to their's may show.
7 That they on the same mighty GOD
   their confidence might set,
   God's works and his commandments keep,
   and never might forget.
8 And might not like their fathers be,
   a stiff, rebellious race;
   A race whose heart not right with God,
   nor spirit stedfast was.

[2 Part.]

9 The sons of Ephraim, tho' well arm'd,
   and carrying warlike bows,
   Yet in the day of battle turn'd
   their backs before their foes.
10 GOD's covenant they neither kept,
    nor in his law would go:
11 His works and wonders they forgot,
    which He to them did show.
12 Things marvellous which he perform'd,
    their fathers had beheld;
    Within the land of Egypt wrought,
    and done in Zoan's field.
13 He cut the sea, and made them pass,
    held back the pressing flood;
    While up in heaps on either side,
    the waters firmly stood.

14 He

PSALM LXXVIII.

14 He led them with a wondrous cloud,
 compos'd of shade and light;
A shelt'ring shade it prov'd by day,
 a light of fire by night.
15 While in the thirsty wilderness,
 the solid rock He clave;
And thence, as from the boundless deeps,
 abundant † drink He gave.
16 Yea from the flinty rock He made
 such streams to gush and flow,
That in full rivers down they ran,
 and water'd all below.

[3 Part.]

17 And yet for all, they more and more
 against Him did transgress;
And more provoked the most High,
 while in the wilderness.
18 First in their hearts they tempted God,
 and did his pow'r distrust;
Then meat requir'd, not urg'd by want,
 but to indulge their lust.
19 Yea spake against the mighty GOD,
 and insolently said,
 ' Can God in such a wilderness,
 ' for us a table spread?
20 ' He smote the flinty rock indeed,
 ' and gushing streams ensu'd;
 ' But can He bread and flesh provide,
 ' for such a multitude?'
21 The LORD with indignation heard,
 and kindled was a flame;
On Jacob, on his Israel,
 the burning anger came.
22 Because their unbelieving hearts
 would not in GOD confide,
Nor trust in his salvation, who
 had them so oft supply'd.

[4 Part.]

† *Hebrew* and *Montanus.*

PSALM LXXVIII.

[4 *Part.*]

23 The clouds He order'd ev'ry night,
   their cravings to relieve;
   The doors of heav'n He op'ned wide,
   the choiceſt food to give.
24 On them He manna rained down,
   and round about them ſpread;
   The corn of heav'n He gave to them,
   ev'n for their daily bread.
25 So men the food of angels eat,
   were fed and ſatisfy'd;
   Yea of his bounty them with meat
   He to the full ſupply'd.
26 He causd an eaſt wind through the air
   to blow at his command;
   And then He brought the ſouth wind forth
   by his almighty hand.
27 He rain'd upon them living fleſh,
   like ſummer's duſt for ſtore;
   And ſhow'red down the feather'd fowls
   as ſand upon the ſhore.
28 Ev'n in their camp and round their tents
   He let them gently fall.
29 They eat, were fill'd, and their deſire
   He fully gave to all.

[5 *Part.*]

30 Yet were they not enſtranged from
   their luſt and murm'ring ſin;
   But while their dainty meat was yet
   their loathing mouths within;
31 The wrath of GOD again aroſe,
   in plagues upon them fell;
   Which ſlew their fat ones, and ſmote down
   the flow'r of Iſrael.

32 And yet for all, they ſinned ſtill;
   his gracious ſoul they grieve:
   And though his works moſt wond'rous were,
   yet they would not believe.

33 Therefore

PSALM LXXVIII.

33 Therefore their sinful days He made,
   in vanity to spend;
Short'ned † their years, and made them waste
   in trouble to their end.

34 When He among them slaughters made,
   they sought Him speedily;
Yea they return'd, and after God
   enquired earnestly.

35 For then they to remembrance call'd,
   how GOD, their rock had been;
And how they had the most high God
   their great redeemer seen.

36 But basely flatter'd with their mouths,
   their tongues ev'n to him ly'd.
37 Their heart was false, nor did they in
   his covenant abide.
38 Yet full of mercy, He forgave,
   nor would them wholly slay,
Nor all his anger raise; but oft
   he turn'd his wrath away.

39 For He remember'd they were flesh
   that could not long remain;
A wind that passes quick away,
   and ne'r comes back again!

[6 *Part.*]

40 How oft did they provoke Him there?
   how oft his heart they griev'd,*
In that same wilderness where He
   their fainting souls reliev'd?
41 Yea they perversely turned back,
   and tempted the most High;
And they to Isr'el's holy One
   set bounds, his pow'r to try.
42 They did not call to mind his hand,
   and that most wondrous day,
When from oppressors He them freed
   and brought them all away.

43 Nor

† *Septuagint, Syriack, ancient Latin, New-England.*

PSALM LXXVIII.

43 Nor all the figns in Egypt's land,
    He wrought before their eyes ;
    Nor wonders done in Zoan's field
    upon their enemies.

44 Their fprings and rivers turn'd to blood,
    that they could drink no more ;
45 Vaft fwarms of flies and frogs
    He fent, them to devour.
46 To caterpillars gave their fruit,
    to locufts gave their toil :
47 With hail did He their vines deftroy,
    great hail † their fig-trees ‡ fpoil.

48 To ftorms of hail their cattle gave,
    which greatly them annoy'd,
    And then to fiery thunder-bolts,
    which terribly deftroy'd.
49 He on them his hot anger, wrath,
    and indignation caft,
    By evil angels whom He fent,
    to vex and lay them wafte.

50 He for his further wrath made way :
    their fouls he did not fave
    From death : and to the murrain plague ‖
    their animals ‖ He gave.
51 Then in the land of Egypt He
    did all the firft-born fmite ;
    And in the tents of cruel Ham
    the chief of all their might.

52 But like a flock of fheep He made
    his people forth to go ;
    And in the defart like a flock
    with care He led them too.

53 He

---

† So *Pagnine, Buxtorf,* and the *Englifh Margin.*
‡ So *Syriack, Arabick,* and *Pfal.* cv. 33. as *DeMuis* obferves.
‖ *Heb. Sept. Chaldee, Syriack, Arabick,* and *Englifh Mragin.*

53 He led them safely through the deeps;
    no cause of fear they found :
    But in the sea's returning waves
    their following foes were drown'd.
54 His people brought into the bounds
    of this his sacred land ;
    This mountain which He purchas'd by
    the work of his right hand.
55 Before them cast the nations out,
    and did their lands divide ;
    And in their tents he plac'd the tribes
    of Ifr'el to reside.

[7 *Part.*]

56 Yet still they tempted, still provok'd,
    and griev'd the GOD most High,
    His sacred testimonies they
    would not keep faithfully :
57 But like their fathers turned back ;
    and faithlesness did show :
    They turned quickly back just like
    a bent deceitful bow.
58 For they with altars him provok'd,
    set up in places high ;
    And with their graven images
    inflam'd his jealousy.
59 GOD hearing this, was wroth, and loath'd
    Ifr'el with hatred great :
60 So Shiloh's tent He left, the tent
    He had among men set.
61 Yea He gave up his ark of strength
    into captivity :
    His glory gave into the hand
    of a vile enemy.
62 His people gave up to the sword,
    to its devouring rage ;
    And was exceeding angry with
    his chosen heritage.

63 The

63 The fire of war confum'd their youth,
   their maids unmarried were:
64 Their priests were slaughter'd in the field,
   no widows mourn'd them there.†

65 But when the *Lord* arose as one
   who rous'd from sleep awakes;
   Yea as a giant rais'd by wine,
   a mighty shouting makes.
66 And on his enemies behind
   He made his strokes to fall;
   And put them all to open shame,
   a shame perpetual.

[8 *Part.*]

67 The tents of Joseph He did then
   and Ephraim's tribe refuse:
68 But Judah's tribe and Zion hill,
   which he had lov'd, did chuse.
69 And there his sanctuary built,
   like palaces on high;
   Like to the earth He founded * hath
   to perpetuity.

70 Of David his young servant He
   the choice did kindly make;
   And from the foldings of the sheep
   the royal Shepherd take.
71 From following the * ewes with young,
   He rais'd him up to feed
   Ifra'l his choice inheritance,
   his people, Jacob's seed.

72 So them he as a shepherd fed;
   and guided all the land,
   In his integrity of heart,
   and skilfulness of hand.

PSALM

† i. e. their Widows had no Opportunity to follow them to their Graves in Mourning.

PSALM LXXIX.

PSALM LXXIX. *A Pfalm of* Afaph.

1 BEHOLD, O GOD, how heathen foes
    Thine heritage invade;
Defile thy holy houfe; in heaps
    Jerufalem have laid.
2 Thy fervants bodies lying dead,
    they caft forth to be meat
To rav'nous fowls; and thy faints flefh
    to favage beafts to eat.
3 Like water they pour'd out their blood
    about Jerufalem;
Their mangled bodies lay abroad,
    and none to bury them.
4 We are become a vile reproach
    to all our neighbours near;
Yea a derifion, and a fcoff
    to all who round us are.
5 How long, O LORD? For evermore
    fhall thus thine anger laft?
How long thy burning jealoufy
    like fire go on and wafte?
6 Thy wrath on heathens Thou wilt pour,
    who own Thee not at all;
And on the kingdoms round who on
    thy name refufe to call.
7 For they have cruelly devour'd
    thy fervant Jacob's race;
And have with fire and fword laid wafte
    his pleafant dwelling place.

[2 *Part.*]

8 Mind not againft us former fins;
    thy tender mercies fhow:
Let them prevent us fpeedily;
    for we're brought very low.
9 Help for the glory of thy Name,
    our Saviour God, this day:
For thy Name fake deliver us,
    and purge our fins away.

10 Why fay the heathen, where's your GOD?
  before us they fhall fee,
  When thy dear fervants blood they fhed
  fhall be reveng'd by Thee.
11 O let the captives fighs afcend
  before thy face on high;
  And let thy mighty arm preferve
  thofe who are doom'd to die.
12 But to our neighbour's bofom Thou
  wilt feven-fold repay,
  For their reproach wherewith, O *Lord*,
  reproached Thee have they.
13 So we thy people and thy flock,
  will ever blefs thy name;
  And from our grateful hearts thy praife
  from age to age proclaim.

PSALM LXXX. *A Pfalm of Afaph.*

1 THOU who lead'ft Jofeph as a flock,
  O Ifra'l's Shepherd hear;
  Who dwell'ft between the cherubims,
  fhine forth in glory there.
2 Before † Manaffeh, Benjamin,
  and Ephr'im : O do Thou
  Stir up thy ftrength, and quickly come;
  to us falvation fhow.
3 Turn us, O GOD, to Thee again,
  and caufe thy countenance
  To fhine forth upon us, and we
  fhall have deliverance.
4 LORD GOD of hofts, how long wilt Thou,
  thus in thine anger fmoke,
  Againft thy people and their pray'rs,
  who Thee alone invoke.
5 Thou feedeft them with flowing tears,
  which foak the bread they eat;
  And for their drink Thou giv'ft them tears
  in meafure very great.   6 Thou

---

† The *Tabernacle* including the *Ark*, in the Wildernefs going before the Faces of *Manaffeh*, *Benjamin* and *Ephraim*.

PSALM LXXX.

6 Thou makest us a strife among
  our neighbours on each side;
Our foes with one another vie,
  who shall us most deride.

7 Turn us again, O GOD of hosts,
  and cause thy countenance
To shine forth upon us, and we
  shall have deliverance

[2 *Part.*]

8 From Egypt Thou hast brought a vine,
  the heathen out didst cast;
And in the land where once they spread,
  thy vine Thou planted hast.

9 Before it room Thou didst prepare
  by thy subduing hand:
And causing it deep root to take,
  it spread and fill'd the land.

10 The mountains high and all around,
  were cover'd with her shade;
And like the cedar trees of God *
  her branches were display'd.

11 Yea, she as far as to the sea
  her growing boughs did send;
And to the mighty River ‡ she,
  her branches did extend.

12 O why then hast Thou broken down,
  its hedge, and laid it bare;
That all who pass along the way
  her fruitful branches tear.

13 'Tis wasted by the savage boar,
  that rushes from the wood;
And all the wild beasts of the field
  devour it for their food.

14 O GOD

‡ The River *Euphrates* being the greatest near the Land of *Canaan*, it went by the name of *the River*.

14 O GOD of hosts, we beg of Thee,
   return again, to thine;
   Look down from heav'n, behold and see,
   and visit this thy vine.
15 The vineyard which with thy right hand
   of pow'r Thou planted hast;
   The very branch which for Thy self
   Thou strongly didst set fast.
16 But now thy vine with fire consumes,
   her branches are cut down;
   At thy rebuke they fade away,
   and perish at thy frown.
17 O with the man of thy right hand,
   let thy hand present be,
   And with the son of man whom Thou
   hast made so strong for Thee.
18 So by thy grace, we never will
   revolt from Thee at all:
   O quick'n us now, and on thy Name
   we gratefully will call.
19 LORD GOD of hosts, turn us again,
   and cause thy countenance
   To shine forth upon us, and we
   shall have deliverance.

PSALM LXXXI. *A Psalm of* Asaph.

1 O To the mighty GOD our strength,
     sing with a shouting voice;
   O to the God of Jacob sing,
   and make a joyful noise.
2 Take up a Psalm, the timbrel bring,
   and with your voices join;
   The pleasant harp and psaltery,
   in consort sweet combine.
3 At the new moon, let trumpets blow,
   and joyful voices raise,
   To celebrate th' appointed time,
   the solemn day of praise.

4 For

PSALM LXXXI.

4 For this to Ifrael of old
   a facred precept was,
And by the God of Jacob this
   did for a ftatute pafs. ¶

5 This witnefs He in Jofeph fet,
   when from th' Egyptian fhore
They went, and heard a voice and fpeech,
   they never heard before.
6 I from the heavy burthens took,
   their fhoulders clear away;
And I their fervile hands fet free
   from lab'ring in clay.

7 When thou waft in great trouble, thou
   to Me for aid didft call;
With pity your diftrefs I faw,
   and fet you free from all.
From thunder clouds I anfwer'd thee,
   my fecret place on high,
And at the ftreams of Meribah,
   I throughly did thee try.

[2 *Part*.]

8 Hear, O my people, and my mind,
   I'll teftify to thee;
To thee, O Ifr'el, if thou wilt,
   but hearken now to Me:
9 Then know, that a ftrange God in thee,
   I never will allow;
Never to any other God,
   fhalt thou prefume to bow.

10 I am the LORD thy God who thee
   from land of Egypt led;
Open thy mouth, and thou by Me
   with plenty fhalt be fed.

11 My

¶ i. e. either the *Monthly New-Moon*, as *Numb*. x. 10. and xxviii. 11—15: See *Lamy*; or rather the *Firft New-Moon beginning their Civil Year*. Lev. xxiii. 23—25. and Numb. xxix. 1—6. So the *Chaldee, Godwyn*, &c.

PSALM LXXXII.

11 My people yet would not give ear
    to the kind voice I spake;
   And Israel would not in me
    their full contentment take.

12 So to the bents of their own hearts
    I gave them up a prey;
   And in their foolish counsels then
    I let them go * astray.

13 O that my people Me had heard,
    and did my voice obey;
   That Isr'el had obedient been,
    and walked in my way:

14 I should within a little time,
    have pulled down their foes;
   And should have turn'd my hand upon,
    such as against them rose.

15 The haters of the LORD had then
    submission paid, tho' feign'd; ‡
   But his own people's happy time
    should ever have remain'd.

16 Yea with the finest of the wheat,
    have nourish'd them should He;
   With honey from the Rock I should
    have satisfied thee.

PSALM LXXXII. *A Psalm of* Asaph.

1 IN the assembly of the great, ‖
   our mighty GOD doth stand,
  As judge among our earthly Gods,
   the Rulers of the land.

2 How long [says He] then will ye dare
    wrong judgment to award?
   The wicked person to accept,
    or partially regard?

‡ So the *Hebrew, Septuagint, Chaldee, Syriack, ancient Latin,* Buxtorf, &c.
‖ i. e. Great in Power.

PSALM LXXXIII.

3 Defend the poor and fatherlefs,
  opprefs'd by worldly might;
  Aid fuch as fuffer injuries,
  and fee ye do them right.
4 The weak and poor deliver ye,
  and needy of the land;
  And rid them from the tyranny
  of ev'ry wicked hand.
5 They know not, nor will underftand,
  in darknefs they walk on:
  All the foundations of the earth
  out of their courfe are gone.
6 I call'd you GODS for your high place,
  fons of the Higheft all;
7 But ye fhall die like common men,
  like other princes fall.
8 Arife, O GOD, and judge the earth,
  and bring oppreffors down:
  For Thou all nations fhalt poffefs,
  and rule them as thine own.

PSALM LXXXIII.
A Song or Pfalm of Afaph.

1 NO longer hold thy peace, O GOD,
    no longer filent be;
  O God no longer fit at reft, *
  and our deftruction fee!
2 For lo, thy num'rous enemies
  rife up tumultuoufly;
  And thofe who hate Thee boaft themfelves,
  and lift their heads on high.
3 Againft thy people they confpire,
  and crafty councils join;
  And to deftroy thine hidden ones, †
  they lay their clofe defign.
4 Come let us cut them off, faid they,
  their nation quite efface,
  That no remembrance may remain,
  of Ifr'el or his race.

5 Yea

† Hidden under the Wing of thy Covenant and Care.

PSALM LXXXIII.

5 Yea they together with one heart,
   in council have combin'd;
And diff'ring people clofe in league,
   againſt Thy felf have join'd.
6 The warlike tents of Edom's race,
   and of the Iſhma'lites,
The people of the Hagareens,
   and of the Moabites.

7 Gebal and Ammon join'd, and they
   with Amalek confpire;
With them the Philiſtines agree,
   and thofe who dwell at Tyre.
8 Yea, mighty Aſhur is combin'd
   with them in amity:
And they have been an arm of ſtrength
   to Lot's pofterity.

9 As once Thou didſt to Midian,
   fo Thou wilt do to them;
Or Jabin's hoſt, and Sifera
   at Kiſhon's ancient ſtream.
10 Who near to Endor fuddenly,
   fell down and periſhed;
And all their carcaſſes as dung,
   upon the earth were fpread.

11 Like Oreb and like Zeeb, Thou
   wilt make their nobles fall:
As Zeba and Zalmunnah fell,
   fo ſhall their princes all.
12 For thus prefumptuouſly they faid,
   come on, and let us take
The houfes of their GOD to us,
   and our poſſeſſion make.

13 But Thou wilt make them, O my GOD,
   as rolling things around;
Or like the chaff blown all about,
   when whirlwinds fweep the ground.

14 As raging fire the forest burns,
    with flames the mountains blaze;
15 So shall thy tempest them pursue,
    and them thy storm amaze.

16 Do Thou, O LORD, their faces fill
    with an abasing shame,
That they may happily be brought
    to seek thy blessed name.
17 Or they shall to confusion come,
    and ever troubled be;
Be put to a perpetual shame,
    and perish utterly.

18 That all may know that Thou alone,
    whom we JEHOVAH call,
Art the most High in all the earth,
    and rulest over all.

PSALM LXXXIV.
A Psalm for the Sons of Korah.

1 HOW amiable, LORD of hosts,
    Thy tabernacles are!
[*Wherein the glories of thy face,
    with wondrous pow'r appear!* ‖]
2 My soul, within me longs, ye faints,
    JEHOVAH's courts to see;
My heart and flesh cry out aloud,
    O living God, for Thee!

3 The sparrow finds herself an house;
    the swallow builds her nest,
Where she may lay and feed her young,
    and she and they may rest;
Ev'n near thy holy altars, where
    they make their safe abode:
And why not I---O LORD of hosts,
    my King, my only God!

‖ As these two Lines are taken from *Psal.* lxiii. 2. where the *Psalmist*, in the same Case, expresses these *Motives* of his *Thirst*: they are plainly alluded to, and implied here.

4 But O how bleſſed then are they,
   who all their happy days
Dwell in thy houſe, and ſee Thee there!
   they will Thee ever praiſe.
5 Yea, O how greatly bleſs'd are they,
   whoſe ſtrength and ſtay Thou art;
Who to thy houſe do trace the way,
   with pleaſure in their heart!

6 Who paſſing Baca's thirſty vale,
   they *Thee* † their fountain make;
And from the pools fill'd with thy rain,
   with cheerfulneſs they take.
7 So they go on from ſtrength to ſtrength,
   and joyfully draw near,
Till they before the God of GODS, ‡
   in Zion all appear.

[2 *Part.*]

8 O Thou JEHOVAH, GOD of hoſts,
   my humble pray'r now hear!
Who of thy Jacob art the God,
   O give a bending ear!
9 O GOD, who art our only ſhield,
   look graciouſly on me,
And with thy happy ſmiles the face
   of thy MESSIAH § ſee.

10 For in thy courts one ſingle day,
   'tis better to attend,
Than 'tis in any other place
   a thouſand days to ſpend.

† The *Hebrew* Particle ſignifies both *it* and *Him.* Lud. *De Dieu,*
Ainſworth, Geir & *Gloſſius* tranſlate it *Him,* (i. e. JEHOVAH)
and by a uſual Figure the Word may ſignify *Thee.*
‡ *Heb.* ÆL ÆLOHIM, i. e. The *God of Gods.*
§ So the *Heb. Septuagint, Chaldee, ancient Latin,* and *Arabick :*
i. e. *David* the *Typical* MESSIAH, and CHRIST the *Real.*

PSALM LXXXV.

In my God's house I rather would,
 ev'n at the threshold ‡ sit, ‖
Than dwell in grand pavillions with
 the wicked and the great.

11 Because the LORD GOD is a sun,
 He is a shield also;
JEHOVAH on his people grace,
 and glory will bestow.
From them who walk in uprightness,
 no good with-hold will He.
12 O LORD of hosts, the man is blest
 who puts his trust in Thee.

PSALM LXXXV.
A Psalm for the Sons of Korah.

1 LORD, Thou didst signal favours show,
 to thine afflicted land;
Jacob's captivity Thou didst
 bring back with mighty hand.
2 Yea Thou thy people didst forgive
 their great iniquities;
And all their aggravated sins
 didst cover from thine eyes. (*Selah.*)
3 Thou all thine anger didst withdraw,
 which on them heavy lay;
And from the fierceness of thy wrath,
 didst wholly turn away.
4 O God of our salvation, now
 return us by thy grace;
And tow'rds us thy displeasure sore,
 O cause Thou quite to cease.
5 Or shall thine anger thus endure,
 against us without end?
And ev'n to generations all,
 wilt thou thy wrath extend?

---

‡ *Hebrew, Pagnine, Montanus, Munster, Junius* and *Tremelius, English Margin. Ainsworth, Bythner,* and Dr. *C. Mather.*
‖ *Castalio, Tigurine* Version, *Piscator, Tirinus, Bythner.*

6 O wilt Thou not return again,
 and us revive, that we
Thy faved people greatly may
 rejoice again in Thee?

7 O great JEHOVAH now to us,
 thy tender mercy fhow;
And thy falvation as a gift
 of grace, on us beftow, *

[2 *Part.*]

8 I'll hear what God the LORD will fpeak
 fpeak to his people peace,
And to his faints: but let not them
 return to foolifhnefs.
9 Sure, his falvation now is nigh,
 to them who Him revere;
That glory may adorn our land,
 and happily dwell there.

10 Mercy and truth have fweet accefs,
 and with great pleafure meet;
And perfect righteoufnefs and peace,
 with mutual kiffes greet.
11 Truth and uprightnefs on the earth,
 out of men's hearts, fhall fpring;
And righteoufnefs from heav'n look down,
 defcend and bleffings bring.

12 Yea ev'ry good thing will the LORD
 give to us bounteoufly:
And then our land fhall her increafe,
 yield with a rich fupply.
13 Before Him righteoufnefs fhall go,
 and all his paths prepare;
And in the way his fteps will guide,
 and place with happy care.

'H 4 [*Six-Line*

PSALM LXXXV.

[Six-Line Long Metre.]

1 LORD, Thou didst favour this thy land;
　Thy Jacob's sad captivity,
．Thou didst return with mighty hand:
2 Yea, Thou forgav'st th' iniquity
　Of this thy flock in former times,
　And thou didst cover all their crimes. *(Selah.)*

3 Thou all thy wrath didst take away:
　From thy hot wrath which flam'd abroad,
　Thou turnedst in that happy day.
4 Of our salvation, O Thou God!
　Convert us now by the same grace,
　And make thy wrath towards us cease.

5 Shall thy wrath on us always lie?
　Wilt thou thy burning wrath extend,
　From generation constantly,
　To generation without end?
6 　Wilt thou not us revive, that we
　Thy people may rejoice in Thee?

7 LORD, let thy mercy now appear;
　And save us in thy boundless grace.
8 What God the LORD will speak, I'll hear:
　For to his people He'll speak peace,
　And to his saints: but they must then
　Ne'er turn to foolishness again.

9 His saving work is nigh at hand,
　Surely, to all that Him revere;
　That glory may dwell in our land.
10 Mercy and truth meet sweetly here,
　Harmonious peace and righteousness,
　Embracing, one another kiss.

11 Truth springs out of the earth below,
　And down from heav'n looks righteousness;
　The LORD will ev'ry good bestow;
　Our land shall yield her great increase.
　Justice shall go before his face,
　And in the way his steps will place.

PSALM LXXXVI.

PSALM LXXXVI.

A Prayer of David.

1 O LORD, bow down thine ear,
  and hearken to my cry;
  For poor and wholly deſtitute
  of other help am I.
2 Preſerve my ſoul, for I
  devoted am to Thee;
  My God, thy ſervant ſave, who makes
  his truſt in Thee his plea.

3 O *Lord* be merciful
  to me, I earneſt pray;
  Becauſe I cry to Thee alone,
  importunate all day.
4 Rejoice thy ſervant's ſoul,
  for I to Thee, O *Lord*,
  Lift up my troubled ſoul, in hope
  that Thou wilt help afford.

5 For Thou, O *Lord*, art good;
  to pardon fully free;
  Yea in thy mercy rich art Thou,
  to all who call on Thee.
6 JEHOVAH to my cry
  O give a gracious ear;
  And to my ſupplications voice
  attend, and kindly hear.

7 In days of my diſtreſs
  I will to Thee complain;
  Becauſe I ſurely know that Thou,
  wilt anſwer me again.
8 Among the GODS, O *Lord*,
  not one is like to Thee;
  Nor any works, that to thy works
  may once compared be.

H 5   [2 *Part.*]

[2 *Part.*]
9 The nations all, O *Lord*,
    whom thy great pow'r did frame,
  Shall come before and bow to thee,
    and glorify thy name.
10 For Thou art high and great;
    the things that Thou haft done,
  Are truly marvellous, and fhow
    that Thou art GOD alone.
11 Teach me thy way of truth,
    and I will walk the fame;
  And LORD, to Thee unite my heart,
    that I may fear thy name.
12 O *Lord* my God, Thee praife,
    with all my heart will I;
  Yea conftantly and evermore,
    thy name will glorify.
13 Becaufe thy mercy is
    exceeding great to me;
  And from the grave and loweft hell,
    Thou haft my foul fet free.

[3 *Part.*]
14 O GOD, the violent
    and proud in troops arife
  Againft me, and they feek my foul,
    nor have Thee in their eyes.
15 But *Lord*, Thou art a God,
    compaffionate and kind;
  Long-fuff'ring Thou, and in thy truth,
    and mercy unconfin'd.
16 O turn to me thy face,
    to me be mercy fhown,
  Thy ftrength, O, to thy fervant give,
    and fave thine handmaid's fon.
17 Shew me a fign for good,
    and let my haters fee
  And be afham'd, becaufe Thou LORD,
    doft help and comfort me.

PSALM LXXXVII.

A Psalm or Song for the Sons of Korah.

1 THE LORD his sacred house doth on
  the holy mountains found;
2 The gates of Zion loves more than
  all Jacob's dwellings round.
3 Exceeding great and glorious things,
  are spoken of abroad,
  Concerning thee, O thou the seat,
  the city of our GOD. *(Selah.)*
4 In those who know me I will name
  Tyre, Rahab, † Babylon,
  In Ethiopia, Palestine,
  were born some of renown;
5 But this of Zion shall be said,
  there many such are born;
  And the most High himself will her
  establish and adorn.
6 Yea when the LORD enrolls their names
  who His own people are,
  To Zion's honour He will say,
  'THIS MAN WAS BORN IN HER.' *(Selah.)*
7 Both those who sing and those who play
  on musick there shall be:
  Yea all my springs of life and grace
  and comfort are in Thee. ‡

PSALM LXXXVII.
[*Six-Line Long Metre.*]

1 HIS sacred dwelling he doth found
  Upon the holy mountain there.
2 To all the tents of Jacob round
  The LORD doth Zion's gates prefer.
3 Most glorious things are spoke abroad
  Of thee, O city of our GOD. *(Selah.)*

4 I'll

† i.e. Egypt. Chald. Munst. Pag. Jun. & Trem. Mol. Ainf. Muis.
‡ i.e. in Thee JEHOVAH, as the original Source; and—in Thee Zion, as the flowing Cistern.

I'll Babylon, and Rahab name,
Who know me, Ethiopia,
Philistia, Tyre: were born in them
Some justly famous in their day.

5 But ZION fam'd for bringing forth
Many renowned for their worth.
The highest will increase her fame,
Establish her and more adorn.

6 And as the LORD writes ev'ry name,
He'll note—THERE SUCH A ONE WAS BORN.

7 Musicians, singers there abound,
And all my springs in Thee are found.

PSALM LXXXVIII.

1 Psalm or Song for the Sons of Korah : Maschil
of Heman *the* Ezrahite.

LORD God, my saviour, day and night
before Thee, loudly cry'd have I:

2 O let my pray'r before Thee come,
And bend thine ear now to my cry.

3 Because my soul's with trouble fill'd,
My life approaches to the grave:

4 Counted with them who to the pit,
Are hastning, and no strength I have.

5 Yea as one free among the dead,
Like to the slain in graves I lie;
Whom by thy hand Thou hast cut off,
And hast no more in memory.

6 Thou lay'st me in the lowest pit,
In darkness as in deepest caves;

7 Thy wrath lies hard on me, and Thou
Afflictest me with all thy waves.

8 My friends thou hast put far from me,
And to them made me loathsome grow;
And I'm in prison shut so fast,
That forth from thence I cannot go.

9 Thro' my affliction great and long,
Mine eye with mourning pines away;
JEHOVAH, loud I call on Thee,
And stretch my hands to Thee all day.

[2 *Part.*]

PSALM LXXXIX.

[2 Part.]

10 Shew wonders to the dead wilt Thou?
  Shall the dead rise and Thee confess?
11 Or doth the grave thy kindness show,
  Destruction tell * thy faithfulness?
12 In darkness are thy wonders known?
  Or are thy acts of righteousness,
  Remember'd or acknowleg'd in
  The land of deep forgetfulness.
13 But LORD to Thee aloud I cry,
  In early morning to Thee pray;
14 Why LORD dost cast my soul from Thee?
  Why from me hide thy face away?
15 I'm poor, afflicted, and to die
  Am ready from my youthful years:
  Distracted and confus'd am I,
  While I endure thy horrid fears.
16 Thy fiery wrath goes over me;
  Thy terrors greatly me dismay;
17 As mighty floods encompass me,
  And rise all round me ev'ry day.
18 My lovers and my choicest friends,
  Thou hast from me removed far:
  And into darkness put away
  Those who my dear acquaintance were.

PSALM LXXXIX.
Maschil of Ethan the Ezrahite.

1 THE mercies of JEHOVAH sing
    for evermore will I:
  I'll with my mouth thy truth make known
    to all posterity.
2 For I have said, Thy mercy shall
    for ever built remain;
  Thou in the heav'ns thy faithfulness
    wilt stedfastly maintain.
3 For with the man whom I did chuse
    a covenant I made,
  And to my servant David swear,
    to what I promised;

4 That

PSALM LXXXIX.

4 That I thy seed establish will
    for ever to endure,
  And will to generations all,
    build up thy throne most sure.
5 And so the heav'ns thy wonders, LORD,
    shall with thy praises ring;
  While thine assembled saints on earth,
    thy faithfulness shall sing.
6 For with JEHOVAH, who is he,
    in heav'n we can compare?
  Who like the LORD among the sons
    of earthly GODS † is there?   † Ælim.

[2 *Part.*]

7 God greatly in the church of saints,
    is to be had in fear,
  And to be reverenc'd of all
    that round about Him are.
8 O LORD of hosts, O mighty * JAH, *
    who like Thee can there be?
  Thy faithfulness on ev'ry side,
    does round encompass Thee.

9 Over the raging of the sea,
    Thou dost dominion bear:
  And when the waves thereof arise,
    by Thee they stilled are.
10 Rahab thou hast in pieces broke,
    and like one slain she lies;
  And with thy mighty arm hast Thou
    dispers'd thine enemies.
11 The heav'ns are thine, the earth is thine,
    which Thou alone hast made;
  The world with all it's fulness; Thou
    hast it's foundations laid.
12 The north and south sides of the world,
    Thou didst extend and frame.
  Tabor and Hermon, mountains high,
    shall triumph in thy name.

[3 *Part.*]

PSALM LXXXIX.

[3 *Part.*]

13 Thou haſt an arm of mighty pow'r,
  thy hand in ſtrength is great,
  And that ſupreme right hand of thine
  aloft on high is ſet.
14 Juſtice and judgment on thy throne,
  have their ſure dwelling place:
  Mercy and truth join'd hand in hand,
  ſhall go before thy face.
15 O bleſſed are the people who
  the joyful ſound do know;
  LORD, in Thy countenance's light,
  they up and down ſhall go.
16 They in thy name ſhall, all the day,
  rejoice exceedingly;
  And in thy righteouſneſs ſhall they
  be lifted up on high.
17 Becauſe the glory of their ſtrength
  they yield alone to Thee;
  And in thy favour ſhall our horn
  of pow'r exalted be.
18 Becauſe JEHOVAH is our ſhield,
  who ſafety gives alone;
  And He who is our ſov'reign King
  is Iſr'el's HOLY ONE.

[4 *Part.*]

19 In viſion then Thou to thy ſaints,
  didſt ſpeak, ' I'll help impoſe,
  ' On One that's mighty, whom I rais'd,
  ' and from the people choſe.
20 ' Among them David I have found,
  ' a ſervant true to Me;
  ' And with my holy oil my King
  ' anointed him to be.
21 ' With whom my hand ſhall firmly be,
  ' mine arm ſhall make him ſtrong:
22 ' On him the foe ſhall not exact,
  ' nor ſon of miſchief wrong.   23 ' And

PSALM LXXXIX.

23 ' And I'll beat down before his face
  ' all his malicious foes ;
  ' And will them greatly plague who shall
  ' in hatred him oppose.

24 ' But lo, my mercy and my truth
  ' with him shall be the same ;
  ' His horn of pow'r shall be on high
  ' exalted in my name.
25 ' His hand of pow'r shall reach afar ;
  ' I'll set it on the sea :
  ' And on the rivers his right hand,
  ' extended wide shall be.

26 ' To me, my father, God, and rock
  ' of safety, he shall cry ;
27 ' I'll place him my first born, above
  all kings in dignity.
28 ' My mercy I will keep for him,
  ' to times which ever last ;
  ' Also my covenant with him,
  ' shall be establish'd fast.

29 ' His offspring also will I make,
  ' ev'n to remain always ;
  ' And I establish will his throne,
  ' as heav'ns eternal days.
30 ' But if his sons forsake my law,
  ' and from my judgments swerve ;
31 ' If they my statutes violate,
  ' my precepts not observe ;

32 ' Their bold transgressions with the rod,
  ' then visit sore will I,
  ' And I with scourges visit will
  ' their cross iniquity.
33 ' My loving kindness yet from him
  ' I'll take not utterly;
  ' Nor suffer will in any wise
  ' my faithfulness to lie.

34 ' The

PSALM LXXXIX.

34 ‘ The covenant I made with him
    ‘ by me shall not be broke ;
    ‘ And what my lips have once pronounc'd,
    ‘ I never will revoke.
35 ‘ Can I to David lie, when by
    ‘ my holiness I've sworn.
36 ‘ Before me last his seed and throne,
    ‘ perpetual as the sun :
37 ‘ And as the moon, by my decree,
    ‘ on high establish'd fast,
    ‘ In heav'n a faithful witness set,
    ‘ for evermore to last.' *(Selah.)*

[5 *Part.*]

38 But now Thou seem'st to cast me off,
   and to abandon me ;
   And with thine own anointed one,
   exceeding wroth to be.
39 Thou seem'st to null thy covenant,
   with him thy servant made :
   His diadem Thou hast profan'd,
   and in the dust hast laid.

40 His hedges all hast broken down,
   his fortresses laid waste ;
41 He's spoil'd by every passenger,
   by neighbours round disgrac'd.
42 His foes right hand Thou hast advanc'd,
   and made them all be glad ;
43 Turn'd his sword's edge, and him to stand,
   in battle hast not made.

44 His glory Thou hast made to cease,
   his throne cast to the ground ;
45 His youthful days made short to be,
   with shame dost him confound.

[6 *Part.*]

46 How long LORD wilt Thou hide thy self ?
   shall it for ever be ?
   How long like as a burning fire
   shall we thine anger see ?

47

47 O call to mind how short a time,
    I shall on earth remain.
  Wherefore hast Thou employ'd thy pow'r,
    to make all men in vain?
48 What man is he that lives on earth,
    who death shall never see?
  Or from the grave's prevailing pow'r,
    what man his soul can free?
49 Thy former loving kindnesses,
    Lord, where do they appear,
  Which in thy truth and faithfulness
    to David thou didst swear? †
50 Remember, Lord, with what reproach,
    thy servants treated are;
  How all the mighty * people's scoffs,
    I in my bosom bear.
51 The scoffs wherewith thy foes, O LORD,
    reproach have laid upon
  The steps of thy MESSIAH ‡ dear,
    thine own anointed one.
52 But bless'd forever be the LORD,
    who doth for ever reign;
  And let the world with one accord
    resound, AMEN, AMEN.

PSALM XC.
A Prayer of Moses, *the Man of GOD.*

1 *L*ORD, Thou hast been our dwelling place,
    our refuge and defence,
  In all the generations past,
    and still our confidence.
2 Before the mountains Thou didst form,
    or earth, and world abroad,
  Thou ev'n from everlasting art
    to everlasting, God.
                                    3 Thou

† So the *Heb. Sept. Chaldee, Syriack, ancient Latin,* and *Arabick.*
‡ So the *Hebrew,* and *all the ancient Versions.*

PSALM XC.

3 Thou to destruction dost reduce
   frail, miserable men;
And to all Adam's * sons Thou say'st,
   return ye back again.
4 For ev'n a thousand years appear
   no more before thy sight,
Than yesterday that now is past,
   or than a watch by night.

5 Thou dost them bear away as with
   a flood that overflows:
Like sleep they are; and as the grass,
   which in the morning grows;
6 Which in the morning flourishes,
   but soon its beauty flies;
When evening comes 'tis all cut down,
   and withers up and dies.

7 For by thy fiery anger we
   consumed are away;
And troubled by thy burning wrath,
   we hastily decay.
8 Thou dost our open trespasses,
   before thy presence place;
And ev'n our secret sins before
   the brightness of thy face.

9 For in thine anger all our days
   away are quickly roll'd;
And all our years we waste away,
   like a short tale soon told.
10 For threescore years and ten the days
   of our short life may be:
Or if by reason of more strength,
   we fourscore years may see;

Yet is this lengthning out * but *sin*,
   toil, *grief* and *vanity*; ∥
And then 'tis speedily cut off,
   and swift away we fly.

∥ The *Hebrew* Word seems to comprehend all these Ideas.

11 O who is he that fully knows
    what pow'r thine anger hath?
   Or who can fully comprehend
    the terror of thy wrath? †

12 O teach Thou us effectually
    to number so our days,
   As that our hearts we may apply,
    to walk in wisdom's ways.

13 JEHOVAH, turn thy self again:
    how long yet shall it be?
   E're thou repent ‡ and comfort ‡ them
    who servants are to Thee?

14 O satisfy us early with
    thy free benignity;
   That so thro' all our days we may
    joy and make melody.

15 According to the days wherein,
    affliction we have had;
   And years of evil we have seen,
    now do thou make us glad.

16 O to thy servants, let thy work,
    thy glorious work appear:
   And show thy glory forth to those
    who their dear children are.

17 The kindness ‖ of the LORD our God,
    let on us ever shine;
   Confirm our handy work for us,
    establish it by thine.

PSALM XCI.

1 HE that does in the secret place
    of the most High reside,
   He under the Almighty's shade,
    securely shall abide.

2 Of

---

† So the *Syriack*.   ‡ Both are implied in the *Hebrew*.
‖ So the *Syriack*; and *all* the *Hebrew Lexicons*, with the *Chaldee* and *ancient Latin*, render it—*the Sweetness* or *Pleasantness*.

2 Of this JEHOVAH, I will say,
   He is my refuge high,
   My strong munition and my God,
   on Him I will rely.
3 Because * He from the fowler's snare,
   will safely keep thee free;
   And from the mortal pestilence,
   will He deliver thee.
4 He with his feathers will thee hide;
   his wings thy trust shall be;
   His truth shall be a certain shield
   and buckler safe to thee.
5 Thou shalt not be with fear dismay'd,
   for terrors in the night;
   Nor for the arrow that by day,
   shoots with the swiftest flight.
6 Nor for th' infection of the plague,
   that does in darkness stray:
   Nor for the slaughter ‖ raging on,
   and wasting at noon-day.
7 Tho' at thy side a thousand fall,
   and at thy right hand lie
   Ten thousand dead; yet none of them
   to touch thee shall come nigh.
8 Only, this awful thing thine eyes
   shall with attention see,
   How they who now live wickedly,
   shall then rewarded be.

[2 *Part.*]

9 Because thou hast JEHOVAH made
   thy dwelling place to be;
   Ev'n the most High, who always was
   a refuge safe to me;
10 Therefore no final injury
   shall ever thee befall,
   Nor any kind of penal plague
   come near thy dwelling shall.   11 For

‖ So *Montanus, Gejer, Grotius,* and the *Lexicons*: i. e. slaughtering Armies.

11 For He'll his angels strictly charge,
   thee ever to attend,
That safely thee in all thy ways
   they ever should defend.
12 They with their hands shall bear thee up,
   lest, if thou be alone,
At unawares thou dash thy foot,
   against a hurtful stone.

13 The lion and the adder fierce
   thou shalt securely tread;
Young lions tread beneath thy feet,
   and crush the dragon's head.
14 'Because he sets his love on Me,
   ' deliver him will I:
' Because he knows and owns my name,
   ' I will exalt him high.

15 ' He shall most freely call on Me,
   ' and I will answer him:
' I will with him in trouble be;
   ' him honour and redeem.
16 ' As best shall be, with length of days,
   ' I will him satisfy:
' And my salvation I will make
   ' him see with joyful eye.'

P S A L M XCII.

A Psalm or Song for the Sabbath-Day.

1 TO Thee, JEHOVAH, thanks to give,
   it is a comely thing;
And to thy name, O Thou most High,
   loud hymns of praise to sing.
2 Thy loving kindness forth to show,
   in early morning light,
And to declare thy faithfulness
   with pleasure ev'ry night.

3 Upon

3 Upon the ten ſtring'd inſtrument,
    and pleaſant pſaltery;
  Upon the harp with ſolemn ſound, ‡
    and high rais'd melody. ‡
4 For Thou JEHOVAH thro' thy work
    haſt made me to rejoice;
  And in thy handy work will I
    triumph with joyful voice.

5 How wondrous are thy works, O LORD!
    how deep are thy decrees!
6 The ſtupid underſtand not this,
    nor fooliſh ſinner ſees;
7 When ſinners ſpring as graſs, and thoſe
    who work iniquity
  Do flouriſh; 'tis that they may be
    deſtroy'd eternally.

8 But Thou, O LORD, as ſov'reign Judge,
    for ever ſhalt remain;
  And Thou, moſt high, ev'n over all
    for evermore ſhalt reign.
9 For lo thy many foes, O LORD,
    Thy foes ſhall quite decay;
  And all who work iniquity
    ſhall be diſpers'd away.

10 My horn of pow'r, as unicorns,
    Thou wilt exalt on high;
  And with freſh oil, from time to time,
    anointed be ſhall I.
11 The downfall of my ſpiteful foes,
    mine eyes ſhall ſee: mine ear
  Of ill men who againſt me riſe,
    the fall ſhall alſo hear.

[2 Part.]

‡ *Hebr. Higaion:* which is thought by ſome to ſignify not only *ſolemn Meditation,* but alſo a *ſolemn Sound* agreable thereto: the *Chaldee* renders it *with Exultation:* and I uſe both the Senſes, agreable to what ſucceeds.

[2 *Part.*]

12 But like the palm-tree flourishing,
 shall be the righteous one;
He shall be like the cedar tree,
 that grows on Lebanon.
13 They that within JEHOVAH's house
 happily planted are,
Within the court-yards of our God,
 shall greatly flourish there.
14 Their fruit they shall when they are grey,
 continue forth to bring;
They shall in fatness grow, and they
 shall still be flourishing.
15 To show JEHOVAH upright is;
 He is a rock to me;
And that He from unrighteousness
 is altogether free.

PSALM XCIII.

1 JEHOVAH reigns: and cloathed is
 with lofty majesty:
JEHOVAH cloaths and girds Himself
 with mighty pow'r on high:
2 The world is so established,
 none move it can but He:
Thy throne is fix'd of old; and Thou
 art from eternity.
3 The floods, O LORD, have lifted up,
 the floods lift up their voice,
The floods have lifted up their waves,
 and make a dashing noise.
4 The LORD on high is mightier far
 than many waters noise:
Yea mightier than the raging seas,
 when all their billows rise.
5 Thy testimonies, LORD, are sure:
 and holiness always
Becomes thy house, and all who there
 assemble for thy praise.

PSALM XCIV.

1 LORD God, to whom alone pertains
   the recompence of wrongs,
O mighty God, shine clearly forth,
   to whom revenge belongs.
2 Thou judge of all the earth wilt rise,
   the proud their wages pay.
3 How long, O LORD, shall wicked men,
   how long triumph shall they?

4 How long shall they break out, and say
   things very hard to bear?
How long shall all those boast themselves,
   who wicked workers are?
5 LORD, they thy people grind to dust,
   thine heritage oppress;
6 The widow and the stranger slay,
   and kill the fatherless.

7 And yet they insolently say,
   JAH * this shall never see,
Nor by the God of Jacob shall,
   these things regarded be.
8 But O ye stupid people, will
   ye never learn to know?
Ye foolish in your hearts and ways,
   wise will ye never grow?

9 He planted ev'ry hearing ear;
   and hear then shall not He?
Who formed ev'ry seeing eye,
   shall He not clearly see?
10 He who the nations doth chastize,
   shall He not chasten you?
He teaches knowledge to all men;
   and shall not He them know?

11 JEHOVAH always clearly sees
   what thoughts men entertain;
He judges and he tries them all,
   and knows they are all vain.

I   [2 Part.]

PSALM XCIV.

[2 *Part.*]

12 O JAH, * how bless'd is he whom Thou
    doft fatherly chaftife ;
    And out of thy moft perfect law
     Thou teacheft to be wife ?
13 That Thou may'ft give him quietnefs,
    till evil times are paft ;
    Until the pit be digg'd, wherein
    the wicked fhall be caft.
14 For fure the LORD will not caft off
    His people utterly;
    Nor his inheritance forfake
    to perpetuity.
15 But judgment fhall to righteoufnefs
    clearly return and reign ;
    And all who are of upright heart,
    fhall follow in her train.
16 Againft the evil doers, who
    will up for me arife ?
    Who ftand for me againft all thofe
    that work iniquities ?

[3 *Part.*]

17 Unlefs the LORD had been my help,
    none other could me fave ;
    My foul had quickly dwelt within
    the filence of the grave.
18 And when I faid, my moving foot
    is ready juft to flide ;
    Thy mercies LORD, then held me up,
    and made me firm abide.
19 Amidft the multitude of thoughts,
    tumultuous in my mind ;
    Still from thy confolations fweet
    my foul delight doth find.
20 What fhall the throne of wickednefs
    have fellowfhip with Thee ;
    Which frameth mifchief by a law,
    and acts it by decree ?

                      21 They

PSALM XCV.

21 They run in crouds againſt the ſouls
  of men both juſt and good ;
  And they condemn to puniſhment,
  thoſe of moſt harmleſs blood.
22 But yet the LORD has always been
  a refuge high * to me ;
  And of my confidence the * rock,
  my God ſhall always be.

23 The LORD our God their miſchief will
  on their own heads repay ;
  In their own malice cut them down,
  yea will them ſurely ſlay.

PSALM XCV.

1 O Come, and let us to the LORD,
  lift up a joyful voice ;
  And to our rock of ſafety ſhout,
  and make triumphant noiſe.
2 Before Him let us early * come
  with thankfulneſs and praiſe ;
  And with the joyful noiſe of hymns
  aloud our voices raiſe. †

3 Becauſe this God JEHOVAH is
  exceeding great and high ;
  And a great King above all GODS,
  in power and majeſty.
4 All the deep caverns in the earth,
  are in his mighty hand ;
  The mountains high in all their ſtrength
  are his, and by Him ſtand.

5 To Him the ſpacious ſea belongs,
  becauſe He made the ſame ;
  And all the land abroad is his,
  for it his hand did frame.

I 2   [2 Part.]

† Inkilemus—as in Montanus.

PSALM XCVI.

[2 *Part.*]

6 O come, and let us all adore,
   bow down, and on Him call;
Come, let us kneel before the LORD,
   the maker of us all.

7 Because He is our God, and we
   his pasture's people are;
And of his hand the sheep, if ye
   to day his voice will hear;

8 ' O let not, as at Meribah,
   ' hardness your hearts possess,
' As in the day of Massah they
   ' did in the wilderness.

9 ' Where your presumptuous ancestors
   ' too boldly tempted Me;
' Where they me prov'd, and where my works
   ' their wondring eyes did see.

10 ' Forty years long I grieved was
   ' with that rebellious race;
' And said, this people err in heart,
   ' and will not know my ways.

11 ' So that to them I sware in wrath,
   ' then kindling in my breast;
' That they should never enter in
   ' my happy place of rest.'

PSALM XCVI.

1 O Sing ye loudly to the LORD
   new songs of sacred mirth;
O sing ye praises to the LORD,
   all people through the earth.

2 O cheerfully sing to the LORD,
   and bless his sacred name;
And his salvation ev'ry day
   to all the world proclaim.

3 His glory in Himself and works,
   among the nations show;
His works that are most marvellous
   let all the people know.

PSALM XCVI.

4 For great, JEHOVAH is indeed,
and greatly prais'd to be;
Above all GODS to be ador'd,
and to be fear'd is He.

5 For of the heathen all the *Gods* † [† Æloni.]
vain and bafe idols are;
But by the LORD, whom we adore,
the heav'ns created were.

6 Glory and comely majefty
appear before his face,
Excelling pow'r with beauty join'd
within his holy place.

7 O to the LORD ye people yield,
and all of ev'ry tribe;
All glory to JEHOVAH yield,
and mighty pow'r afcribe.

8 The glory to JEHOVAH give,
that to his name is due;
Come ye into his courts, and bring
an offering with you.

9 Worfhip the LORD in his abode,
his beauteous, holy place;
And let the univerfal earth
tremble before his face.

10 Thro' nations fay, JEHOVAH reigns,
the world confirm'd fhall be;
It fhall not move, but righteoufly
the people judge will He.

11 O let the heav'ns be glad,
and let the earth rejoice;
The fea and fulnefs of the fame
with roaring make a noife.

12 O let the fields and all therein
with joyful triumph fing;
Then all the trees throughout the woods
with fhouts of joy fhall ring.

13 Before

13 Before the LORD; for lo He comes,
   He comes the earth to try;
   He'll judge his people with his truth,
   the world with equity.

PSALM XCVII.

[*The glorious* Reign *of* CHRIST *on* Earth, *both* at
and after *the* Conflagration, *Heb.* i. 6. *Mal.* iv.]

1 JEHOVAH reigns! O let the earth
   exult with joyful voice:
   And all the multitude of isles
   exceedingly rejoice.
2 Thick clouds and darkness round Him spread;
   and yet the world must own,
   That righteousness and judgment sit
   for ever on his throne.

3 Fire goes before Him; and it burns
   His foes up ev'ry where:
4 His light'nings lighten thro' the world;
   earth sees and shakes for fear.
5 Before JEHOVAH's face, behold
   the mountains melting down;
   Like wax before the *Lord*, who all
   the earth doth rule and own.

6 The heav'ns on high his righteousness
   to all abroad declare;
   And to all people through the earth
   his glory doth appear.
7 All who serve graven images,
   shall now confounded be;
   And all who of their idols boast:
   all GODS † HIM worship ye!

8 Mount

† The *Hebrew* is ÆLOHIM: And the *Septuagint*, *ancient Latin*,
Syriack, and *Arabick*, translate it *Angels*; and so does the
Apostle, and applies the following Word—HIM, to THE
SON of GOD, *Heb.* i. 6.

PSALM XCVII.

8 Mount Zion hears and fees with joy;
   all Judah's daughters are
   Exceeding glad; becaufe O LORD,
   thy judgments now appear.
9 For over all the earth abroad,
   JEHOVAH, Thou art high;
   Supream above all other GODS
   exalted wondroufly.
10 All ye who truly love the LORD;
   all evil hate: for He
   The fouls of all his faints will keep,
   and from the wicked free.
11 For fuch as righteous are, is fown
   a feed of fhining light,
   And of immortal joy for thofe
   who are in heart upright.
12 Rejoice ye righteous in the LORD,
   your joy in Him exprefs;
   And give Him thanks in mem'ry of
   his glorious holinefs.

[*Hallelujah Metre.*]

1 JEHOVAH reigns! the earth
    O let hereat rejoice,
   The num'rous ifles with mirth
   Lift up on high their voice.
2   About Him round
     Dark clouds there went;
     Right and judgment
     His throne do found.
3 Fire goes before his fight,
   Burns up his foes about:
4 The world is fill'd with light,
   By light'nings He fends out.
     The earth doth fear,
     And greatly fhake;
5   The mountains quake,
     And melting are,

PSALM XCVII.

As wax before the LORD,
Before the *Lord*, who is
O'er all the earth ador'd.
6 That righteousness of his
  The heav'ns high shew;
  That all may know,
  On earth below
  His glory view.

7 Who graven images
  Adore, on them abide
  Shall utter shamefulness,
  Who in their idols pride:
  But worship HIM;
  Down to HIM bow,
  Ev'n all of you,
  Whom GODS they name.

8 Zion heard and was glad,
  Glad Judah's daughters were;
  This cause O LORD, they had,
  Thy judgments did appear.

9   For LORD Thou high
  All earth art o'er,
  All GODS before
  In dignity.

10 All ye who love the LORD,
  All evil hate do ye:
  To his saints souls afford
  Protection safe does He;
    Yea He'll command,
    And timely see
    They shall be free
    From wicked hand.

11 For those who righteous are,
  Is sown a shining light,
  And gladness for their share,
  Who are in heart upright,
12   Joy in the LORD;
    With thankfulness
    His holiness
    Ye just record.

PSALM

PSALM XCVIII. *A Pfalm.*

1 O Sing a new fong to the LORD;
 for wonders he hath done,
His right hand and his holy arm
 the victory have won.
2 His great falvation to the world
 JEHOVAH hath made known;
And to the nations all abroad
 his righteoufnefs hath fhown.
3 His mercy to his Ifra'l's houfe
 and truth, remembers He;
And now the ends of all the earth
 Our God's falvation fee.
4 O, to JEHOVAH all the earth,
 make ye a joyful noife;
With raifed voices fhout aloud,
 fing praifes and rejoice.
5 With tuneful harps, and hymns of praife,
 now to JEHOVAH fing.
6 With trumpets and loud cornets fhout,
 before the LORD the King.
7 Let the fea rife, and roar for joy,
 and all that is therein;
The world and all who therein dwell,
 let them be joyful feen.
8 Let the floods clap their lifted hands,
 their waves to praife employ;
And let the mountains fpring aloft,
 as leaping all for joy;
9 Before the LORD: for lo he comes
 the earth, as judge to try;
With juftice He'll the people judge,
 the world with equity.

PSALM XCIX.

1 JEHOVAH reigns as King fupreme;
 let all the nations quake:
He fits enthron'd on cherubims,
 let all the earth then fhake.

2 JEHOVAH great in Zion is,
  above all people high.
3 Thy great and dreadful name let them
  praise for its sanctity.
4 This mighty King does judgment love,
  and equity ordain:
  Both judgment Thou and righteousness
  in Jacob dost maintain.
5 Do ye the LORD our God exalt;
  and bowing worship ye
  Before the footstool of his throne:
  the HOLY ONE is He.
6 When Moses, Aaron, with his priests,
  and Samuel with all
  Who sought his name, cry'd to the LORD,
  He kindly heard their call!
7 He from the cloudy pillar spake,
  and shew'd to them his will:
  The laws and statutes He them gave
  they labour'd to fulfil.
8 Thou didst them hear, O LORD our God;
  a sparing * God Thou wast;
  Tho' for their bold inventions Thou
  didst vengeance take at last.
9 Exalt the LORD our God; and in
  his holy mount adore,
  Because the LORD, who is our God,
  is holy evermore.

PSALM C. *A Psalm of Praise.*

1 SHOUT to JEHOVAH all the earth:
2 With joyfulness the LORD serve ye:
  Before his presence come with mirth,
  And with exulting * melody.
3 Know ye, the LORD is GOD alone;
  Without our aid He did us make;
  We are the people He does own,
  And for his pasture-sheep does take.

4 O enter then his gates with praise;
  And in his courts aloud proclaim
  Your thankfulness to Him always,
  And ever bless his holy name.
5 Because the LORD is ever good;
  His mercy is for ever sure;
  His truth has through all ages stood,
  And will eternally endure.

[*Common Metre.*]

1 O To the LORD a joyful noise,
    now make ye all the earth;
2 With joyfulness JEHOVAH serve;
  before Him come with mirth.
3 Know that the LORD is GOD; and He
  made us without our aid:
  His people and the sheep are we
  in his rich pasture fed.

4 O enter then his gates with praise;
  and in his courts proclaim
  Your thankfulness to Him always,
  and ever bless his name.
5 Because the LORD is ever good,
    His mercy ever sure;
  His truth has thro' all ages stood,
    and ever will endure.

PSALM CI. *A Psalm of* David.

1 OF mercy and of judgment I
    will tune my voice to sing:
  To Thee JEHOVAH both are due,
    to Thee the praise I'll bring.
2 I shall the perfect way discern, †
    when Thou wilt come to me;
  And I'll in uprightness of heart
    walk in my house with Thee.
3 No wicked thing before mine eyes
    will I endure to have:
  I hate their work who turn aside;
    to me it shall not cleave.

4 The

† *Heb,* Understand in the perfect way.

4 The stubborn and the froward heart
   away from me shall go:
I'll make no friendship with the bad,
   nor intimately know.

5 I'll cut him off whose lies defame ‖
   his neighbour secretly:
I will not bear the proud of heart,
   nor him whose looks are high.

6 I'll eye the faithful of the land,
   that they may dwell with me:
And who walk in an upright way,
   shall my attendants † be.

7 But he who acts deceitfully,
   in my house shall not dwell;
Nor shall he stay before my eyes,
   who lies allows to tell.

8 Yea all the wicked of the land,
   early suppress will I;
From the LORD's city cut off all
   who will do wickedly.

PSALM CII.

*A Prayer of the afflicted, when he is overwhelmed,
and poureth out his Complaint before the* LORD.

1 O LORD, now hear my mournful pray'r,
   And let my cry come up to Thee!

2 In this the day of my distress,
Hide not thy face away from me:
Thine ear to me O do thou bend;
In this my time of pressing need,
Wherein I cry aloud to Thee:
O hear and answer me with speed!

3 For as the smoke my days consume,
My bones burnt like an hearth decay;

4 My heart with sorrow smitten is
And with'red like the grass away.

So

‖ Heb.—*who slanders*: which is to defame by Lying.
† See *Pool's Synopsis* and *Bytbner*.

PSALM CII.

So swallow'd up with grief am I,
That I my bread forget to taste.
5 By reason of my groaning voice
My bones ev'n to my skin cleave fast.

6 I'm like a mourning pelican,
In the sad wilderness alone;
Or bittern † in a desart place,
Who nightly makes a dismal moan.

7 I keep awake all night and am
Like to a sparrow all alone,
That on the house-top watching sits,
And for her company hath none.

8 All day my foe reproaches me,
And mad with rage against me swears;
9 That for my bread I ashes eat,
And mix my drink with streaming tears.

10 Thine anger is the cause of all,
Thy wrath which on me dreadful frown'd;
For Thou didst raise me up aloft,
And now hast cast me to the ground.

[2 *Part.*]

11 Like shadows are my days declin'd;
And like the wither'd grass I fall:
12 But LORD, Thou ever dost abide,
Thy memory to ages all.
13 Thou wilt arise; to Zion dear
Wilt now thy tender mercy show;
For now 'tis time to favour her,
Yea the appointed time is Now.

14 For in the very stones thereof
Thy servants take a great delight,
And even her despised dust
Is ever precious in their sight.
15 So all the heathen nations round,
Shall fear JEHOVAH's holy name;
And all the Kings on earth shall see
Thy glory, and revere the same.

† *Eckart in Pol. Synopsis,* and Dr. *Cotton Mather,*

PSALM CII.

16 For when the LORD shall Zion build,
   He in his glory will appear;
17 The poor's petition He'll regard,
   And He will not despise their pray'r.
18 This shall in writ enrolled be,
   For every succeeding race;
   That so the people to be form'd
   Th' eternal JAH * may ever praise.

19 From heav'n his height of holiness,
   The LORD looks down on earth to see,
20 To hear the pris'ners dismal groans,
   And the bound sons of death to free:
21 JEHOVAH's name in Zion-hill,
   His praise in Salem to declare;
22 When people meet to serve the LORD,
   And kingdoms to adore Him there.

[3 *Part.*]

23 Weak in the way my strength He made,
   And of my life cut short the day.
24 In midst of my few days, I cry'd,
   My God, O take me not away.
   Thy years throughout all ages stay:
25 Thou hast the earth's foundations laid
   In elder time: and heav'ns above
   Are works that thine own hands have made.

26 They perish shall: but Thou shalt last,
   And they shall old like garments wear:
   Thou as a vesture shalt them change,
   And they shall changed quite appear.
27 But Thou the same abidest still,
   And of thy years no end shall be: ‖
28 Thy servants race continue shall,
   Their seed establish'd be with Thee.

PSALM

‖ These three Verses, viz. 25, 26, 27, are expresly applied to the SON of GOD, in *Heb.* i, 10, 11, 12.

PSALM CIII.

P S A L M CIII. *A Pfalm of* David.

1 O Thou my foul, JEHOVAH blefs,
his praife aloud proclaim,
Let all my pow'rs in me confpire,
to blefs his holy name.

2 Still O my foul, JEHOVAH blefs,
and ne'er do thou forget
His benefits fo undeferv'd,
fo num'rous and fo great.

3 He who moft gracioufly forgives
all thine iniquities;
He all thy ficknefses removes,
and thine infirmities.

4 Who from the pit * thy life redeems,
when ready to go down;
Does thee with loving-kindnefses,
and tender mercies crown.

5 Who with good things abundantly
doth fatisfy thy mouth;
That like reviving eagles, fo
renewed is thy youth.

[2 *Part.*]

6 Judgment and juftice ftill the LORD,
for all th' opprefs'd will do:

7 His ways to Mofes, and his acts
to Ifra'l's race did fhew.

8 Moft merciful JEHOVAH is,
moft gracious to be found;
To anger He is very flow,
in mercy does abound.

9 Tho' He contend with us a while,
He will not always chide;
Nor keep his anger in his breaft
for ever to abide.

10 He hath not dealt with us in wrath
according to our fin;
Nor has He recompenced us
as our deferts have been.

11 But

PSALM CIII.

11 But as the heav'n above the earth
   in height surpasses far;
His mercy so transcends to all
   who Him supreamly fear.

12 As far as east is from the west
   in their vast distances,
So far hath He remov'd away,
   from us our trespasses.

[3 Part.]

13 The pity of a father's heart
   which he his sons doth bear,
The LORD such pity has for all
   who Him, as children, fear;

14 Because He knows this frame of ours,
   He minds that dust are we;

15 Man's days like grass; like a field-flow'r,
   so flourishing is he;

16 But as the wind swift o'er it moves,
   so quick away it goes;
And thence the place where it appear'd
   no more it ever knows.

17 But yet on * them who fear the LORD,
   His mercy ever is;
And on their children's children, so
   descends his righteousness.

18 On such as keep his covenant
   with strict integrity,
And his commandments bear in mind,
   to do them faithfully.

[4 Part.]

19 The LORD hath in the heav'ns on high
   established his throne:
And as the world his kingdom is;
   He reigns o'er all, alone.

20 O ye his angels that excel
   in strength, bless ye the LORD;
Who his commandments always do,
   and hearken to his word.

PSALM CIV.

21 O all ye armies of the LORD,
  to blefs JEHOVAH join;
 His minifters, who to perform
  his will, with joy combine.
22 O praife the LORD, all ye his works
  with which the world is full,
 In his dominion every where:
  the LORD blefs, O my foul!

PSALM CIV.

1 O Thou my foul, JEHOVAH blefs;
  for Thou art great and high,
 O LORD my God, with honour cloath'd,
  and comely majefty.
2 With fhining robes of light
  Thou doft thy felf array;
 And like a curtain to thy throne
  Thou doft the heav'ns difplay.
3 His chamber-beams on waters lays,
  and clouds his chariot makes,
 And on the wings of mighty winds
  his fteps ferenely takes.
4 His angels active fpirits makes,
  who glad before Him ftand;
 His minifters as lightning fly
  to compafs his command.
5 The deep foundations of the earth
  fo firmly did he lay,
 That never from their fixed place
  fhall they be mov'd away.
6 As with a robe Thou o'er the earth
  didft fpread the fpacious flood:
 Above the mountains higheft head,
  the mighty waters ftood.
7 But then at thy rebuke they fled,
  they dare no longer ftay,
 And at thy thunders dreadful voice
  they hafted quick away.

PSALM CIV.

8 As down they rush, the mountains rise, *
   the vallies sink below; *
   And to the deeps Thou mad'st for them
   tumultuously they flow.

9 There hast Thou set their certain bound,
   which they may not pass o'er;
   That they to overwhelm the earth
   may turn again no more.

[2 Part]

10 He sends the springs and streaming rills
   along the vales to glide;
   Which running all among the hills,
   refresh on every side.

11 Thence drink to the field-beasts he gives,
   their thirst wild asses slake:

12 And on their bord'ring boughs the birds
   their sweetest musick make.

13 From his high chambers plenteous stores
   He waters all the hills;
   And with the fruits of those his works
   the earth He richly fills.

14 For beasts He makes the grass to grow,
   and herbs for human use;
   He makes the earth for ev'ry one
   their various food produce.

15 To glad man's heart He make the earth
   to bring forth grapes for wine;
   Heart-strengthing bread, and suppling oil
   to make his face to shine.

16 JEHOVAH's great and lofty trees
   with sap thence filled are;
   The cedars of mount Lebanon,
   which He hath planted there.

17 Upon their branches cheerful birds
   quite fearless build their nest;
   And lodg'd aloft on stately firs
   the storks securely rest.

18 The

PSALM CIV.

18 The tow'ring mountains for wild goats
   places of refuge are;
   The clefts of rocks for feebler tribes,
   who make their dwelling there.

19 The changing moon He conſtitutes
   the ſeaſons forth to ſhow;
   The ſun his time of going down
   exactly makes to know.

20 Thou doſt the earth with darkneſs ſpread,
   and night ſucceeds the day;
   When wild beaſts creeping from the woods,
   are bold through fields to ſtray.

21 Young lions then range here and there,
   and hunt for prey abroad:
   But when they find no prey, they roar,
   and call for meat to God.

22 But when the ſun begins to riſe,
   and makes the ſhades to fly,
   They all retire to hide themſelves
   and cloſe in dens they lie.

23 Then man goes forth with chearfulneſs
   his labours to begin;
   And plies his work throughout the day,
   till evening calls him in.

[3 *Part.*]

24 How various are thy works, O Lord!
   and with what wiſdom made!
   Thy riches fill the earth within,
   and ev'n all over ſpread.

25 So is this great and ſpacious ſea,
   where ſwarms of creatures creep;
   And ſhoals of fiſh both ſmall and great,
   which traverſe through the deep.

26 There ſail the ſhips amidſt the waves,
   [thy winds give them their way.]
   And there's the great Leviathan,
   Thou mad'ſt therein to play.

27 All

27 All thefe on thee fubmiffive wait,
    and on thy care depend,
  That Thou their Vigour to renew
    may'ft food in feafon fend.
28 That which Thou kindly giv'ft to them,
    they gather for their food;
  Thy lib'ral hand Thou op'neft wide,
    and they are fill'd with good.
29 But when from them Thou hid'ft thy face,
    they troubled are and mourn;
  Thou tak'ft away their breath, they die,
    and to their duft return.
30 Thou fend'ft thy fpirit forth, and we
    a new creation view;
  And with frefh animals the earth
    doft conftantly renew.

[4 *Part.*]

31 The glory of JEHOVAH fhall
    laft to eternity:
  JEHOVAH fhall in all his works
    rejoice exceedingly.
32 If on the earth He turns his eye,
    it trembles at his look:
  If He the mountains does but touch,
    they rife into a fmoke.
33 I'll to the LORD fing chearfully
    throughout my life always;
  Yea, while I have my being, I
    will to my God fing praife.
34 With meditations upon Him
    I fhall be fweetly fed;
  And ever in JEHOVAH I
    fhall be exceeding glad.
35 Sinners from earth fhall be confum'd,
    no more the wicked be:
  O thou my foul JEHOVAH blefs:
  fing HALLELUJAH,* ye.

PSALM

PSALM CV.

PSALM CV.

1 O To JEHOVAH give ye thanks,
   and call upon his name;
   Among the people show his deeds
   and spread abroad his fame.

2 To Him with raised voices sing,
   sing psalms to Him with joy:
   In telling all his wondrous works
   your grateful tongues employ.

3 To glory in his holy name
   with due respect accord:
   And let the hearts of all rejoice
   who humbly seek the LORD.

4 Seek ye the LORD most earnestly,
   his saving pow'r implore:
   O seek the shinings of his face,
   and seek them evermore!

5 Recall to mind what He hath wrought,
   each admirable deed,
   His wonders, and the judgments which
   did from his mouth proceed.

[2 *Part.*]

6 O ye the seed of Abraham,
   his servant and his friend,
   And ye the chosen race who from
   his Jacob dear descend.

7 JEHOVAH the Almighty is
   by covenant our God:
   And his most righteous judgments are
   in all the earth abroad.

8 His covenant He ever minds,
   the word He did command,
   Ev'n to a thousand ages down,
   unshaken still to stand.

9 The covenant which first He made
   with faithful Abraham;
   And then to Isaac with an oath
   He did renew the same;

10 And

10 And then to Jacob for a law,
    He made it firm and sure,
  A covenant to Israel
    which ever should endure.
11 Wherein He said, ' I will to you
  ' the land of Canaan give,
  ' The lot of your inheritance,
  ' where you and your's shall live.'

12 And when in number they were small
    against their foes to stand;
  Yea, at the first but very few,
    and strangers in the land;
13 When they thro' various nations went,
    from realm to realm remov'd;
14 He suffer'd none to do them wrong,
    but kings for them reprov'd.

15 He said to those who sat on thrones,
    let no presumptuous arm
  Dare touch my dear anointed ones,
    nor do my prophets harm.

[3 *Part.*]

16 He call'd a famine on the land,
    and break the staff of bread.
17 But he before had sent a man
    by whom they should be fed:
  Joseph was into Egypt sold,
    and there a slave was made;
18 Whose feet with fetters hurt, his soul
    was pierc'd, in irons laid.

19 Till in due time the blessed word
    of inspiration came,
  A revelation from the LORD,
    that try'd and clear'd his name:
20 And then the king commandment gave,
    that he enlarg'd should be;
  The sov'reign of the nation sent
    and set him fully free.

21 Yea

PSALM CV.

21 Yea made him ruler of his houfe,
    the chief of all his land;
    And all the fubftance he poffefs'd
    committed to his hand.
22 With full commiffion, at his will
    his princes to controul,
    And teach his wifeft fenators
    the wifdom how to rule.
23 His father Ifr'el, with his houfe,
    then into Egypt came;
    And Jacob was a fojourner
    within the land of Ham.

[4 *Part.*]

24 His people then exceedingly
    He multiplied there,
    And made them mightier than thofe
    who their oppreffors were.
25 Their hearts then turn'd that they to hate
    his people, did arife;
    And with his fervants craftily
    to deal, did they devife.
26 His fervant Mofes then He fent,
    Aaron his chofen too;
27 Who did within the land of Ham
    His figns and wonders fhow.
28 He darknefs fent, and made it dark:
    all things his word obey:
29 He turn'd their waters into blood,
    and He their fifh did flay.
30 Great fwarms of frogs fpread o'er their land;
    yea chambers of their kings:
31 His word all forts of flies and lice
    in all their borders brings.
32 For rain he pour'd down ftorms of hail;
    flames on their land he fent:
33 When He their vines and fig-trees fmote,
    yea all their trees He rent.

34 He

34 He spake, and caterpillars came,
   and locusts swarm'd around;
35 Which eat the herbs of all their fields,
   and fruits of all their ground.
36 Then in one dreadful night He slew
   their first-born thro' the land,
   The chief of all their strength, ev'n by
   a mighty angel's hand.

[5 *Part.*]

37 But thence with gold and silver He
   His people made to pass;
   Nor had they one among their tribes
   that faint or feeble was.
38 All Egypt was exceeding glad,
   to see them thence depart;
   So great a fear of Jacob's race,
   had seiz'd on ev'ry heart.
39 By day he for a cov'ring spread
   a cloud; and in the night
   He made it like a shining fire,
   to give them kindly light.
40 He brought them living quails for food,
   when flesh they ask'd to have;
   And satisfy'd them with the bread
   which then from heav'n He gave.
41 He open'd wide the flinty rock,
   there gushed out a stream;
   Which through the dry and desart land
   in rivers follow'd them.
42 He on his holy promises,
   and servant Abr'ham thought:
43 With joy his people, and with songs
   He forth his chosen brought.
44 And then to them the pleasant lands
   He of the heathen gave,
   That of the nations labours they
   inheritance might have.

45 That

45 That they his statutes might observe
   in perfect purity;
   And in full freedom keep his laws:
   sing HALLELUJAH * ye!

PSALM CVI.

1 SING HALLELUJAH! to the LORD
   give thanks; for good is He,
   Because his mercy doth endure
   ev'n to eternity.
2 Who can the LORD's great pow'rs † declare,
   or set forth all his praise?
3 Blessed are they who judgment keep,
   and justice do always.

4 LORD mind me with the favour Thou
   dost to thy people bear;
   And with thy great salvation me
   to visit now appear.
5 That I may see thy nation's good
   which Thou hast made thy choice;
   And glory with thy heritage,
   and in their joy rejoice.

[2 *Part.*]

6 We with our fathers sinned have,
   have sinned ev'ry one,
   Have trespassed exceedingly,
   and wickedly have done.
7 The mighty wonders Thou hast wrought
   in the Egyptian land,
   Our fathers saw, but did not mind
   or duly understand:

Nor did they mind the multitude
   of thy benignities; *
But at the sea, at the red sea,
   they made thy wrath to rise.

† *Hebrew*, *Septuagint*, ancient *Latin*, and *Arabick*.

8 Neverthelefs He faved them
   ev'n for his own name's fake;
That thereby He his fov'reign pow'r
   moft manifeft might make.
9 For He the mighty fea rebuk'd,
   and made before Him fly;
And through the depths He led them fafe,
   as through a defart dry.
10 From his high hand who hated them
   He timely did them fave;
And from the hand of mighty foes
   a full redemption gave.
11 The waters overwhelm'd their foes,
   not one was left alive;
12 Then they his word believ'd, and praife
   to Him in fongs did give.

[3 *Part.*]

13 Yet foon did they his mighty works
   ungratefully forget;
Nor for his fov'reign counfel would
   with due fubmiffion wait.
14 But journeying in the wildernefs,
   they lufted fhamefully;
And in the defart would prefume
   the glorious God to try.
15 And yet the things which they requir'd
   He gave them to the full;
But leanefs at the fame time fent
   into their pining foul.
16 They envy'd Mofes in the camp,
   tho' their great prophet known;
And with him Aaron their high prieft,
   JEHOVAH's holy one.
17 The earth her mouth then op'ned wide,
   and Dathan did devour,
With proud Abiram's company,
   and hid with dreadful roar.

PSALM CVI.

18 Among the reſt who mutiny'd,
   a fire was kindled then,
  Whoſe flame purſu'd and ſoon conſum'd
   thoſe daring impious men.

19 They made a calf of melted gold,
   while they at Horeb were;
  And ſtupidly they worſhipped
   the molten image there.

20 Thus they moſt fooliſhly exchang'd
   Him that their glory was,
  For the baſe likeneſs of an ox,
   that feeding lives on graſs.

21 They quite forgot the glorious God,
   who had their ſaviour been;
  By whom ſuch mighty things perform'd
   they had in Egypt ſeen:

22 The wondrous works which He had done
   in Ham's aſtoniſh'd land,
  The fearful things at the red ſea
   wrought by his ſov'reign hand.

23 He ſaid then, He would them deſtroy,
   if Moſes in that day
  Had not ſtood in the dreadful breach,
   and turn'd his wrath away.

[4 *Part.*]

24 Yea they deſpis'd the pleaſant land,
   and would not truſt his word;

25 But murm'ring in their tents, refus'd
   to hearken to the LORD.

26 To make them in the deſart fall,
   He lifted up his hand;

27 Among the nations to diſperſe
   their race in ev'ry land.

28 To Baal-peor they join'd themſelves,
   made off'rings to the dead;

29 With theſe devices Him provok'd;
   the plague among them ſpread.

30 But Phineas rofe, and judgment wrought,
    whereon the plague did ceafe:
31 Which to all ages is to Him
    accounted righteoufnefs.
32 Yea at the ftreams of Meribah
    they there incens'd Him fo,
That ev'n with Mofes for their fakes
    it grievoufly did go:
33 Their provocations were fo great,
    his patient fpirit ftir'd,
That with his lips he fpake in hafte
    an unadvifed word.

[5 *Part.*]

34 They did not, at the LORD's command,
    the impious nations flay;
35 But with the heathen mix'd themfelves,
    and learnt their works and way.
36 They ferv'd their idols, which to them
    a fatal fnare became;
37 Their fons and daughters facrific'd
    to devils in the flame.
38 The blood of innocents they fhed,
    to Canaan's idols vile;
Their children's blood they facrific'd,
    and did the land defile.
39 Then with their deteftable works
    themfelves polluted they;
And with devices of their own
    a whoring went aftray.
40 JEHOVAH's wrath was kindled then
    againft his people more;
So that his own inheritance
    He greatly did abhor.
41 He gave them to the heathen's pow'r,
    into their haters hand;
42 Their foes opprefs'd them, and they were
    enflav'd to their command.

43 He

PSALM CVII.

43 He many a time deliver'd them;
    but with their councils so
They Him provok'd, that for their sins
    again He brought them low.

44 Yet He regarded their distress,
    whene'er He heard their cry;
45 And He his covenant for them
    recall'd to memory :
46 Yea, in his mercies multitude
    did He repent; and made
Them to be pity'd of all those
    who them had captive led.

47 O save us in this darksome day,
    O LORD our mighty God;
Thy people gather where dispers'd,
    in gentile lands abroad :
That so we to thy holy name
    may render thanks always,
And all together joyfully,
    may triumph in thy praise.

48 The LORD, the God of Israel
    be bless'd eternally;
And let all people say, AMEN :
    sing HALLELUJAH * ye.

PSALM CVII. [*The Goodness of the* LORD]

[1. *To Captives and Travellers.*]

1 O To JEHOVAH give ye thanks,
        because most good is He,
Because his mercy doth endure
    ev'n to eternity.
2 Let the redeemed of the LORD
    thus of his mercy say;
Whom He hath from the hand of foes
    redeem'd and brought away.

3 From all the lands wherein they were
     disperfed and diftrefs'd,
   Hath gather'd from the north, the fea, *
     the eaft and from the weft.
4 They wandred thro' the wildernefs
     in an untrodden way;
   No habitable town they found,
     nor place wherein to ftay.
5 With hunger were they famifhed,
     with thirft extremely dry;
   Their fouls were in them overwhelm'd,
     and ready were to die.
6 But then they to JEHOVAH cry'd
     in their extreme diftrefs;
   And He them fet at liberty
     from all their arguifhes.
7 For then along He led them in
     a right tho' tracklefs way,
   Glad to a town inhabited,
     where they might fafely ftay.

8 O that men would JEHOVAH praife
     for his great goodnefs then,-
   And for his many wondrous works
     wrought for the fons of men.
9 For he the thirfty, longing foul
     refrefhing fatisfies:
   And He the hungry foul with good
     — ev'n to the full fupplies.

[2. *To Prifoners.*]

10 Such as fhut up, in darknefs dwell,
     and in death's fhade abide;
   Who are in great affliction bound,
     and faft in irons ty'd.
11 Becaufe againft the words of God
     they did as rebels rife,
   And counfels of the higheft One
     did daringly defpife:

12 Therefore

12 Therefore with flavish labour * He
    their hearts brought wholly down :
    Under their burdens down they fell,
    and helper there was none.
13 But then they to JEHOVAH cry
    in their extreme diftrefs ;
    And He them fets at liberty,
    from all their anguifhes.
14 He them out of their darknefs brought,
    and from death's fhade He took ;
    And all the chains which bound them faft
    He all to pieces broke.
15 O that men would JEHOVAH praife
    for his great goodnefs then,
    And for his many wondrous works
    wrought for the fons of men.
16 For He hath into fhivers broke
    the gates of folid brafs,
    Afunder cut the iron bars,
    and let the pris'ner's pafs.

[3. *To the Sick.*]

17 Fools for their bold iniquities
    and fins, afflicted are :
18 Their fouls all meat abhor,
    to gates of death draw near.
19 But then they to JEHOVAH cry
    in their extreme diftrefs ;
    And He them fets at liberty
    from all their anguifhes.
20 He fent his word of fov'reign pow'r,
    and to them healing gave ;
    And gracioufly deliver'd them
    from death and from the grave.
21 O that men would JEHOVAH praife
    for his great goodnefs then,
    And for his many wondrous works
    wrought for the fons of men.

22 And of their thanks the sacrifice
   let them with pleasure bring;
And while his works they tell abroad,
   with gladness shout and sing.

[4. *To those who go to Sea.*]

23 All those who down into the seas
   in floating ships descend,*
And venture on the waters great,
   their business to attend;
24 They there JEHOVAH's mighty works
   with waking eyes behold,
And in the moving deeps they see
   his wonders manifold.
25 For He commands, and instantly
   the stormy winds arise,
Which drive the swelling waves along,
   and raise them to the skies.
26 They mount to heav'n, and down they rowl
   to dreadful depths again;
Their souls quite faint and melt away
   with anxiousness and pain.
27 As drunkards stagger to and fro,
   they reel, with tempests toss'd;
They are as men of sense bereft,
   and all their skill is lost.
28 But then they to JEHOVAH cry
   in their extreme distress,
And He then brings them speedily
   from all their anguishes.
29 He turns the storm into a calm,
   at his almighty will;
So that the raging waves thereof
   grow peaceable and still.
30 Then they rejoice, because at rest
   they find themselves to be:
So them He to the haven brings,
   which they had long'd to see.

PSALM CVII.

31 O that men would JEHOVAH praise,
    for his great goodness then,
  And for his many wondrous works,
    wrought for the sons of men.
32 In all the congregation great
    Him let them highly raise;
  And where th' assembled elders sit
    unite to spread his praise.

[5. *To Husbandmen.*]

33 He to a desart turns a land
    where rivers did abound;
  And where the springs of water flow'd,
    into a thirsty ground.
34 A fruitful land to barrenness
    He turns because of sin,
  For the provoking wickedness
    of those who dwell therein.

35 Then He the barren wilderness
    with pools enriching fills,
  And turns the dry and thirsty land
    to springs and flowing rills.
36 And there for dwelling He a place
    does to the hungry give;
  Where they may social towns prepare,
    and pleasantly may live.
37 Where they may fruitful vineyards plant,
    and sow the fertile fields,
  And may receive the rich increase,
    which ev'ry harvest yields.
38 Yea he so greatly blesses them,
    He multiplies their race,
  And in his goodness suffers not
    their cattle to decrease.
39 And when they are diminished,
    and for their sins brought low,
  Beneath oppression, tyranny
    and grief are made to bow;

40 Then He on princes pours contempt,
   and caufes them to ftray,
   And wander in a wildernefs,
   wherein they find no way.
41 But he from deep affliction makes
   the poor on high to rife;
   And like to multiplying flocks
   He makes their families.
42 All this the righteous fhall behold,
   and will rejoice to view:
   But all, afham'd, fhall ftop their mouths,
   who wickednefs will do.
43 Whofo is wife and will obferve
   thefe things attentively,
   He fhall the goodnefs of the LORD
   with pleafing wonder fee.

PSALM . CVIII.
A Song, or Pfalm of David.

1 O GOD, my heart is fix'd; I'll fing,
   yea with my glory praife:
2 Awake my pfaltery and harp;
   my felf I'll early raife.
3 Thy praife, O LORD, will I proclaim
   among the people round;
   Among the nations I with fongs
   thy praifes will refound.
4 For thy benignity is great,
   ev'n to the heav'ns on high;
   And thy eternal truth extends,
   up to the cloudy fky.
5 Above the ftarry firmament
   exalt thy felf, O GOD;
   And o'er the fpacious earth difplay
   thy glory all abroad.
6 That thofe who thy beloved are
   may quite deliver'd be:
   O do Thou fave with thy right hand,
   and anfwer give to me.

7 GOD

PSALM CIX.

7 GOD in his holiness hath spoke,
   and I'll triumph with joy;
   Shechem divide, and Succoth's vale,
   measure for mine will I.

8 Gilead is mine, Manasseh mine,
   who both espouse my cause;
   Ephraim is of my strength the head,
   and Judah gives my laws.

9 Moab I will my washpot make ‖;
   my shoe o'er Edom fling ‖;
   And over Palestina's land
   I will in triumph sing.

10 Who will me to the city lead,
    so strongly fortify'd?
    And who will into Edom's land
    me and my army guide?

11 Didst Thou not cast us off, O GOD?
    yet still we look to thee:
    Wilt Thou not with our armies go,
    and GOD our leader be?

12 O from our trouble give us help;
    for man's help vain is known;

13 Thro' GOD we shall do valiantly;
    and He'll our foes tread down.

PSALM CIX. *A Psalm of* David.

1 HOLD not thy peace, O GOD my praise;
  2 For op'ned wide at me
  Are wicked and deceitful mouths,
    with tongues of falsity.

3 With words of spiteful hatred they
    encompass me around;
    And fight against me, tho' no cause
    in me they ever found.

4 They for my love became my foes;
    yet I for them did pray;

5 Ill they reward me for my good,
    and hate for love repay.

[2 *Part.*]

‖ See the Notes on *Psalm* lx. 8.

PSALM CIX.

[2 *Part.*]

6 But Thou wilt set a wicked one
   o'er him to have command;
And at his right hand always shall
   the troubler Satan stand.
7 When he to judgment comes, he shall
   be wicked found therein;
His pray'rs shall aggravations be
   of his presumptuous sin.

8 His days shall be but few; his charge
   another man shall take;
9 Thou wilt his children fatherless,
   his wife a widow make.
10 His children shall be vagabonds,
   and beg continually;
And from their places desolate
   shall seek for a supply.

11 Extortioners shall seize on all
   that to him appertains;
And strangers spoil the fruits of all
   his labours, care and pains.
12 None to him favour shall extend,
   nor to his orphans show;
13 His race shall fail, nor shall their names
   the age succeeding know.

14 Their fathers wickedness shall be
   remembred by the LORD;
And how their mother did transgress,
   shall still be on record.
15 They shall before JEHOVAH's face
   appear continually,
Until he wholly from the earth
   cuts off their memory.

16 Because he did no mercy mind,
   but persecute the poor;
That he might slay afflicted ones
   whose hearts were broke before.

PSALM CIX.

17 As he did bitter curſing love,
    curſes ſhall on him lie ;'
As he delighted not to bleſs,
    bleſſing ſhall from him fly.
18 As he with curſes cloath'd himſelf;
    like water they ſhall flow
Into his bowels, and like oil
    into his bones ſhall go.
19 Like an encloſing garment, they
    ſhall. compaſs him around ;
And as a girdle conſtantly
    they ſhall on him be bound.
20 Thus will JEHOVAH deal with * thoſe
    my ſpiteful enemies ;
Who evil ſpeak againſt my ſoul, ‡
    againſt my life ‡ deviſe.

[3. Part.]

21 But *Lord* JEHOVAH, * deal Thou well
    for thy name ſake with me :
Becauſe thy mercies. tender are,
    O ſet me quickly free.
22 For I afflicted am and weak,
    and helpleſs and oppreſs'd ; ||
My heart moſt deeply wounded is,.
    and pained in my breaſt.
23 Like to the ſhadow far declin'd,.
    ſo far away I'm gone ;
And as the locuſt with the wind;.
    am toſſed up and down.
24 By faſting long and frequently
    my knees are feeble grown ;
And ſo much waſted is my fleſh,
    that all its fat is gone.

25 I'm

‡ The *Hebrew* ſignifies *Life* as well as *Soul*, and *Both* may be intended.

|| The *Hebrew* ſeems to comprize all theſe Ideas ;. See *Schindler* and *Martin Albert*,

25 I'm a reproach among my foes,
   who mock me as forlorn;
And always when they look on me,
   they shake their heads with scorn.
26 Help me JEHOVAH, O my God,
   in mercy save Thou me.
27 That all may know this is thy hand,
   that, LORD, 'tis done by Thee.

28 When me they curse, do Thou me bless:
   let them asham'd be made,
When they rise up; but O then let
   thy servant's heart be glad.
29 So shall my spiteful enemies
   be cloathed all with shame;
And their confusion shall like as
   a mantle cover them.

30 But I will greatly thank the LORD,
   and with my mouth aloud,
Will joyful praises to Him sing
   among the multitude.
31 For at the right hand of the poor
   He stands to rescue them
From those who judge unrighteously,
   and would their souls condemn.

PSALM CX. *A Psalm of* David.
[*The Exaltation, Reign, Priesthood and Victories of* CHRIST.]

1 JEHOVAH to my *Lord* † hath said,
   Sit Thou on high at my right hand,
Till I thy foes thy footstool make,
On which Thou shalt in triumph stand.
2 JEHOVAH out of Zion-hill
The sceptre of thy strength will send:
And in the midst of all thy foes
Thou shalt thy reigning pow'r extend.

                               3 But

---

† The *Hebrew* is ADONAI; and signifies, The MESSIAH: *Mat.* xxii. 42—44.

3 But in thy day of conqu'ring pow'r
Thy people shall be made most free;
And will most freely Thee obey
In all the joys of liberty. ‡
And as from early morning's womb
The drops of dew shine o'er the ground,
So shall thy num'rous youths be seen
In holy beauties all around.

4 JEHOVAH never will repent
Of what resolvedly He swore;
In likeness of Melchizedek.
Thou art a priest for evermore.

5 This sov'reign and almighty *Lord*, †
Who sits on high at thy right hand,
Shall in his day of wrath strike through
The haughty kings that Him withstand.

6 He shall among the heathen judge,
And fill their places with the slain,
And wound to death the cruel heads
Who over many regions reign.

7 He, of th' enlivening brook shall drink,
As in his way to victory;
Then with fresh ardour shall go on. ‖
Triumph, and lift his head on high.

PSALM CXI.

1 SING Hallelujah! praise the LORD
I will with all my mind,
Where upright ones in private meet,
and are in publick join'd.

2 JEHOVAH's

‡ In *Hebrew* 'tis—*Thy People shall be* WILLINGNESSES *in the Day of thy Power*: Which Words are so full of Sense as to intimate all these delightful Sentiments.

† In *Hebrew* 'tis Adonai—to signify 'tis the same Person mentioned in the *latter Part* of the *first Line* of the *Psalm*, who is placed *at the Right Hand of* Jehovah: and all this is therefore implied.

‖ The Words plainly signify, That on his drinking of the Brook in the Way, He should be wondrously refreshed and enlivened.

2 JEHOVAH's works are wondrous great,
    and show his boundless might;
  And are sought out by ev'ry soul,
    who views them with delight.

3 His work is glorious majesty,
    and comely honour is;
  And to perpetual ages stands *
    that righteousness of his.
4 His works most marvellous He made
    still to be kept in mind:
  Full of compassion is the LORD,
    most merciful and kind.

5 A portion of fit food He gives
    to all who fear his name;
  And ever will He bear in mind
    his covenant with them.
6 He of his work the mighty pow'r
    did to his people show,
  In that the heathens heritage
    He did on them bestow.

[2 *Part.*]

7 Unshaken truth and judgment are
    the working of his hands,
  Sure all his threatnings, promises,
    and sure all his commands. ‖
8 They firmly are established
    to perpetuity;
  And are fulfill'd and perfected
    in truth and equity.

9 He to his flock redemption sent:
    that covenant of his
  For ever He ordain'd: his name
    holy and rev'rend is.

10 The

‖ As the judicious *A. Jackson* observes—GOD's *Commands* in the *Scripture Sense* of the *Word* include his Statutes, Promises and Threatnings, all inseperably joined together.

10 The LORD's fear the beginning is
of wifdom : they are wife
Who do his will : and evermore
endures his higheft praife.

PSALM CXII.

1 SING Hallelujah ! * O how blefs'd,
   The man who doth Jehovah fear ;
Who alfo takes a great delight
In keeping his commands with care.
2 His feed fhall multiply on earth,
Be great and profper mightily :
The righteous race of righteous men
Shall bleffed be abundantly.

3 Riches and wealth fhall fill his houfe ;
His righteoufnefs no end fhall find ;
4 Light in his darknefs fhall arife ;
He's juft, compaffionate and kind.
5 A good man lends, and favour fhews,
And his affairs with judgment * guides :
6 Surely he never fhall be mov'd ;
For ever dear his name abides.

7 Ill tydings fhall not him difmay ;
His heart fix'd, on the LORD relies ;
8 His heart fo firm, he never fears
While he looks on his enemies.-
9 He kindneffes difperfes round,
And gives the poor a meet fupply ;
His righteoufnefs fhall ever laft ;
His horn in honour rife on high.

10 The wicked this fhall fee and grieve,
And gnafh their teeth and melt away ;
While all their ill defires and aims,
Shall fail and utterly decay.

PSALM

PSALM CXIII. CXIV.

PSALM CXIII.

1 SING Hallelujah ! sing his praise,
 O all ye servants of the LORD:
 JEHOVAH's great and glorious name
 O praise ye all with one accord.
2 O blessed be JEHOVAH's name,
 From this time to eternity:
3 From sun-rise to his going down
 JEHOVAH's name shall praised be.

4 O'er all the nations of the world
 The great JEHOVAH reigns on high:
 Yonder his brightest glory shines,
 Yonder above the starry sky.
5 To God our LORD who dwells above,
 Who ever can compared be?
6 Who all that is in heav'n and earth
 Humbles himself to mind and see.

7 Out of the dust he raises up
 The slighted man of low degree;
 And from the dunghill needy men
 Surprizingly lift up doth He.
8 That He may them advance on high,
 And ev'n along with princes seat;
 Yea those who of his people are
 The princes chief in pow'r and state.

9 He makes the barren woman keep
 Her house with pleasure, and to be
 Of babes a mother full of joy.
 Sing therefore Hallelujah * ye.

PSALM CXIV.

1 WHEN Isr'el Egypt left,
  and Jacob's family
 Did from a barb'rous † people there
  march forth triumphantly;
2 Then Judah was ordain'd
  to guard his holy place;
 But the whole host of Israel
  His choice dominion was.

3 The

† So the *Hebrew*, and *all* the *ancient* Versions.

PSALM CXV.

3 The sea it saw, and fled;
   and Jordan back did flow;
4 Like rams the mountains, and like lambs
   the hills leap'd to and fro.
5 Thou sea! what made thee fly?
   thou Jordan back to flow?
6 Ye mountains leap like rams? ye hills
   like lambs leap to and fro?

7 Before the mighty *Lord*, †   [† *Adon.*]
   tremble O earth for fear,
   While the dread presence of the God
   of Jacob doth appear!
8 Who made the solid rock
   melt into pools below;
   To springs of water turn'd the flint,
   and made the flint to flow.

PSALM CXV.

1 O Not to us, LORD, not to us,
     but all the glory take
   To thine own name, both for thy truth
   and sov'reign mercy's sake.
2 Why should the taunting heathen cry,
   " where is the God they own?"
3 Our God in heav'n sits high enthron'd,
   and what he pleas'd hath done.

4 Their idols silver are and gold;
   men's handy work are they,
5 Mouths have they, but they cannot speak
   and eyes, but cannot see.
6 Ears have they, but they cannot hear;
   noses, but favour not:
7 Have hands and feet, but cannot move;
   nor murmur * in * their throat.

8 Such senseless stocks are they themselves,
   who did these idols frame.;
   And such are all who to them pray
   and put their trust in them.

                              [2 *Part.*]

PSALM CXVI.

[2 *Part.*]
9 O Ifr'el, truſt ye in the LORD;
 your help and ſhield is He:
10 O Aaron's houſe, truſt in the LORD;
 your ſhield and help He'll be.
11 Who fear the LORD, truſt in the LORD;
 He is your help and ſhield.
12 The LORD hath mindful been of us;
 his bleſſing He will yield.

 The houſe of Iſra'l bleſs He will;
 the houſe of Aaron bleſs.
13 He will bleſs all who fear the LORD,
 the greater and the leſs.
14 To you JEHOVAH will, to you
 and to your children add:
15 You are the bleſſed of the LORD,
 that heav'n and earth has made.

16 The heav'ns of heav'ns are all the LORD's,
 where He his glory ſhows:
 But ev'n on Adam's * offspring He
 the ſpacious earth beſtows.
17 Not any praiſe to JAH * on high
 can from the dead aſcend;
 No praiſe from thoſe who to the place
 of ſilence deep deſcend.

18 But we th' eternal JAH * will bleſs,
 who yet alive are ſeen,
 From this time forth for evermore,
 ſing HALLELUJAH then!

PSALM CXVI.

1 I Love, becauſe JEHOVAH doth
 my voice and pray'r * ſtill hear;
2 And all my days will call on Him,
 who bow'd to me his ear.
3 The cords of death on ev'ry ſide
 begirt me faſt around:
 The pains of hell laid hold on me:
 grief and diſtreſs I found.

        4 Then

PSALM CXVI.

4 Then on JEHOVAH's name I call'd,
  and earneftly did cry;
  'O LORD! deliver Thou my foul
  'in my extremity.'
5 JEHOVAH juft and gracious is;
  our God moft kind alfo.
6 The LORD the fimple keeps, and He
  me fav'd when I was low.

7 O now my foul, do thou return
  to thy delightful reft,
  Becaufe the LORD hath bounteoufly
  Himfelf to thee exprefs'd.
8 Becaufe Thou haft my foul from death
  now fet at liberty:
  Mine eyes from tears, my fliding feet
  from falling haft fet free.

9 Therefore I'll walk before the LORD,
  in his appointed ways,
  While in the land of living ones
  He lengthens out my days.

[2 Part.]

10 I did believe, and therefore fpake,
   I great affliction bear;
11 Then in diftrefs and hafte I faid,
   that all men liars are.
12 But O JEHOVAH! what returns
   fhall I now make to Thee?
   For all the many benefits
   Thou haft beftow'd on me.

13 I'll take the cup of faving health
   and on the LORD's name call:
14 I'll pay the LORD my vows, yea now,
   before his people all.
15 In prefence of JEHOVAH is
   efteem'd exceeding dear
   The death of ev'ry one of thofe
   his gracious faints who are.

16 I verily thy servant am,
  thy servant, LORD, am I,
 And of thy handmaid am the son,
  my bands Thou did'st untie.

17 The sacrifice of thankfulness
  I'll offer up to Thee;
 And I upon JEHOVAH's name
  will call continually.
18 The vows which in distress I made,
  I to the LORD will pay,
 In presence of his people all,
  without the least delay.

19 Within *Jehovah*'s courts therefore
  I gladly pay my vow,
 In midst of thee, Jerusalem!
  sing HALLELUJAH * now!

PSALM CXVII.

1 O All ye nations of the world,
   JEHOVAH praise always!
 And all ye people ev'ry where,
  set forth his highest praise!
2 For great his kindness is to us,
  and flows for ever free;
 JEHOVAH's truth will never fail,
  sing HALLELUJAH * ye!

[*Long Metre.*]

1 O All ye nations of the world,
   To praise the LORD with joy combine!
 And all ye people ev'ry where
  To Him in songs of praises join!
2 For his most wondrous grace abounds,
  And flows to us for ever free;
 JEHOVAH s truth will never fail,
 Therefore sing HALLELUJAH * ye!

PSALM CXVIII.

PSALM CXVIII.

1 O Praise the LORD, for He is good,
    his mercies ne'er decay:
2 And that his mercies ever last,
    let thankful Isr'el say.
3 Their sense of his eternal love
    let Aaron's house declare:
4 And that it fails not, let all say,
    all who *Jehovah* fear.

5 To the almighty JAH * I cry'd
    in my extreme distress;
And JAH * on high me heard, and brought
    into this happy place.
6 The LORD is for me; I'll not fear
    what man to me can do:
7 The LORD is with my helping friends;
    and I will face ‡ my foe.

8 'Tis better on the LORD to trust,
    than trust in man's defence;
9 Better to trust the LORD than place
    in princes confidence.

[2 *Part.*]

10 All nations round environ'd ‖ me,
    design'd my fatal fall;
But in JEHOVAH's mighty name
    I overcame them all.
11 They compass'd me, again, again,
    and try'd my utter fall;
But in JEHOVAH's mighty name
    I did subdue † them all.

---

‡ So the *Hebrew* and *Syriack*: i. e. Face with Courage, and Confidence of Victory. The *Septuagint* renders it—*disdain*; and the *Arabick*—overcome.

‖ The *Sept. Syr. Arab. Æthiop.* and *Jerom*, as also *Tremelius* and *Junius, Piscator, Ainsworth, De Muis, Rivet* and *Geir*, render these Conquests as being *past*, and here mentioned as Encouragements to hope for *future* Victories.

† So the *Æthiopick*: or, *cut them down*; as *Montanus, Piscator, Ainsworth, Rivet* and *Geir*,

PSALM CXVIII.

12 Like angry bees they round me swarm'd,
    rag'd like a thorny flame;
   Yet quenched and destroyed were,
    but in JEHOVAH's name.
13 When they push'd hard to beat me down,
    JEHOVAH helped me.
14 The mighty JAH * my strength, my song,
    and saving help is He.
15 In tents of righteous men is heard
    the voice of health and joy:
   The LORD's right hand gives mighty strength ‡
    and works most mightily. ‡
16 JEHOVAH by his mighty pow'r
    advances them on high: ‡
   The Lord's right hand gives mighty strength ‡
    and works most mightily. ‡

[3 Part.]

17 I shall not die, but longer live,
    and gratefully declare
   The works of our almighty JAH, *
    how wonderful they are.
18 For JAH hath sorely me chastiz'd,
    till just of life bereav'd:
   But kindly from the gates of death,
    my fainting life repriev'd.
19 O set wide open now to me
    the gates of righteousness;
   And I will enter them, and there
    the praise of JAH * confess.
20 This gate, JEHOVAH's blessed gate,
    into his house doth lead:
   The righteous love to enter in;
    and entering in are glad.
21 Among these righteous ones I'll be,
    and praise on Thee bestow;
   For Thou hast heard me, and to Thee
    I my salvation owe.

22 The

‡ See the *Hebrew, Septuagint, Syriac*

PSALM CXVIII.

22 The stone ‖ the builders did despise,
  and utterly disclaim,
 Is now the chief and corner stone,
  which bears up all the frame.
23 This work JEHOVAH's mighty pow'r
  hath brought to pass alone;
 And we in great amazement stand,
  to see what He hath done.

[4 *Part.*]

24 This is the great and blessed day
  the LORD himself hath made;
 And we will all therein rejoice,
  and be exceeding glad.
25 JEHOVAH we † now Thee beseech
  SALVATION TO AFFORD: ‡
 We † humbly Thee entreat now send
  prosperity, O LORD!
26 He that comes in JEHOVAH's name
  O let him blessed be.
 Out of JEHOVAH's house to you
  a blessing wish do we.
27 God is JEHOVAH, who to us
  hath made his light to rise:
 Bind therefore to his altar's horns
  with cords, our sacrifice.
28 Thou art my God, and I'll proclaim
  for evermore thy praise:
 Thou art my God, and thy great name
  my thankful song shall raise.
29 O to JEHOVAH give ye thanks;
  immensely good is He,
 Because his mercy doth endure
  ev'n to eternity.

‖ Applied to CHRIST, Mat. xxi. Acts iv. Eph. ii, 1 Pet. ii.
† So the *Chaldee.* The Word—*Ana*—which I here render —*We*—is an *Adverb*; and applicable both to the *Singular* and *Plural* Number.
‡ This Line in *Hebrew* is HOSANNA—and this *Word* and *Verse* are plainly alluded to by the exulting Multitude applying it to CHRIST in *Mat.* xxi. 9.

PSALM CXIX.

[Every Verſe of this Pſalm repreſents the ſuperiour Excellency of the written Word of God: and under the wiſe Conduct of Inſpiration it w. s compos'd with the greateſt Plainneſs, without Poetical Ornaments. It muſt be therefore our Wiſdom to repreſent the Original in its inſpir'd Simplicity, both of Sentiments and Style, with all the Exactneſs poſſible.]

1 HOW bleſs'd the upright in the way!
  Who in JEHOVAH's law will go:
2 Who keep his records bleſs'd are they,
  With all their heart who ſeek him too:
3 And who work not iniquity,
  But in his ways ſtrict walkers are.
4 Thou haſt commanded us to keep
  Thy precepts with our utmoſt * care.
5 O that my ways eſtabliſh'd * were
  To keep thy ſtatutes heedfully!
6 When I all thy commands regard,
  Then be aſhamed ſhall not I.
7 When thy juſt judgments I ſhall learn,
  Thee with an upright heart I'll praiſe.
8 Me utterly forſake not Thou;
  And I'll thy ſtatutes keep always.

[2 Part.]

9 By what may youth make pure their way?
  Thy word by ſtrict attending to.
10 With all my heart I ſought for Thee:
   From thy commands ne'er let me go!
11 I hid thy word within my heart,
   Leſt I ſhould give offence to Thee.
12 O Thou, JEHOVAH, bleſſed art;
   Thy ſtatutes therefore teach Thou me!
13 I all the judgments of thy mouth
   Did with my faithful lips declare.
14 My joys more in thy records way,
   Than in all earthly riches are.
15 I'll on thy precepts meditate,
   And on thy ways mine eyes will ſet:
16 Thy ſtatutes ſhall be my delight;
   And I thy word will not forget.

[3 Part.]

PSALM CXIX.

[3 *Part.*]

17 O to thy servant give this grace,
  that I may live thy word to keep:
18 Unveil mine eyes, that I may see
  Within thy law the wonders deep.
19 I am a stranger in the earth;
  O never hide thy laws from me.
20 My soul is broken with desire,
  Thy judgments at all times to see.

21 Thou hast rebuk'd the proud accurs'd,
  Who from thy sacred statutes swerv'd.
22 Reproach and shame roll off * from me;
  For I thy records have observ'd.
23 The great against me sit and speak,
  But I thy laws my study make:
24 Thy records are my great delight,
  And them my councellors I take.

[4 *Part.*]

25 Down to the dust my soul cleaves fast;
  After thy word revive me now:
26 I told my ways, and Thou didst hear;
  Thy statutes teach Thou me to know.
27 Thy precepts way O learn Thou me;
  Thy wonders then * will I declare:
28 My soul with grief dissolves away;
  O by thy word my strength repair!

29 The way of lies from me remove;
  Grant me thy law's enlight'ning aid:
30 For I have chose the way of truth;
  Thy judgments I before me laid.
31 I to thy testimonies cleave;
  O LORD shame on me never cast:
32 I'll run thy precepts way with joy,
  When Thou my heart enlarged hast.

L 2　　　　　[5 *Part.*]

[5 *Part.*]

33 O teach me, LORD, thy statutes way;
 And I will from it ne'er depart:
34 Instruct me; and I'll keep thy law,
 And it observe with all my heart.
35 In thy laws path make me to go;
 Because therein my pleasure lies:
36 O to thy records bow my heart,
 And leave it not to avarice.

37 From all vain objects turn mine eyes;
 Me in thy way revive and chear.
38 O to thy servant keep thy word,
 Who is devoted to thy fear.
39 The slander which I fear remove;
 Good are the judgments Thou dost give.
40 See how I for thy precepts long;
 Me in thy righteousness revive.

[6 *Part.*]
41 LORD, let thy mercies come to me;
 After thy word, salvation show:
42 So I my sland'rers shall refute;
 Because thy word I trusted to.
43 The word of truth keep in my mouth,
 For on thy judgments I depend.
44 So I with care will keep thy law,
 With constancy, ev'n to the end.

45 Yea I will walk at liberty;
 Because I thy commandments seek;
46 And I before the greatest kings
 Will boldly of thy records speak.
47 In thy commands which I have lov'd
 My self I'll greatly recreate.
48 To thy lov'd precepts lift my hands,
 And on thy statutes meditate.

[7 *Part.*]

[7 *Part.*]

49 Good to thy servant make thy word,
   By which Thou mad'st me rest on Thee :
50 My comfort in distress is this,—
   Thy faithful word hath quick'ned me.
51 Tho' proud ones greatly me deride,
   I have not from thy law declin'd. *
52 Thy judgments, LORD, which were of old,
   I have review'd, and comfort find.
53 I'm struck with horror, to behold
   How impious men thy law forsake :
54 But in my house of pilgrimage,
   Thy statutes are the songs I make.
55 By night remembred I thy name,
   O LORD, and kept thy laws have I :
56 This comfort I receiv'd ‡ because
   I kept thy precepts heedfully.

[8 *Part.*]

57 The LORD my chosen portion is :
   I said that I will keep thy word.
58 I sought thy face * with all my heart :
   After thy word, * me grace afford.
59 I view'd my ways and turn'd my feet,
   Into thy testimonies way ;
60 I hast'ned thy commands to keep,
   And made not any more delay.
61 Tho' bands of wicked men me spoil,
   Thy laws I think on with delight.
62 I'll rise at midnight Thee to praise,
   Because thy judgments all are right.
63 Companion to them all am I,
   Who keep thy laws, and rev'rence Thee :
64 O LORD, thy mercy fills the earth,
   Thy statutes kindly teach Thou me.

L 3   [9 *Part.*]

‡ The *Syriack* renders it—*This is a Consolation to me :* and so *Junius* and *Tremelius*, *Rivet* and *Glassius*.

[9 *Part.*]

65 O LORD, Thou with thy servant well
  According to thy word hast done:
66 Good taste and judgment teach Thou me,
  For I thy laws have rested on.
67 Before I was chastiz'd, I stray'd;
  But now to keep thy word I learn.
68 Both good Thou art, and good Thou dost;
  Thy statutes cause me to discern.

69 The proud against me forge their lies;
  Thy laws I'll keep with heart upright:
70 Their heart is grown as fat as grease;
  But in thy law is my delight.
71 That I might well thy statutes learn,
  'Tis good that Thou didst me chastise.
72 Laws of thy mouth I far above
  Thousands of gold and silver prize.

[10 *Part.*]

73 Thy hands have made and fashion'd me;
  Wisdom to learn thy laws afford:
74 Who fear Thee shall see me with joy,
  Because I've hoped in thy word.
75 Thy judgments, LORD, are right I know,
  And in thy truth * Thou chastnest me:
76 After thy word, thy servant to,
  Now let thy grace my comfort be!

77 Thy kindness show, that I may live!
  Thy law with pleasure I peruse.
78 Shame proud ones who me causeless wrong,
  While on thy precepts I will muse.
79 Let such as fear thee, and who know
  Thy testimonies, turn to me:
80 My heart make in thy laws entire,
  That I may not ashamed be.

[11 *Part.*]

[11 Part.]

81 Looking for thy salvation long,
  My soul faints; yet I trust thy word:
82 Mine eyes fail for thy word; and cry,
  When wilt Thou comfort me afford?
83 I'm like a skin † dry'd in the smoke;
  Yet I thy laws do not forget!
84 How long thy servant's days? when wilt
  Thou judge the men who me beset?

85 For me the proud have digged pits,
  Which never would thy law allow:
86 For all thy laws are truth *; help me,
  Whom they unrighteously pursue.
87 They almost me consum'd on earth;
  Yet from thy laws I did not swerve.
88 O in thy mercy me revive;
  And thy mouth's records I'll observe.

[12 Part.]

89 Made fast thy word in heav'n, O LORD,
  It doth eternally endure:
90 Thy truth for ever lasts; and Thou
  The earth hast founded, and 'tis sure:
91 By thy decree they stand this day;
  For they all servants are to Thee.
92 Were not thy law my joy, I soon
  Had perish'd in adversity.
93 Thy laws I'll ne'er forget; for Thou
  By them hast quickning to me brought:
94 O save me; for I'm wholly thine,
  And careful have thy precepts sought.
95 To ruin me the wicked watch;
  But I thy testimonies mind:
96 Of all perfection ‡ bounds I see;
  But Thy command is unconfin'd. ||

L 4 [13 Part.]

† The *Hebrew* signifies a *Vessel* made of a *Skin* in the *Form* of a large *Bottle*.
‡ i. e. The Perfection of all Creatures in this lower World.
|| In it's Excellencies, Influences, Benefits.

PSALM CXIX.

[13 *Part.*]

97 How greatly do I love Thy law !
  It daily my sweet study grows :
98 By thy laws, ever with me, Thou
  Hast made me wiser than my foes.
99 More than my teachers all, I know ;
  Because thy laws my study are :
100 I know more than the ancient do ;
  Because I keep thy laws with care.

101 From all ill ways I kept my feet ;
  That I might well thy word obey :
102 Because thou hast instructed me,
  I did not from thy judgments stray.
103 How sweet thy words are to my taste !
  More to my mouth than honey they :
104 I from thy precepts wisdom gain ;
  And therefore hate each lying way.

[14 *Part.*]

105 Thy word is to my feet the lamp,
  A shining light to show my way :
106 I sware, and to perform, resolve
  Thy right'ous judgments to obey.
107 I'm sore distress'd ; LORD me revive,
  According to thy faithful word :
108 My mouth's free off'rings, O accept ;
  And me thy judgments teach, O LORD.

109 My soul is always in my hand,
  Yet did I not thy law forget :
110 Nor from thy precepts have I stray'd,
  Tho' snares for me the wicked set.
111 Thy word my endless heritage
  I chuse, as of my heart the joy :
112 My heart to do thy will I bow,
  And therein all my life employ.

[15 *Part.*]

[15 Part.]

113 Proud, wav'ring and vain ‡ thoughts I hate;
    But dearly love thy law do I:
114 My covert and my shield art Thou;
    And on thy word I firm rely,
115 Depart from me ye wicked men;
    For, keep my God's commands I must:
116 By thy word stay me; and I live,
    Nor am ashamed of my trust.

117 Uphold me and I shall be safe;
    And I thy laws will always eye:
118 Who leave thy laws Thou treadest down;
    For their deceit is all a lie.
119 Earth's lewd, as dross Thou throw'st away;
    To love thy law I'm therefore led:
120 My flesh all shakes for fear of Thee,
    And I thy judgments greatly dread.

[16 Part.]

121 O, to oppressors, leave me not;
    I judgment do and righteousness:
122 For good, thy servant's surety be;
    And let not proud ones me oppress.
123 Mine eyes for thy salvation fail,
    And for thy word of equity.
124 In mercy with thy servant deal;
    And all thy statutes teach Thou me.

125 I am thy servant; make me wise,
    Thy testimonies all to know:
126 'Tis time for Thee, O LORD, to work,
    For men thy law abolish * now.
127 Hence above gold, the finest gold,
    Thy law I love and estimate:
128 And all thy precepts right esteem,
    And ev'ry way of falshood * hate.

L 5   [17 Part.]

‡ The *Hebrew* seems to signify *all these*; See *Glassius, Ainsworth, Leigh*, &c.

[17 *Part.*]

129 Replete with wonders are thy words;
　　Therefore my foul keeps them with care:
130 The op'ning of thy word gives light;
　　And makes them wife who fimple were.
131 With open mouth for thy commands
　　I pant, with longings for the fame.
132 Look on; in judgment † pity me,
　　As Thou doft thofe who love thy name.
133 By thy word, order all my fteps;
　　Let no fin over me bear fway.
134 Save me from being opprefs'd by man;
　　And I will all thy laws obey.
135 Thy face let on thy fervant fhine,
　　And me to learn thy ftatutes caufe:
136 While tears in floods run down mine eyes,
　　To fee men violate thy laws.

[18 *Part.*]

137 Stedfaftly juft Thou art, O LORD;
　　Thy judgments art upright alfo:
138 Thy records which Thou doft command
　　Are right'ous and moft * faithful too.
139 My zeal confumes me to behold
　　Mine enemies thy words forget:
140 Thy word is moft refin'd; * therefore
　　Thy fervant's love thereon is fet.

141 Tho' I am little and defpis'd;
　　My foul thy precepts yet retains:
142 Thy righteoufnefs for ever lafts;
　　Thy law eternal truth remains.
143 Diftrefs and anguifh on me feize;
　　Yet great delight thy precepts give:
144 Thy records ever right'ous laft;
　　O make me wife, and I fhall live.

[19 *Part.*]

† So *Sept.* ancient *Latin, Arab. Munfter, Ver.* 149, and the *Hebrew Lexicons*; i, e, *the Judgment* given in thy Word,

[19 *Part.*]

145 To Thee with all my heart I cry;
   LORD hear, and I'll thy word obey:
146 To Thee I cry, O save Thou me;
   And I will keep thy records way.
147 Before the morning dawn I cry;
   And for thy word in hope ‖ I wait, ‖
148 Mine eyes prevent the midnight watch,
   Upon thy word to meditate.

149 My voice, LORD, in thy mercy hear,
   Revive me in thy judgment ‡ too:
150 They who seek mischief near me come;
   But from thy law far off will go.
151 But, O JEHOVAH, thou art near;
   All thy commands are verity.
152 Of old I know, thou founded haft
   Thy records for eternity.

[20 *Part.*]

153 My griefs consider, and me save;
   For I do not forget thy laws:
154 For thy word's sake revive Thou me,
   Deliver me, and plead my cause.
155 Salvation is from sinners far,
   Since for thy laws they will not strive:
156 Thy tender mercies, LORD, are great:
   After thy judgments § me revive.

157 Many my persecuting foes;
   Yet from thy laws I do not swerve:
158 I sinners see, and greatly grieve;
   For they thy word do not observe.
159 Consider how I love thy laws;
   In mercy LORD revive Thou me:
160 Thy word is ever perfect truth,
   Thy judgment just eternally.

[21 *Part.*]

‖ The *Hebrew* includes both Ideas.
‡ i.e. *thy Judgment* given in thy Word in Favour of thy People.
§ i.e. thy *Sentences as my Judge* declared in thy Word.

PSALM CXIX.

[21 Part.]

161 Great men me causeless persecute;
    But more thy word o'er-awes my mind;
162 And yet I in thy word rejoice,
    As they who stores of riches find.
163 I falshood utterly-abhor,
    But dearly love thy law always:
164 And for thy right'ous judgments I
    Ev'n seven times a day Thee praise.

165 Great peace have they who love thy law;
    No stumbling stone shall them offend:
166 For thy salvation, LORD, I hope;
    And thy commands with care attend.
167 My soul thy testimonies keeps;
    And them I love exceedingly.
168 I keep thy records and commands;
    For all my ways before Thee lie.

[22 Part.]

169 O let my cry, LORD, come to Thee;
    After thy word me prudent make:
170 Let my request before Thee come;
    And save Thou me for thy word's sake.
171 To Thee my lips shall utter praise,
    When Thou thy statutes teachest me:
172 My tongue shall forth thy word resound,
    For all thy laws are just, I see.

173 O help me by thy mighty hand;
    For I thy precepts make my choice.
174 LORD I for thy salvation long;
    And greatly in thy law rejoice.
175 Let my soul live; and I'll Thee praise;
    And from thy judgments succour find:
176 Thy servant seek, who like stray sheep
    Am lost; yet I thy precepts mind.

PSALM CXX, CXXI.

PSALM CXX. *A Song of Degrees.* ||

1 IN diſtreſs cry'd to the LORD;
  and kind, He heard my cries.
2 LORD, ſave my ſoul from guileful tongues
  and lips inur'd to lies.
3 What ſhall to thy falſe tongue be done?
  or giv'n, thou ſlanderer?
4 Sharp arrows of the Mighty one,
  and coals of Juniper.

5 Ah! wo is me, that I am forc'd
  in Meſhech to reſide;
  And muſt in the ungodly tents
  of Kedar ſtill abide!
6 My ſoul has long been forc'd to dwell
  with them who peace abhor:
7 I am for peace; but when I ſpeak,
  they all declare for war.

PSALM CXXI. *A Song of Degrees.*

1 TO thoſe mountains lift mine eyes,
  from whence muſt come mine aid:
2 Mine help muſt from JEHOVAH come,
  who heav'n and earth has made.
3 He will not let thy foot be mov'd,
  nor ſlumber who thee keeps:
4 Lo, He who keeps his Iſrael,
  He ſlumbers not, nor ſleeps.
5 The LORD thy keeper is; the LORD
  thy ſhade on thy right * hand:
6 The ſun ſhall not ſmite thee by day,
  nor moon by night offend.
7 JEHOVAH will preſerve thy ſoul;
  he'll keep thee from all ill:
8 Thy going out and coming in,
  the LORD keep ever will.

PSALM

|| *Heb. Aſcenſions*: and perhaps the *Titles* of theſe *fifteen* Pſalms may mean—the *Aſcenſions* of the *Soul* to GOD.

PSALM CXXII. *A Song of Degrees of* David.

1 IT was my joy to hear them say,
  come to the LORD's house go:
2 O dear Jerusalem, our feet
  thy gates shall pass into.
3 Jerusalem is builded up
  into a city frame:
  Quite uniform and beautiful
  and compact is the same.
4 Whither the tribes, the tribes of JAH *
  to Isr'el's witness go;
  That there they to JEHOVAH's name
  their thankfulness may show.
5 And there the thrones of judgment rais'd
  established remain;
  The thrones that to the royal house
  of David appertain.
6 Pray for Jerusalem's firm peace:
  they prosper who love thee:
7 Be in thy walls and palaces
  peace and prosperity.
8 Now, * for my friends and brethren sake,
  I wish thee perfect peace;
9 And for our God JEHOVAH's house,
  I'll seek thy happiness.

PSALM CXXIII. *A Song of Degrees.*

1 O Thou who in the heav'ns dost dwell,
  I lift mine eyes to Thee.
2 Behold, as servants eyes intent
  their masters hand to see;
  As maids eyes to their mistress hand;
  to Thee our eyes are so;
  To Thee the LORD our God, till Thou
  wilt mercy on us show.
3 O LORD, be merciful to us,
  to us, O gracious be!
  For filled with contempt and scorn
  exceedingly are we.

4 Our souls are fill'd exceedingly
    with scoffs of men at ease;
And with the scorns of proud men who
    from scoffing never cease.

PSALM CXXIV. *A Song of Degrees of* David.

1 HAD not the LORD been on our side
    may Isr'el now confess;
2 Had not the LORD appear'd for us,
    in our extreme distress;
3 When men against us rose, inflam'd
    with rage and cruelty;
Like rav'nous beasts they us alive
    had swallow'd instantly.

4 Or like o'erflowing waters, they
    had rag'd without controul;
5 The waters proud, the mighty streams,
    had overwhelm'd our soul.
6 Then ever praised be the LORD,
    who sav'd from instant death;
And would not give us up a prey
    to their devouring teeth.

7 Our soul escap'd is as a bird
    out of the fowler's snare:
The snare asunder broken is,
    and we escaped are.
8 Our sure and alsufficient help
    is in JEHOVAH's name;
Who all the glorious heav'ns around,
    and all the earth did frame.

PSALM CXXV. *A Song of Degrees.*

1 ALL those who in JEHOVAH trust
    shall like mount Zion be;
Which shall not be remov'd, but stands
    to perpetuity.
2 See how around Jerusalem,
    the mountains stand on high;
The LORD his people so surrounds
    hence to eternity,

3 For

PSALM CXXVI.

3 For, sinners rod upon the lot
 of just men shall not lie;
Lest righteous men stretch forth their hands
 to do iniquity.
4 To all who are sincerely good
 thy goodness LORD impart;
And let it freely flow to all
 who are of upright heart.

5 But those who turn to crooked ways,
 the LORD will make to go
With workers of iniquity,
 but Isr'el peace shall know.

PSALM CXXVI. *A Song of Degrees.*

1 WHEN from captivity the LORD
 his Zion did redeem:
We in an extacy of soul
 were like to them who dream.
2 Then were our mouths with laughter fill'd,
 our tongues with shouts did sound:
'The LORD hath done great things for them,'
 the heathen freely own'd.

3 Great things and marvellous for us,
 the LORD hath done indeed;
In the surprizing view whereof
 our hearts with joy exceed.
4 LORD, our remaining captives bring
 home from the barb'rous foe,
Like cooling streams which in the south
 to thirsty regions flow.

5 Who sow in tears shall reap in joy,
6 Who going forth, did mourn,
Bearing choice seed; shall fill'd with joy,
 bringing full sheaves return.

PSALM

PSALM CXXVII.
A Song of Degrees of Solomon.

1 UNlefs JEHOVAH builds the houfe,
vain is the workman's pain:
Unlefs the LORD the city keeps,
the watchmen watch in vain;
2 'Tis vain for you to rife betimes,
and late from reſt to keep,
Or eat the bread of care: 'tis He
gives his beloved fleep.
3 Lo, children are an heritage,
the LORD alone beſtows:
Poſterity is a reward
which from his bounty flows.
4 As arrows in a mighty hand
when enemies are near;
So children grown up in their youth
to their glad parents are.
5 How happy is the man who hath
his quiver full of thofe!
For he undaunted in the gate,
will fpeak to all his foes.

PSALM CXXVIII. *A Song of Degrees.*

1 HOW greatly bleſſed is the man,
how bleſſed all his days,
Who fears JEHOVAH, and who walks
uprightly in his ways.
2. For thy hands labour thou ſhalt eat
and happy ſhalt thou be:
In all the changes of thy life,
it ſhall be well with thee.
3 Thy wife ſhall like a fruitful vine
by thy houfe fide be found;
Thy children like fair olive plants
adorn thy table round.
4 Lo thus the man who fears the LORD
ſhall greatly bleſſed be!
5 Yea more, the LORD from Zion will
his bleſſing fend to thee.

The good of our Jerusalem,
  her great felicity,
Thou shalt thro' all thy lengthned life
  with raised pleasure see.
6 Yea of thy children's children thou
  shalt see a glad increase,
And our dear land of Israel,
  in all the joys of peace.

[*Long Metre.*]

1 HOW bless'd is he who fears the LORD
  And walks in his appointed ways.
2 For thy hands labour thou shall eat,
  And shalt be happy all thy days.
3 Thy wife shall like a goodly vine
  By thy house side be fruitful found:
Thy children like fair olive plants,
  Adorn thy cheerful table round.

4 Lo, thus the man who fears the LORD,
  With earthly good shall blessed be:
5 Yea more, the LORD from Zion hill
  Will heav'nly blessings send to thee.
The good of our Jerusalem,
  Thou all thy happy life shalt view.
6 Thy children's children thou shalt see,
  And peaceful times on Isr'el too.

PSALM CXXIX. *A Song of Degrees.*

1 OFT from my youth they me distress'd,
  may Isr'el say with joy;
2 Oft from my youth, they me distress'd,
  but never could destroy.
3 My back as ploughers, oft they plough'd,
  and furrows long did make;
4 But the just LORD, the wicked's cords
  did all asunder break.

5 All those who Zion hate shall be
  confounded and o'erthrown;
6 Shall be as grass on houses tops,
  which fades before 'tis grown.

7 Whereof

7 Whereof enough to fill his hand,
   the mower cannot find;
Much less can he his bosom fill,
   whose work is sheaves to bind.

8 Nor those who pass by say—' On you
   ' JEHOVAH's blessing rest !'
Nor these reply—' In the LORD's name
   ' we wish you to be bless'd !' ‖

PSALM CXXX. *A Song of Degrees.*

1 LORD ! from the deeps I cry to Thee !
   2 My voice Lord do thou hear !
And to my supplications voice,
   O give attentive ear !
3 Lord, who can stand, if thou O JAH *
   shouldst mark iniquity ?
4 But with Thee there forgiveness is
   that feared thou may'st be.

5 Therefore for Thee, O LORD, I wait,
   my soul still waits for Thee ;
And on thy known and faithful word
   I hope continually.
6 My soul looks out more for the *Lord*,
   than watchers in the night ;
Yea more than watchers weary'd out,
   look for the dawning light.

7 Let Isr'el then wait hopefully,
   and on the LORD confide ;
For boundless mercies with the LORD
   continually reside :
8 Yea plenteous redemption is
   eternally with him ;
And Isr'el He from all their sins,
   will perfectly redeem.

[*Long*

‖ These two Verses represent the ancient, pious, mutual *Salu-*
tations of Mowers, Reapers and Passengers in *Israel.*

PSALM CXXX, CXXXI.

[*Long Metre.*]

1 LORD, from the deeps I cry to Thee;
2 My voice, *Lord*, do Thou kindly hear!
And to my supplications voice,
O give thou an attentive ear.
3 O JAH! if thou shouldst mark our sins,
Who can before Thee stand, O *Lord?*
4 But there forgiveness is with Thee,
That Thou may'st humbly be ador'd.

5 I for the LORD wait; my soul waits,
And I hope in his faithful word:
6 Than watchers for the dawning look,
My soul more looks out for the *Lord.*
7 Let Isr'el then wait hopefully,
And ever on the LORD confide;
For boundless mercies with the LORD
To perpetuity abide.

8 Yea plenteous redemption is
Ev'n to eternity with him;
And Isr'el He from all their sins
Will to eternity redeem.

PSALM CXXXI.
A Song of Degrees of David.

1 JEHOVAH, see my open heart,
if it is haughty grown;
Or if mine eyes are rais'd aloft,
unless to Thee alone;
If I in any things too great
and high for me aspire,
To exercise my self; or if
too high is my desire.

2 Or if I do not now compose
my soul to quiet rest,
Ev'n as a young and weaned child,
wean'd from the mother's breast.
3 Let Isr'el then look to the LORD,
and his kind aid implore;
And on his tender care rely,
henceforth and evermore.   [*Short*

PSALM CXXXI, CXXXII.

[*Short Metre.*]

1 MY heart's not haughty, LORD,
    nor lofty are mine eyes:
In things too great or high for me
    is not mine exercife.
2 I as a child behave
    wean'd from the mother's breaft:
My foul ev'n as a weaned child,
    fubmits and lies at reft.

3 Let Ifr'el on the LORD,
    reft therefore quietly:
Yea henceforth ever hope and wait,
    his faving help to fee.

PSALM CXXXII. *A Song of Degrees.*

1 DAVID, and all his troubles, LORD,
    O do Thou kindly think upon:
2 How to the LORD he fware, and how
    He vow'd to Jacob's mighty one;
3 Into my tent I will not go,
    Nor to my bed for fweet repofe;
4 No fleep will to mine eyes afford,
    Nor flumber fhall my eye-lids clofe;

5 Until I for the LORD have found
    And for his ark a dwelling place;
For Him who is the mighty One,
    Of Jacob, and his favour'd race.
6 Behold at Ephrata we heard
    The place of it's retir'd abode;
And fearch'd till it we found with joy,
    In a dark field enclos'd with wood.

7 We'll go into his facred tents,
    Our worfhip at his footftool pay.
8 Arife, O LORD, into thy reft,
    And with thine ark of ftrength there ftay.

9 Let righteousness thy priests adorn,
  Thy saints with shouts their joy display:
10 And for thy servant David's sake ‖
  Turn thy MESSIAH ‡ not away.

[2 *Part.*]

11 The LORD to David sware in truth;
  The oath he never will disown;
  " I one descended from thy loins
  " Will surely set upon thy throne:
12 " And if my covenant and law,
  " That to thy children teach shall I,
  " They always keep, then shall their race
  " Sit on thy throne perpetually.

13 " Because the LORD hath Zion chose,
  " And there desir'd to have his seat;
14 " This is my rest for ever; here
  " I'll dwell, for I desired it:
15 " I'll her provision greatly bless,
  " And satisfy her poor with food:
16 " Her priests with my salvation cloath,
  " Her saints with joy shall shout aloud.

17 " There David's horn I'll make to spring,†
  " There my MESSIAH's * lamp ordain:
18 " With shame I'll cloath his foes: on Him
  " His crown shall flourish and remain."

PSALM CXXXIII.
A Song of Degrees of David.

1 BEHOLD, how good it is,
  and what a joy to see,
When brethren with each other dwell
  in love and unity.
2 'Tis like the precious oil,
  they pour'd on Aaron's head;
Which down his hair and garment flow'd,
  and fragrant odours spread.

3 Or

‖ i. e. Thy Promise made to *David*. ‡ *Heb.*—MESSIAH: and so the *Sept. Chaldee,* ancient *Latin* & *Arab* i. e. either *David* (or *Solomon,* as the *Chaldee*) the *Typical* MESSIAH, or CHRIST the *Real.* † See the *Hebrew Lexicons.*

PSALM CXXXIII, CXXXIV.

3 Or as refreshing dew
  on Hermon's mount distills;
  Or like the pearly drops that shine
  on Zion's joyful hills.
  For there the LORD commands,
  and doth his blessing give,
  The foretaste of that blessedness
  which shall for ever live.

[*Hallelujah Metre.*]

1 BEHOLD how good it is,
  and what a pleasing sight,
  When brethren dwell in love,
  and cordially unite;
     When all agree
     to act their part
     as with one heart
  In charity.

2 'Tis like the precious oil,
  that gave a fragrant smell;
  Which pour'd on Aaron's head,
  adown his locks it fell;
     From whence it shed
     along his breast
     down to his vest,
  And odours spread.

3 Or as refreshing dew
  on Hermon's mount distills;
  Or like the drops that shine
  on Zion's joyful hills.
     The LORD on high
     there blessing gives,
     and bliss that lives
  Eternally.

PSALM CXXXIV. *A Song of Degrees.*

1 BEHOLD, bless ye the LORD,
  ye the LORD's servants all,
  Who in the LORD's house stand by night,
  and there upon Him call.
2 Lift up your hands; the LORD
  bless in his holy place.
3 The LORD, who heav'n and earth has made,
  thee out of Zion bless.   [*Hallelujah*

PSALM CXXXIV, CXXXV.

[*Hallelujah Metre.*]

1 YE servants of the LORD,
   who in the LORD's house wait,
And keep your watch before
the threshold of his gate;
   The LORD's praise sing
   by silent night,
'till cheerful light
Of morning spring.

2 Lift in his holy place,
   your joyful hands on high;
And say, the LORD we bless,
who made the earth and sky.
3   And may he still
   thee greatly bless
   with joy and grace,
From Zion-hill.

PSALM CXXXV.

1 O Sing ye HALLELUJAH * now,
   And praise JEHOVAH's holy name;
O all ye servants of the LORD,
His praises all abroad proclaim.
2 Ye who within the house do stand,
Wherein the LORD has his abode;
And in the court-yards of his house,
Who is by covenant our God.

3 Sing HALLELUJAH *; for the LORD
Is good: sing praises to his name;
For it is sweet to be employ'd
His praise in singing to proclaim.
4 For the eternal JAH * hath chose
Jacob for his propriety;
And his peculiar treasure hath
He taken Israel to be.

5 For well we know, the LORD is great,
And that this sov'reign *Lord* of ours
Transcends all that are called GODS,
And reigns o'er all created pow'rs.

6 In

PSALM CXXXV.

6 In heaven and earth the LORD hath done,
Whatever his own mind did pleafe ;
In the deep caverns of the earth,
And in the great and fwelling feas.

7 From the wide furface of the earth
He makes the vapours to arife ;
He makes the lightning for the rain,
And winds brings from his treafuries.

[2 *Part.*]

8 Egypt's firft born, both man and beaft
9 He flew : and wondrous tokens He
On Pharaoh and his fervants fent,
O Egypt in the midft of thee.
10 Great nations fmote, great kings he, flew,
11 Sihon, who was of Hefhbon king,
And Og of Bafhan ; and to nought
All Canaan's kingdoms he did bring.

12 And gave their land an heritage
To his own people Ifrael.
13 O LORD, eternal is thy name,
LORD, endlefs thy memorial.
14 JEHOVAH will his people judge,
And for his fervants turn again.
15 The heathen idols filver are
And gold ; the handy work of men.

16 Mouths have they, yet they cannot fpeak ;
And they have eyes, but never faw ;
17 Ears have they, yet they nothing hear ;
Their mouths no breath can ever draw.
18 Such fenfelefs ftocks are they themfelves,
Who did thefe fenfelefs idols frame ;
And fuch are all who to them pray,
And put their confidence in them.

19 O houfe of Ifr'el blefs the LORD :
The LORD blefs—who of Aaron's are :
20 The LORD, O houfe of Levi blefs :
The LORD blefs ye, the LORD who fear.

21 From Zion-hill his sacred seat,
O let JEHOVAH blessed be;
Who dwells within Jerusalem:
O sing, sing HALLELUJAH * ye.

PSALM CXXXVI.

1 O Thank the LORD; for he is good,
For ever are his mercies sure:
2 Thanks give ye to the God of GODS;
His mercies evermore endure.
3 Thanks give ye to the *Lord* of *Lords*; †
For ever are his mercies sure:
4 Him who alone does wonders great;
His mercies evermore endure.

5 To Him whose wisdom made the heav'ns;
For ever are his mercies sure:
6 Who o'er the waters spread the earth;
His mercies evermore endure.
7 To Him who made great lights to shine;
For ever are his mercies sure.
8 The sun to rule and guide the day,
His mercies evermore endure.

9 The moon and stars to rule the night;
For ever are his mercies sure.
10 Who the first-born of Egypt smote;
His mercies evermore endure.
11 Who from among them Isr'el brought;
For ever are his mercies sure.
12 With a strong hand and stretch'd out arm;
His mercies evermore endure.

13 Who the red sea asunder clave;
For ever are his mercies sure.
14 And through the midst made Isr'el go;
His mercies evermore endure
15 But there drown'd Pharoah and his host;
For ever are his mercies sure.
16 His people through the desart led,
His mercies evermore endure.

† *Adoni Adonim.*

17 To Him who mighty kings did smite;
    For ever are his mercies sure.
18 And famous kings in battle slew;
    His mercies evermore endure.
19 King Sihon of the Amorites;
    For ever are his mercies sure.
20 And Ogg of Bashan mighty king;
    His mercies evermore endure.
21 And gave their land an heritage;
    For ever are his mercies sure.
22 To his dear servant Israel;
    His mercies evermore endure.
23 Who minds us in our low estate;
    For ever are his mercies sure.
24 And who redeems us from our foes,
    His mercies evermore endure.
25 Who to all flesh gives proper food;
    For ever are his mercies sure.
26 O to the God of heav'n give thanks;
    His mercies evermore endure.

PSALM CXXXVII.

1 AS by the streams of Babylon
    We captives sat with anxious fears;
  Then we dear Zion thought upon,
  And melted into streams of tears.
2 Our harps, our instruments of joy,
  Which us'd with chearful songs to sound,
  We hung upon the willow trees,
  Which on the shaded banks abound.

3 Because * our foes, who all conspir'd
  To triumph in our slavish wrongs,
  Musick and mirth of us requir'd;
  'Come sing us one of Zion's songs'
4 But, ah! how could we guide our hands
  To play, with hearts so full of woes?
  Sing Zion's songs in heathen lands,
  JEHOVAH's hymns to chear his foes?

5 O dear Jerusalem! if I
  Ever of thee forgetful grow;
  Let me the skill of my right hand
  For ever wholly cease to know.
6 Let my tongue to my palate † cleave,
  If thee remember should not I,
  Or don't prefer Jerusalem,
  Above my highest earthly joy.

7 LORD, Thou remembrest Edom's sons,
  Who on Jerusalem's sad day,
  'To the foundation raze her!' cry'd;
  'Raze, raze her!' out aloud cry'd they.
8 O Babel's daughter! doom'd to fall!
  That conqueror ‖ shall blessed be,
  Who, just as thou hast done to us,
  Will do in righteousness to thee!

9 Yea, he shall blessed be by heav'n,
  Who shall by heav'n employed be,
  Upon the stones to dash thy race,
  And end thy cruel progeny.

PSALM CXXXVIII. *(A Psalm)* of David.†

1 WITH all my heart I'll Thee confess,
    to Thee my thanks will bring.
  And openly before the GODS, ‡
    I'll praises to Thee sing.
2 Towards thy house of holiness *
    I'll bow and worship Thee;
  And thy great name to celebrate,
    shall my employment be.

  But chiefly for thy love and truth
    thy praises I'll proclaim;
  For over all, Thou, by thy word,
    hast magnify'd thy name.

‡ i. e. *The Roof of the Mouth*—as all the *Versions, Lexicons,* and *Writers* of *Anatomy,* both in *Latin* and *English,* testify.
‖ Who proved to be that glorious Conqueror CYRUS.
† *Chaldee*—By the Hand of *David.*
‡ It may mean both *Mighty Men* and *Angels.*

3 The very day I cry'd to Thee,
    Thou kindly didft reply ;
  And Thou didft fortify my foul
    with ftrength in full fupply.
4 All kings throughout the joyful earth,
    fhall give Thee praife, O LORD,
  When of thy mouth they come to hear
    the true and faithful word.
5 Yea, they with raifed joy fhall fing
    along JEHOVAH's ways;
  For great the glory of the LORD,
    and great is all his praife,
6 The LORD, tho' high, yet kindly looks
    on thofe who lowly are ;
  But thofe exalted high with pride,
    he knows and keeps afar.
7 Although I walk amidft diftrefs,
    Thee quick'ning me I have ;
  Thine hand fhall fmite my raging foes,
    and thy right hand me fave.
8 The LORD will perfect what I want :
    thy mercy ever ftands ;
  JEHOVAH, O forfake thou not
    the works of thine own hands,

PSALM CXXXIX. *A Pfalm of* David.

1 O LORD, thou doft me fearch and know :
2   Thou know'ft my fitting down ;
  My rifing up, and all my thoughts
    to Thee far off are known.
3 Thou compaffeft my path and bed,
    and knoweft all my ways :
4 And ev'ry word that moves my tongue,
    O LORD, thine eye furveys.
5 Thou haft befet me round about,
    and on me laid thy hand.
6 Such knowledge wondrous is to me,
    too high to underftand.

M 3   7 Where

7 Where shall I from thy spirit go;
   or from thy presence fly?
8 If heav'n I climb, lo, Thou art there;
   There if in hell I lie.
9 If morning wings I take, and dwell
   where utmost sea coasts are;
10 Ev'n there thy hand shall lead me on,
   and thy right hand me bear.
11 Or if I say, the darkness shall
   conceal me from thy sight;
   The darkest night shall then to Thee
   around me, all be light.

12 For darkness darkens not to Thee;
   but night as day shines clear:
   Thick darkness and the shining light
   to Thee alike appear.

[2 *Part.*]

13 Because thou hast possest my reins,
   and safely cover'd me
   Within my tender mother's womb;
14   my praise shall be to Thee:
   For fearfully and wondrously
   Thou didst my frame compose;
   Thy works in me are marvellous;
   and that my soul well knows.

15 When first I was in secret made,
   my substance Thou didst know;
   While I most curiously was wrought,
   as in dark caves below.
16 Thine eyes my shapeless substance saw:
   and written in thy book
   Were all my members, tho' not made,
   which after fashion took.

17 How precious also to my soul
   are thy sweet thoughts become?
   O God, how numerous they grow,
   how vast their growing sum?

18 If

18 If I should number them, their sum
   more than the sand would be :
   And still whenever I awake
   I present am with Thee.
         [3 *Part.*]
19 O God, Thou surely wilt them slay,
   who wicked persons are :
   And therefore all ye men of blood,
   depart from me afar.
20 For they against Thee wickedly
   speak out with tongues profane :
   And they who are thine enemies,
   take thy great name in vain.
21 JEHOVAH ! hate I not all those,
   who hatred show to Thee ?
   And those who up against Thee rise,
   am I not griev'd to see ?
22 Yea I abhor them utterly,
   who up against Thee rise ;
   And all who show themselves thy foes,
   I count mine enemies.
23 O gracious God, I beg Thee make,
   a thorough search of me ;
   And know my heart, me strictly try,
   my thoughts within me see.
24 And see if any way of sin ‡
   in me indulged be ;
   And in thy way to endless bliss
   for ever lead Thou me.

P S A L M CXL. *A Psalm of* David.

1 LORD, save me from malicious men,
      such as injurious are ;
2 Who mischief in their hearts contrive,
   and daily meet for war.
3 Like serpents they make sharp their tongues
   for piercing calumnies ;
   Conceiv'd beneath their guileful lips
   the adder's poison lies.

‡ So the *Septuagint* and *Arabick*.

4 LORD,

4 LORD, keep me from ungodly hands,
　　from vi'lent men me save;
　Who to o'erthrow me in my steps
　　a wicked purpose have.
5 The proud for me have hid their snares,
　　and cords to draw their net,
　Which they have spread across my paths,
　　and traps for me have set.

6 O LORD, Thou art my God, I cry'd;
　　whom I love, chuse and fear;
　O to my supplications voice,
　　LORD, give a gracious ear.
7 O *Lord* JEHOVAH, thou the strength
　　of my salvation wast;
　And in the day of battle Thou
　　my head safe cov'red hast.

[2 *Part.*]

8 Grant not O LORD, what wicked men
　　desire unrighteously;
　Nor further Thou their ill designs,
　　lest they triumph on high.
9 But for the leading heads of those
　　who round encompass me;
　Ev'n with the mischief of their lips
　　they quite shall cover'd be.

10 On them shall burning coals be cast;
　　and He will make them fall,
　Into deep pits and glowing fire,
　　to rise no more at all.
11 The man of evil tongue shall not
　　at peace on earth arrive:
　Evil shall chase the violent
　　and to destruction drive.

12 The LORD, I know, for the oppress'd
　　and poor will judgment give.
13 Surely the just shall praise thy name,
　　and in thy presence live.

PSALM

PSALM CXLI.

PSALM CXLI. A Psalm of David.

1 O LORD, to Thee I call aloud!
   O make Thou haste to me,
And hearken to my earnest voice,
   now while I cry to Thee!

2 O let my pray'r before thy face *
   as fragrant incense rise; †
The lifting of my hands accept
   as ev'ning sacrifice.

3 O set a constant watch before
   my hasty mouth, O LORD;
And of my lips keep Thou the door,
   against each evil word.

4 Let not my heart incline to ill;
   nor let me ever share
With evil men in evil deeds;
   nor on their dainties fare.

5 Me, let the righteous kindly smite,
   and that I'll kindly take;
Their just reproofs shall fall so soft,
   my head they shall not break.
But as an oil of great esteem,
   I shall it highly prize;
And in requital pray for them
   in their calamities.

6 And when by ‖ judges they shall be
   in stony places cast;
My kind words they shall hear, and they
   shall sweet be to their taste.

7 About the grave's wide open mouth,
   our bones are scatter'd round,
As wood which hewers cut and cleave,
   lies scatter'd on the ground.

8 But O JEHOVAH, *Lord*, to Thee
   directed are mine eyes:
My soul, O leave not destitute:
   on Thee my hope relies.

---

† *Arab.* ‖ This seems to be the true Version: and both the *Chaldee*, and *Gejer*, in *Pol. Synop.* seem to favour it.

9 O keep me from the hands of those
   who snares have laid for me ;
And from the secret net of those
   who work iniquity.
10 Into the nets which they have set
   shall the ungodly fall ;
While I, for whom they were prepar'd,
   pass *. and escape them all.

PSALM CXLII. *Maschil of* David.
A Prayer when he was in the Cave.

1 To JEHOVAH with my voice
   express'd aloud my cry ;
In supplications to the LORD,
   I rais'd my voice on high.
2 Before his face * I poured out
   my sorrowful complaint ;
Before his presence I declar'd
   the grief I underwent.
3 In me my spirit was o'erwhelm'd ;
   my path was known to Thee :
And in the way I was to go
   they hid a snare for me.
4 On my right hand I look'd and view'd,
   but none would know me there ;
All human refuge failed me ;
   none for my soul would care.
5 Then to the LORD I cry'd, and said ;
   Thou shalt my refuge be,
And in the land of living ones,
   my portion is in Thee.
6 Because I'm brought exceeding low,
   O listen to my cry ;
Me from my persecutors save,
   who stronger are than I.
7 From out of prison bring my soul,
   to sing loud praise to Thee ;
The just will circle me with joy,
   when Thou shalt favour me.

PSALM CXLIII.

PSALM CXLIII. *A Pfalm of* David.

1 LORD, hear my humble pray'r to Thee,
and to my cries attend;
And in thy truth and righteoufnefs
a gracious anfwer fend.
2 O with thy fervant enter not
in judgment me to try;
For in thy fight no man alive
himfelf can juftify.
3 The foe purfues my foul, my life
down to the ground doth tread,
In darknefs makes me dwell as thofe
that ages have been dead.
4 Therefore my foul is overwhelm'd
with great perplexity;
My heart, of joy and comfort is
made defolate in me.
5 I call'd to mind the days of old,
on all thy works I thought;
I meditated on the deeds
thy mighty hands have wrought.
6 And now I earneftly to Thee
reach mine out-ftretched hands;
My foul for Thee with ardour longs,
like dry and thirfty lands.

[2 *Part.*]

7 LORD hear with fpeed, my fpirit fails:
hide not thy face from me;
Left I like thofe who in the grave
defcend, fhould quickly be.
8 Let me thy kindnefs early hear;
in Thee my hope I place:
Shew me the way wherein to go;
my foul to Thee I raife.
9 JEHOVAH, from mine enemies
quickly deliver me:
To hide me safe beneath thy wings,
in hafte I fly to Thee.

10 Teach

PSALM CXLIV.

10 Teach me to do thy will, becauſe
   Thou art my GOD indeed:
Let thy good ſpirit to the land
   of uprightneſs me lead.
11 Yea for the ſake of thy great name,
   O LORD, revive Thou me;
And in thy right'ouſneſs do Thou
   my ſoul from trouble free.
12 Yea in thy mercy Thou my foes
   wilt quite ſuppreſs; ‖ and them
Thou wilt deſtroy who vex my ſoul,
   for I thy ſervant am.

PSALM CXLIV. *(A Pſalm) of* Davd. †

1 O Let JEHOVAH bleſſed be,
   who is my rock of might;
My hands he teaches how to war,
   my fingers how to fight,
2 My goodneſs, fortreſs, my high tow'r,
   ſaviour and ſhield is He;
In whom I truſt, and who ſubdues
   my people under me.
3 LORD, what is man, that Thou of him
   ſhouldſt any knowledge take;
Or ſon of man, that Thou of him
   ſo great account doſt make?
4 For man is like to vanity,
   uncertain here to ſtay;
His days like ſhades of flying clouds
   paſs haſtily away.
5 LORD, bow thy heav'ns above, come down;
   and with thy thunder's ſtroke
Do Thou but once the mountains touch,
   and they will riſe in ſmoke.
6 Caſt forth thy lightnings, and diſperſe
   thine enemies around;
And make thy piercing arrows fly,
   and all their pow'r confound.   7 Thine

‖ *Ainſworth.*   † *Chaldee*—By the Hand of *David.*

PSALM CXLIV.

7 Thine hand O send Thou from above,
  redeem and rescue me;
  From mighty waters, from the hand
  of strangers set me free.
8 Whose evil mouths are wont to speak
  falshood † and vanity; †
  And whose right hand a right hand is
  of fraud and perfidy.

[2 *Part.*]

9 O God, new songs I'll sing to Thee,
  upon the psaltery;
  And on a ten-string'd instrument
  to Thee sing praise will I.
10 It is He only who to kings
  salvation doth afford;
  And who his servant David saves
  from the destroying sword.
11 Free me from hands of strangers sons,
  whose mouths speak vanity,
  And whose right hand a right hand is
  of fraud and perfidy.
12 But let our sons in youthful age
  as thriving plants appear;
  Daughters like polish'd corner stones
  which grace a palace fair.
13 That to afford all kinds of stores,
  our garners may be fill'd;
  Our cattle thousands in our streets,
  yea may ten thousands yield.
14 Our oxen for their labour strong;
  no enemy invade;
  No leading captive; no complaint
  in all our streets be made.
15 O happy people they, who are
  in such a case as this;
  But far more happy people they
  whose God JEHOVAH is.

PSALM

† The *Hebrew* signifies *Both*,

PSALM CXLV.

PSALM CXLV. David's (*Psalm of*) *Praise*.‡

1 MY God and king, I'll Thee extol,
    thy name I'll ever bless;
2 For ever will I praise thy name
    in daily thankfulness.
3 Great is the LORD, most worthy praise;
    his greatness search exceeds:
4 Age shall to age extol thy works
    and show thy mighty deeds.
5 Of thy transcendent comeliness, *
    thy glory, majesty, ‖
  And of thy admirable works
    with pleasure speak will I.
6 Yea, they shall of thy mighty works
    discourse, which dreadful are;
  And I will thy magnificence
    to all the world declare.
7 The mem'ry of thy goodness great
    they largely shall express;
  And shall in joyful hymns of praise,
    sing of thy right'ousness.

[2 Part.]

8 Most gracious our JEHOVAH is,
    most merciful is He;
  Slow is to anger, and He is
    great in benignity.
9 The LORD is good, and ev'n to all
    his goodness does appear;
  And over all his works behold
    his tender mercies are.
10 LORD, all thy works shew forth thy praise;
    and Thee thy saints shall bless:
11 Shall of thy kingdom's glory speak,
    and thy great power express.
12 That so the sons of men abroad
    thy mighty acts may know;
  And that thy kingdom's majesty
    and glory they may show.   13 Thy

‡ *Chaldee—A Hymn of* David.
‖ Few of the Authors of the metrical Versions seem to have
look'd on this noble Verse in the *Original*.

PSALM CXLVI.

13 Thy kingdom firm eſtabliſh'd is,
    never to know an end;
    And thy ſupreme dominion ſhall
    through ev'ry age extend.

[3 *Part.*]

14 Thoſe who juſt ready are to fall,
    JEHOVAH doth ſuſtain;
    And thoſe he ſees are bowed down
    He raiſes up again.
15 All eyes wait on Him, and their food
    He in fit ſeaſon gives:
16 His open hand fills the deſire
    of ev'ry thing that lives.
17 The LORD is juſt in all his ways,
    his works are holy all:
18 He's near to all who call on Him,
    in truth that on him call.
19 He will of them who Him revere,
    the juſt deſire fulfil;
    And He will hear their cry to Him,
    and ſave them then He will.

20 All who the LORD ſincerely love
    his ſafe-guard ſhall enjoy;
    But He all thoſe who wicked are
    will utterly deſtroy.
21 My mouth the praiſes of the LORD
    ſhall gratefully expreſs:
    And let all fleſh his holy name
    ever and ever bleſs.

PSALM CXLVI.

1 Sing HALLELUJAH! * praiſe the LORD,
2 I'll praiſe JEHOVAH all my days:
    O thou my ſoul! I'll to my God,
    While I a being have, ſing praiſe.
3 Truſt not in princes, nor mens ſons,
    Who can no ſuccour to you ſend;
4 Their breath expires, to earth they turn,
    And all their thoughts that moment end.

PSALM CXLVII.

5 O bless'd is he who hath the God
Of Jacob for his constant aid;
Whose lively confidence upon
The LORD his God is firmly stay'd.
6 Who heav'n, earth, sea, all in them made;
Who ever doth his truth make good;
7 Who for th' oppressed judgment does;
And kindly gives the hungry food.

8 JEHOVAH sets the pris'ners free,
JEHOVAH sight gives to the blind,
The LORD lifts up the bowed down,
The LORD is to the righteous kind.
9 The LORD the strangers doth preserve,
The widows and the orphans raise; *
But He of them who wicked are
Intirely overthrows the ways.

10 The LORD shall reign for evermore:
Thy mighty God, O Zion, He
To generations all shall reign:
Therefore sing HALLELUJAH, * ye.

PSALM CXLVII.

1 Sing HALLELUJAH: * for 'tis good
    praise to our God to sing;
For the employment is most sweet,
    and praise a comely thing.
2 The LORD Jerusalem rebuilds,
    though level'd with the ground;
And Isr'el gathers, tho' dispers'd
    through all the nations round.

3 The broken hearted ones He heals,
    binds up their breaches all:
4 The numbers of the stars He tells,
    and each by name doth call.
5 Great is our *Lord*, and great in pow'r;
    his knowledge has no bound:
6 The LORD lifts up the meek; but casts
    the wicked to the ground.

PSALM CXLVII.

7 With thankfulnefs then to the LORD
 your chearful voices raife:
 And on the harp to Him our God,
 fing grateful hymns of praife.
8 Who over-fpreads with clouds the fky;
 who for the earth below
 Prepares his rain, and makes the grafs
 upon the mountains grow.
9 To all the beafts of fields and woods
 He gives a full fupply;
 Yea fees and hears the ravens young,
 and feeds them when they cry,
10 In horfes ftrength † or fortitude, †
 is none of his delight;
 Nor in the fprightly limbs of men,
 moft active in the fight.
11 The LORD in all who fear him takes
 a pleafure very great;
 And in all thofe who humbly hope
 and on his mercy wait.

[2 *Part.*]

12 The LORD praife, O Jerufalem,
 thy God, O Zion praife;
13 Who made thy gates and bars fo ftrong,
 and blefs'd in thee thy race.
14 Who caufes in thy borders peace;
 thy ftore fo rich to be,
 He gives the fineft flower of wheat
 a full fupply to thee.
15 He forth on earth fends his decree,
 his word is fwiftly paft.
16 He gives the fnow like wool, and doth
 hoar froft as afhes caft.
17 His ice in hail, like morfels down,
 He cafts as with his hand:
 Before the fharpnefs of his cold
 who can endure to ftand?

18 But

† The *Hebrew* fignifies *Both.*

PSALM CXLVII.

18 But then sends forth his mighty word,
   bids his warm wind to blow,
Which soon dissolves the parts congeal'd
   and makes the waters flow.
19 To Jacob He, as his belov'd,
   his heav'nly word hath shown:
His statutes and his judgments He
   to Isr'el hath made known.

20 With none of all the nations round
   so kindly dealt hath He:
For they his judgments have not known;
   sing HALLELUJAH,* ye.

[*Hallelujah Metre.*]

1 LOUD HALLELUJAH * sing;
    for to our God 'tis meet;
Praise is a comely thing,
   and is exceeding sweet.
2   The LORD doth rear
   Jerusalem,
   and gather them
  That outcasts are.

3 The broke in heart he heals,
   binds up their breaches all;
4 The stars by number tells,
   and each by name doth call.
5   Our *Lord* we bless,
   is great in might,
   and infinite
  In wisdom is.

6 The LORD the meek doth raise
   the proud brings to the ground:
7 O to the LORD sing praise,
   on harps our God's praise sound:
8   Who clouds the skies,
   . rains on the ground;
   on mountains round
   Makes grass to rise.

PSALM CXLVIII.

9 Ev'n beasts and ravens young
   He feeds whene'er they call:
10 In horse or foot-men strong
   takes no delight at all:
11   The LORD doth place
      His pleasure where
      men with his fear
   Hope in his grace.
12 Salem and Zion praise
   the LORD your God in song;
13 Who blesses your lov'd race
   and makes your gates so strong.
14   Thy borders stills
      with peace so sweet:
      with finest wheat
   Thy stores He fills.
15 On earth his orders go
   his word is swiftly past:
16 Like wool doth give the snow,
   hoar-frost as ashes cast.
17   His ice doth send
      like morsels too:
      in his cold who
   Can steady stand?
18 His word sends, and them thaws:
   blows winds, and water flows:
19 Jacob his word, his laws
   and judgment Isr'el shows:
20   So done hath He
      to nations none
      his judgments shown.
   JAH, then praise ye. † († *Hallelujah.*)

PSALM CXLVIII.

1 SING HALLELUJAH *: praise the LORD,
   ev'n from the heav'ns on high:
   Ye in the heights his praise resound
   above the starry sky.
2 O all his angels, gladly join
   your voices Him to praise,
   And all ye heav'nly hosts conspire
   his glorious name to raise.

PSALM CXLVIII.

3 Praise Him ye shining sun and moon,
    that rule the day and night:
  Praise Him in all your various orbs,
    ye glitt'ring stars of light.
4 Praise Him ye heav'ns of heav'ns, which all
    the rest in height exceed;
  And all ye wat'ry clouds above
    the airy heav'ns out-spread.
5 O let them all conspire to praise
    JEHOVAH's glorious name:
  For He commanded, and at once
    they into being came.
6 He hath establish'd each of them
    for ever in it's place:
  And he hath made a firm decree,
    which none shall ever pass.

[2 Part.]

7 O praise JEHOVAH from the earth,
    ye dragons, deeps and seas;
8 Fire, hail, snow, vapour, stormy wind;
    fulfilling his decrees.
9 All mountains, hills, and fruitful trees;
    and all ye cedars high:
10 Wild beasts, all cattle, creeping things,
    and all ye fowls that fly.
11 Kings and all people on the earth,
    princes, earth's judges all;
12 Young men and maidens ev'ry where,
    old men and children small.
13 Let all the LORD's name praise, because
    his name alone, on high
  Exalted is; his glory shines
    above the earth and sky.
14 His people's HORN,† the praise of all
    his saints, exalt will He;
  Ev'n Isr'el's SEED † to Him most near,
    sing HALLELUJAH,* ye.   [*Hallelujah*

† It may especially look to the MESSIAH. *Luk.* 1. 69.
  Gal. iii. 16.

PSALM CXLVIII.

[*Hallelujah Metre.*]

1 LOUD Hallelujah * sing
   from heav'n JEHOVAH praife
On high ‡ his honours ring,
   and with the higheft lays. ‡
2   Ye angels lead ;
       and all his hofts
      round heav'ns wide coafts
      His glory fpread.

3 Praife Him ye fun and moon,
   to whom ye owe your light:
Praife Him ye ftars, who run
   your glitt'ring courfe by night ;
4   His praife declare
      ye heav'ns on high,
      ye clouds that fly
     On fluent air.

5 Let all in this accord
   to praife JEHOVAH's name ;
For He but fpake the word,
   and they from nothing came :
6   And from the place
      where fix'd they be
      by his decree
     They cannot pafs.

[2 *Part.*]

7 On earth all praife the LORD ;
   ye dragons from your caves ;
And deeps that none can ford,
   with all your roaring waves ;
8   Fire, hail and fnow ;
      and mifty air ;
     and ftorms that where
     He bids them, blow.

9 All hills and mountains high,
   trees that with fruit are crown'd,
Cedars that touch the fky ;
10   wild beafts that range around ;

‡ The *Hebrew* including Both.

All cattle tame,
   things low, and high,
   that creep, that fly,
His praise proclaim.
11 Kings who on earth preside,
   and all of meaner birth;
   Princes who nations guide,
   and judges of the earth;
12   Ye young men strong,
   and virgins fair,
   heads with grey hair,
   And children young.
13 Let all JEHOVAH's name
   with praises celebrate;
   His name alone proclaim
   as excellent and great:
   His glories far
      above earth rise,
      yea utmost skies,
   And ev'ry star.
14 Yea He on high doth raise
   His people's horn of might,
   And thus inspires with praise
   His saints, his soul's delight.
   Bless'd Isr'el's race,
      a people near
      and to him dear:
   To JAH sing praise. † († *Hallelujah*.)

PSALM CXLIX.

1 SING HALLELUJAH *: to the LORD,
   a new song to Him sing:
   In the assembly of his saints,
   make ye his praises ring.
2 Let Isr'el in his makers ‡ be
   exceeding glad and sing:
   And all who Zion's children are,
   exult ‖ in Him their king.

‡ So the *Hebrew*—in the Plural Number.
‖ i. e. Rejoice exceedingly: So the *Hebrew*, *Septuagint*, ancien. *Latin*, *Chaldee*, *Arabick*, and *P*

PSALM CXLIX.

3 O let them with a leaping * joy
   give praises to his name;
   The harp and timbrel join and sing,
   aloud his praise proclaim.
4 For in his people whom He chose
   JEHOVAH pleasure takes;
   And with salvation all the meek
   most beautiful He makes.
5 In glory let his holy ones
   triumphantly rejoice;
   And ev'n aloud upon their beds
   in songs lift up their voice.
6 Let the high praises of our God
   their mouths with gladness yield;
   And let a two-edg'd sword be put
   into their hands to wield.
7 Vengeance and judgments to dispense
   among the heathen lands;
8 To bind their haughty kings in chains,
   and peers with iron bands.
9 The judgment written in his word
   justly on them to bring:
   This honour is for all the saints:
   then HALLELUJAH * sing.

[*Six Line Long Metre.*]

1 SING HALLELUJAH * to the LORD,
   Let Him for ever be ador'd:
   Amidst the saints assembled sing
   New songs of praise for mercies new:
2 Joy in his maker, Isr'el shew;
   And Sion triumph in their King.

3 Exult in Him ye sacred Quire, †
   With the sweet timbrel and the lyre ‡
   Sing forth and sound aloud his praise.
4 The LORD doth in his flock delight,
   Will save with his resistless might
   The meek, and them to honour raise.

5 Triumph

† i. e.—a Body of Singers.   ‡ i. e. the Harp.

PSALM CL.

5 Triumph ye faints with cheerful voice,
With fhouts for glory gain'd rejoice,
   And on your beds exprefs your joy:
6 To God your mouths high praifes yield,
A two edg'd fword let your hands wield,
7   His foes and heathen to deftroy.

8 To bind their haughty kings in chains,
In iron-bands their noble trains;
   On them his wrath decreed to pour.
9 The faints fhall this great honour have
To quell his foes and Zion fave.
   Sing HALLELUJAH * evermore.

PSALM CL.

1 SING HALLELUJAH ! * praife ye God
    Within his place of fanctity;
Praife Him all round the firmament,
Which fhows his wondrous pow'r on high.
2 O praife Him for his mighty deeds:
Praife for his greatnefs without bound,
His excellencies infinite. ‖
3 Praife Him with trumpets lofty found.

Praife with the pleafant pfaltery,
And with the harp's melodious noife:
4 Praife Him with timbrel's virgin airs,
And pipes exciting leaps of joys:
With harpficords and organs praife:
5 Praife, praife, with cymbals loud and high.
6 Praife JAH, O ev'ry living thing:
And HALLELUJAH * fhout for joy.

‖ The *Hebrew* literally fignifying *the Multitude of his Greatnefs*; and fo the *Septuagint, Syriack*, ancient *Latin, Chaldee, Arabick,* and *Montanus*; and as Greatnefs applied to God extends to *all* his Attributes, thefe Ideas are doubtlefs here comprized.

The

(265)

The *Song* of *Songs*, which is SOLOMON's.

Being Poetical Dialogues, in the most admirable Strains, between the CHURCH *and* CHRIST, *which the* ancient Jewish *Church, to whom the inspired Apostle* Paul *tells us were committed* [*i. e. by her inspired Prophets*] *the Oracles of God, received and carefully kept, with the other* Scripture *of the Old Testament; and the same Apostle assures us,* That all Scripture is given by Inspiration of God, and is profitable for Doctrine, *&c. And in this inspired Song the Pious and Learned of all Ages have viewed King* Solomon *as the* Typical MESSIAH, *and King* Pharoah's *Daughter, the most beautiful and accomplish'd Princess of her Age, as a lively Type of the* Church *of the* MESSIAH, Israelitish *Then, and* Christian *Now :* Psalm xlv. *being an happy Key to* This Divine Treasury—*full of the most pure, tender and sublime Hints, which holy Souls have had a most grateful Relish of, in all Ages.* See 1 King. iv. 32. Isai. liv. 5. lxii. 4, 5. Jer. ii. 2, 3. Hos. ii. 7. 16—20. Mat. ix. 15. Mark ii. 19, 20. Luke v. 34, 35. Joh. iii. 29. ‖ 2 Cor. xi. 2. Eph. v. 29—32. Rev. xix. 7—9. xxi. 2.

CHAP. I.

[*The* CHURCH.]

2 LET Him with kisses of his mouth,
be pleased me to kiss : (1)
For better than the choicest wine
thy loving kindness is.

3 Thy name as ointment poured out :
for that most fragrant smell
Of thy choice ointments (2) therefore do
the virgins (3) love Thee well.

4 O draw Thou me, and readily
we will run after Thee :
Into his secret chambers hath
the King conducted me. (4)
We will be glad, and will in Thee
exceedingly delight ;
Thy love remember more than wine :
love Thee do the upright.

(1) i. e. Give me the kind Expressions of his peculiar and dear Affection : as He does in ver. 8. 11. and other Places. (2) Thy Names, Endowments, Graces, Offices, Word, Ordinances, Titles, Influences, Benefits. (3) i. e. Pure and holy Souls. (4) i. e. Led me into retired, holy, and intimate Communion with Him.

Solomon's SONG.

5 O daughters of Jerusalem!
   I'm black; and yet you own
I'm comely as the Kedar tents,
   and beds (5) of Solomon.
6 Because I blackish am, therefore
   upon me look not ye;
Because the sun with scorching beams
   has looked fierce on me. (6)
My mother's sons displeas'd with me, (7)
   vineyards did me assign
To keep: whereas I scarce could keep
   the vineyard singly mine. (8)
7 Tell me Thou whom my soul does love
   where Thou thy feed dost take;
And where at noon-time Thou thy flock
   to rest dost kindly make.
For wherefore should I be as one,
   who vailed, turns away
From thy companions (9) and their flocks,
   and sadly goes astray?
[*CHRIST.*]
8 Most fair of women, know'st thou not?
   then by the flock-steps go,
Till to the shepherds tents (10) you come:
   and feed thy kids there too.
9 To troops (11) in Pharaoh's chariots I
   will Thee my love compare.
10 Thy neck with chains; with rows of gems
   thy comely cheeks appear.

11 [Yet

(5) If the *Hebrew* signifies *Curtains*; then, by a usual Figure, it seems to mean, the beautiful *Coach-Beds* of *Solomon*, somewhat in the Form of *Tents*, with all their *Curtains, Canopies*, and *other Furniture*, from Top to Bottom; and tho' she is *black* with Taints of Sin, yet *comely* in her Graces. (6) The Glory of *this lower World*, with it's blackening Influence, tho' it could have no such Influence on CHRIST, *Mat.* iv. 8—11. (7) For my professing the true and pure Religion. (8) They made me promote *their earthly Delights*, which are THEIR *Vineyards*; when I could not duly keep MY OWN *Vineyard*, which is my *Heart*, *Prov.* iv. 23. (9) Thy faithful Under-Shepherds. (10) The Places of pure and perfect Worship. (11) Beautiful for Shapes, Colours, Ornaments, Liveliness, Air and Majesty.

11 [Yet that thou mayſt be comelier ſtill,
and as becoming mine,]
WE'll make thee ornaments of gold,
with ſilver ſpangles ſhine. (12)
[*The* CHURCH.]
12 While the King at his table ſits
my ſpikenard-ointment (13) ſends
And ſpreads its fragrance all around,
to pleaſe Him and his friends.
13 As a freſh bunch of fragrant myrrh,
is my belov'd to me ;
Which conſtantly between my breaſts
ſhall my companion be.
[*CHRIST.*]
14 As a ripe camphire-cluſter in
Engedi's vineyard grown ; (14)
So my beloved is to me
a perfect, lovely one.
15 Lo fair, my Love, lo fair art Thou !
thine eyes as doves eyes are :
16 Lo fair tranſcendently Thou art, (15)
and ſweet as Thou art fair !

Our bed of reſt is richly green,
moſt grateful to the eyes : (16)
17 Our houſes * beams of cedar are,
of firr our galleries. (17)

(12) Notwithſtanding all your preſent Ornaments, Gifts and Graces; WE (my FATHER, I, and the HOLY SPIRIT) will make you ſtill more glorious. (13) i. e. an odoriferous Ointment made of *Spikenard*, a fragrant Root of *India :* and may ſignify the *Graces* of her *Heart* flowing forth in her Lips, Countenance, Behaviour, gracious Exerciſes, Speeches, Prayers, Thanks, Praiſes, &c. (14) It ſeems to be a Cluſter of the fineſt Fruit, for Beauty, Taſte and Flavour, in the exceeding rich Vineyards of *Engedi*. (15) The *Hebrew* ſtrongly implies all This. (16) As *Green* is a Colour very pleaſing to the Eyes, ſo our *retired* Place of holy Reſt and Communion is eſpecially delightful. (17) *Red Cedar* and *White Firr*, or *Cypreſs* ; both of them odoriferous, uncorrupt, and beautiful : and may mean the *Divine Inſtitutions* in the Places of *Publick Worſhip*.

Solomon's SONG.

CHAP. II.

[*CHRIST.*]

1 I Sharon's rose, and lilly am,
  which in the valley grows:
2 As lillies among thorns, my Love
  among the daughters shows.

[*The* CHURCH.]

3 As th' apple-tree among the woods,
  which fruit most beauteous bears;
  So my most dear beloved one
  among the sons appears:
  I with great joy sat in his shade;
  his fruit most sweet did prove:
4 He brought me to his banquet-house;
  his banner o'er me love.
5 With flaggons stay, with apples cheer,
  for faint with love am I.
6 Under my head his left hand doth,
  his right above me lie. (1)
7 O daughters of Jerusalem,
  wake not my Love, nor raise,
  By roes and hinds of all the fields,
  I charge you, till He please.
8 O 'tis the voice of my Belov'd!
  upon the mountains He,
  As roes or fawns bound o'er the hills,
  so leaping comes, I see!
9 But now behind our wall He stands,
  and thro' the window views?
  I see Him thro' the Latices; (2)
  how lovelily He shews!
10 Then my Beloved call'd to me,
  to me did kindly say;

[*CHRIST.*]

  ' Arise my Love, my fairest one,
  ' make haste and come away! 11 ' For

---

(1) i. e. He upholds and protects me as his own. (2) Through his Word and Ordinances, by divine Illumination, and the open Eye of Faith.

Solomon's SONG.

11 ' For lo the winter now is paſt,
    ' the rain entirely gone :
12 ' The flow'rs appear all o'er the earth,
    ' the ſinging birds come on !

    ' The turtle's ſoft and melting voice
    ' thro' all the land I hear:
13 ' The fig-tree, ſee, puts forth her figs ;
    ' the young and green appear !
    ' The vines with their young tender grapes
    ' around perfume the air: (3)
    ' Ariſe my love, my faireſt one ;
    ' come, ſtay no longer there !'

14 O Thou my dove, in clefts of rocks,
    in ſecret ſtairs ! let me
    Hear thy ſweet voice ! thy comely face
    O let me gladly ſee ! (4)

[*The* CHURCH.]

15 The foxes take for us away,
    the little foxes (5) there,
    Who ſpoil the vines ; and then the vines
    their tender grapes will bear.

16 My moſt beloved one is mine,
    and I am wholly his :
    Among the lillies of the vales
    his pleaſant feeding is. (6)
17 Till the day break, and ſhades fly hence,
    turn my Belov'd to me ;
    And like a roe or fawn upon
    the Bether mountains be !

(3) A ſpring-like Revival of lively and pure Religion. (4) Who hides herſelf from meeting Him in ſome publick Ordinances, thro' Shame for her Unfitneſs. (5) Little, but ſubtil, lurking and deceitful Enemies ; who greatly hinder the flouriſhing of Truth and Holineſs in the Vineyards or Churches of Chriſt. (6) He more delights in innocent and holy Souls, than ever any did in the whiteſt and ſweeteſt Lillies of the Valley.

CHAP. III.

[*The* CHURCH.]

1 BY night as on my bed I lay,
   when I awak'd, I fought
For the Beloved of my foul;
   I fought, but found Him not! (1)
2 Now I'll arife, and in the ftreets,
   and all broad places round,
Him I will feek whom my foul loves:
   I fought, but had not found.

3 The watchmen, as I went about
   the city, met with me;
Of them I afk'd; HIM whom my foul
   moft loves, O did you fee?
4 But 'twas a very little fpace
   that I from them had paft,
E'er Him whom my foul loves I found,
   I feiz'd and held Him faft.

Nor would I let Him go till I
   had brought Him in to fee
My mother's houfe, her chamber too,
   who had conceived me.
5 O daughters of Jerufalem,
   wake not my Love, nor raife;
By roes and hinds of all the fields,
   I charge you, till He pleafe.

[*Daughters of* Jerufalem.]

6 Who's fhe * that from the defart comes, (2)
   as incenfe-pillars rife?
Perfum'd with myrrh and frankincenfe,
   and powders all of fpice? (3)
7 Behold the ftately bed of reft
   which is King Solomon's,
And round it threefcore valiant men
   of Ifr'el's valiant fons.

(1) When I had indulged myfelf in earthly Eafe and Negligence.
(2) The *Defart* was in her way from *Egypt* to the *Holy Land*.
(3) *Syriack*—with all the fine Powders of Spices.

8 So dreadful to their enemies,
all warriours skill'd in fight;
Their ready swords girt on their thighs
becaufe of fear by night.
9 Of wood of Lebanon the King
a stately couch has made: (4)
10 It's pillars are of silver form'd,
gold for it's bottom laid.

Of purple is the canopy,
arch'd over all above.
For daughters of Jerufalem,
the midst is fpread with love.
11 O Zion's daughters, go ye forth,
with rais'd delight behold
King Solomon all glorious with
his diadem of gold:

The crown which on his nuptial day
his mother on him plac'd;
The day when gladnefs fills his heart,
and all around are blefs'd.

CHAP. IV.
[CHRIST.]

1 LO fair thou art, lo fair my Love!
doves-eyes in thy locks are;
Thy hair like flocks of goats that on
mount Gilead high appear.
2 Thy teeth are like the whit'ned flock
which from the wafhing rofe,*
New fhorn,* and ev'ry one bear twins,
and none without them goes.

3 Thy lips are like a fcarlet thread,
whence graceful accents flow:
Within thy locks, thy temples like
pomgranates in their blow. (1)

(4) A ftately Couch rais'd on Pillars with an arched Canopy
fpreading over it.
(1) So the *Hebrew* may fignify according to *Caftellus*,

4 Thy neck like David's tow'r appears,
   built for a magazine;
  Wherein a thousand bucklers hang,
   all shields of mighty men.
5 Thy two fair breasts are like two fawns,
   twins of a roe, who feed
  Among the lillies of the vale;
   but thine in charms exceed.
6 Till morning's fragrant breath shall rise, *
   and all the shades fly hence,
  I'll get me to the mount of myrrh,
   and hill of frankincense.
7 All fair thou art, my lovely one,
   there is no spot in thee!
8 My spouse, O come from Lebanon,
   from Lebanon with Me!
  Look from the top of Amana,
   from Shenir's summit high;
  From Hermon's top; from lions dens,
   from leopards mountains fly. (2).
9 My sister (3), spouse! thou hast my heart
   quite ravished from Me,
  With one of thy chaste eyes, with one
   chain of thy neck I see.
10 How fair thy loves (4) my sister, spouse,
   how far they wine excel!
  How far above all spices is
   thy od'rous ointments smell!
11 Thy lips drop like the honey-comb:
   my spouse, beneath thy tongue
  Honey and milk: thy cloaths perfume
   like scents from Lebanon.
12 My sister, spouse, a garden is,
   fenc'd for security;
  And as a precious spring enclos'd,
   a fountain seal'd for Me.   13 Thy

(2) In *Arabick*—make haste. (3) He may call her *Sister*; as a Term of tender and pure Affection, and as she was the Daughter of a King, &c. (4) Heb.—*Loves*, or *Lovingkindnesses*, as in Chap. i. 2.

Solomon's SONG.

13 Thy cions, of pomgranates, are
   the sprouts of paradise * ;
   With all the most delicious fruits,
   camphire and spikenard choice.
14 Where calamus and cinnamon,
   with saffron, spikenard too,
   All incense-trees, aloes and mirrh,
   with all chief spices grow. (5)
15 A fountain there, of gardens is
   in thee, and springs that run
   Yea living springs that send their streams
   all round from Lebanon. (6)

[*The* CHURCH.]

16 Awake, O north wind, come thou south,
   and on my garden blow ;
   That all the spice and odours there
   may forth abundant flow.
   And then let my beloved one
   into my garden come,
   Partake of his delicious fruit,
   and of his choice perfume.

CHAP. V.
[*CHRIST.*]

1 I Am into my garden come,
   my sister, and my spouse:
   I gather'd have my myrrh and spice
   for our delightful use:
   My honey-comb with honey eat,
   my wine with milk drank I:
   Eat, O ye friends, drink, O belov'd,
   yea drink abundantly. (1)

---

(5) All the Varieties of fragrant, healthful and chearing Graces.
(6) I think, a plain Hint that the *Land* and *Church* of *Israel* were at that Time chiefly meant by the admired Spouse.
(1) The *first Verse* of this Chapter should have been the *last* of the preceeding; being an Answer to the Church's Prayer: and the *Hebrew* was not divided into *Chapters* till above 1400 Years after CHRIST's Ascension.

[*The* CHURCH.]
2 I sleep; but yet my heart awakes:
   the voice 'tis of my Love,
Who knocks and kindly calls to me;
   and all my bowels move;
[*CHRIST.*]
' Open to Me, my sister-Love,
' my dove, my undefil'd;
' My head with dew, my locks with drops,
' the night distills, is fill'd!'
[*The* CHURCH.]
3 My coat I have put off; how shall
   I put it on again?
And I my feet have washed clean;
   how shall I them distain?
4 But when I my Beloved's hand
   upon the latch discern'd;
Griev'd that I should so long delay,
   my bowels stronger yearn'd.

5 I rose to open to my Love:
   my hands myrrh dropped down;
And on the handles of the lock
   myrrh from my fingers run. *
6 But when the door I open'd wide
   to my Beloved one;
My Love had then withdrawn Himself,
   and out of sight was gone!

When as He spake, my soul did fail;
   and now I sought Him have,
But found Him not; I call'd to Him,
   yet He no answer gave!
7 The city-watchmen met me then,
   they smote and wounded me,
The keepers of the wall ev'n took
   from me my vail away.

8 O daughters of Jerusalem,
   I charge you, to Him say,
If my Belov'd ye find, that I
   for love shall faint away.

[*Daughters*

[*Daughters of Jerusalem.*] (2)
9 O faireſt thou of all the fair !
what's thy Beloved, ſhow :
What more than others is thy Love,
that thou doſt charge us ſo ?
[*The* CHURCH.]
10 My Love is white and ruddy; chief
above ten thouſands fair :
11 His head is fineſt gold ; his locks
curl'd, black as ravens, are !
12 His eyes are like the eyes of doves
looking on water-ſtreams ;
As if they waſhed were with milk,
and fitly ſet as gems !
13 His cheeks like garden-beds of ſpice,
with flowers of ſpices crown'd :
His lips like lillies, dropping myrrh,
diffuſing odours round !
14 His hands adorn'd (3) with rings of gold,
with precious ſtones (4) inlaid :
His bowels (5) like bright ivory,
with ſaphires overſpread !
15 His legs (6) like marble pillars ſtand,
on golden ſockets plac'd ;
His countenance like Lebanon,
with ſtately cedars grac'd.
16 His mouth is all of ſweetneſs made ! (7)
He's perfect lovelineſs ! (8)
O daughters of Jeruſalem !
my Love and Friend is this ?

C H A P.

(2) They may ſignify the Children of the Church, by Birth, religious Education, and towardly Carriage. (3) So the *Sept.* (4) So the *Syriack, Mercer* and *Munſter* ; and 'tis likely that all the Rings were ſet with precious ſtones of various and ſparkling Colours. (5) Including his *Breaſt* ; *(Ainſworth.)* (6) His Legs, including his *Attire* from his *Bowels* to his Feet, *(Ainſworth)* the Sockets being at his *Knees* and *Ankles.* (7) Heb. *The Roof of his Mouth is Sweetneſſes ;* by a uſual Figure, a Part is named for the Whole. (8) Heb.—*He is all Deſires !*

CHAP. VI.

[*Daughters of Jerusalem.*]

1. O Faireſt Thou of all the fair!
  if Thou canſt tell us, do,
Whither thy ſoul's Belov'd is gone,
  that we may ſeek Him too.

[*The* CHURCH.]

2 My Love is to his garden gone, (1)
  down to the beds of ſpice;
To feed in gardens, and collect
  his flowers of lillies choice.

3 I'm my beloved's, He is mine;
  our hearts in one agree;
And feed among the lilly-flowers
  with great delight doth He.

[*CHRIST.*]

4 O Thou my Love, as Tirza fair,
  fair as Jeruſalem,
Majeſtick * as a marching hoſt.
  we ſee with banners ſtream.

5 O turn away thine eyes from Me!
  they have Me overborn.
Thine hair is like a flock of goats
  which Gilead's mount adorn.

6 Thy teeth are like a flock of ſheep
  up from the waſhing gone;
Whereof ev'n, ev'ry one bear twins,
  and deſtitute is none.

7 So gracefully within thy locks
  thy temples formed are,
That to pomgranates in their bloom, (2)
  I may them well compare.

8 Tho' round thee there are threeſcore Queens,
  and concubines fourſcore,
And of fair virgins more there are
  than can be number'd o'er;

9 Yet

(1). To the Aſſembly of all his Saints.   (2) See *Caſtellio.*

Solomon's SONG.

9 Yet is my dove my perfect one, (3)
   the only one to Me;
   Yea of the mother that her bare
   the choicest one is she.
   The daughters, as they her beheld,
   admir'd, and call'd her bless'd;
   The queens and concubines were charm'd, (4)
   and thus her praise confess'd;
10 " O, how she looks forth like the morn,
   " fair as the moon on high,
   " Clear as the sun, majestick as
   " an host whose banners fly!"
       [*The* CHURCH.]
11 To the nut-garden I went down, (5)
   the valley fruit to see;
   See if the vines did bud, if bloom
   did the pomgranate tree.
12 And then my soul quick mounted me,
   before I was aware,
   As on the char'ots of those who
   my willing people are.
     [*Daughters of Jerusalem.*]
13 But O thou lovely Shulamite,
   gone to thy secret place;
   O turn, make haste, and come again,
   that WE may view thy face!
       [*CHRIST.*]
   What see you in the Shulamite?
   what like her has there been?
     [*Daughters of Jerusalem.*]
   She's like the choir of angel-hosts
   at Mahanaim seen! (6)

(3) So the *Hebrew, Septuagint,* ancient *Latin, Syriack, Arabick, Montanus.* (4) i. e. The most illustrious Persons of the Nations round her. (5) To her Retirement, to examine how her Graces flourished. (6) Heb.---*Like the Chorus,* or double Hosts *at Mahonaim. Gen.* xxxii. 1, 2.---alike for Number, Beauty, Majesty and Brightness; and may comprize the double Church both of *Israelites* and *Gentiles.*

CHAP. VII.

[*Daughters of Jerusalem.*]

1 HOW beautiful thy feet with shoes,
O prince's daughter, are!
Thy joints (1) like jewels finely wrought
by an artificer.

2 Thy navel like a cover'd cup, (2)
with liquor full, and round;
Thy bowels like a heap of wheat
about with lillies crown'd.

3 Thy breasts are like two new wean'd roes,
twins of one fruitful dam.

4 Thy neck like a fair tow'r appears,
of iv'ry shining frame
Thine eyes like Heshbon-fish pools bright,
Bethrabbim-gate fast by:
Thy nose like Lebanon's fine tow'r
which doth Damascus eye.

5 Like Carmel is thy head on thee;
the hair like purple is;
And thy rare beauty holds the King
in th' open galleries.

[*CHRIST.*]

6 O how delightful thou my Love!
how pleasant and how fair.

7 Thy stature stately like a palm,
thy breasts as clusters are.

8 I said, I'll to this stately palm,
to its high top ascend,
And seize the pleasant fruit (3) thereof
which from its boughs extend. Thy

---

(1) The *Hebrew* signifies the Joints of the Thighs and Knees, and the learned *Sanctius* and Bp. *Patrick* show, that the external Ornaments only, are in the five First Verses, described. (2) A Cup of a Globular Form, with a Crown-work Cover over it. See *Avenarius, Schindler,* and *Buxtorf*'s great *Chaldee, Talmudick* and *Rabbinick* Lexicon. (3) This *Hebrew* Word is no where used but *here,* as *Avenarius* observes. The *ancient Latin* renders it the *Fruits;* the *Syriack*---the *Boughs;* the *Septuagint* and *Arabick*---the *Tops,* where they all grow; and are all included; as by seizing the *Boughs,* the pleasant *Fruits* called *Dates,* are seized with them.

Solomon's SONG.

Thy full grown breasts like clusters are,
  full clusters of the vine : (4)
Thy breath (5) sweet, as ripe apples, smells (6)
  no breath so sweet as thine.

[*The* CHURCH.]

9 Like choicest wine to my Belov'd,
  that move most pleasantly,
And makes the sleeper's lips to speak,
  so thy mouth's roof (7) to me.

10 I am my Love's ; and his desire
   moves to me as his own.

11 Come my belov'd, let us go forth
   to see the fields new sown :
Lodge let us in the villages ;

12 then early let us rise,
Go to the vineyards, and there see
   if the vine flourishes ;
If yet the tender grapes appear ;
   if the pomgranates grow,
Or if they bud ; and there my loves
   I'll fully to Thee show.

13 The mandrakes smell : and at our gates
   all pleasant fruits we see ;
Which old and new, O my Belov'd
   I have prepar'd for Thee.

CHAP. VIII.

[*The* CHURCH.]

1 O That Thou as my brother wert,
   sucking * my mother's breasts !
I would Thee find abroad and kiss,
   and none should me disgrace : (1)

2 I'd

(4) Thy *Soul* and *Spirit*, mature in Grace, are like the Clusters of ripe Grapes, and Breasts of Milk, full of holy Beauties, Influences and Consolations ; *Isai.* lxvi. 11, &c. (5) Heb. ---*Nose*, which, by a usual Figure seems to signify the *Breath* commonly passing thro' it : i. e. the gracious *Aspirations* from thy Heart. (6) Heaps of ripe Apples in a Chamber breathe a pleasant Smell. (7) *The enlivening Voice* of thy Word and Spirit, from the *Roof* of thy *Mouth*.

(1) That she might as openly and freely kiss him, and with as pure Affection, as a young Sister kisses her dear and sucking Brother : the purest Affection that was ever imagin'd.

2 I'd lead Thee to my mother's house,
  where skill she would me show:
Spic'd wine of my pomgranate juice,
  to drink I'd make Thee too.
3 His soft left hand should underneath
  my ravish'd neck intwine;
His right hand should around me bend,
  as one most dearly mine.
4 O daughters of Jerusalem,
  I charge you make no noise,
To wake or to disturb my Love,
  till He shall please to rise.

[*Daughter of Jerusalem.*]

5 But who is this that comes up now
  out of the wilderness,
Leaning on her Beloved one?
  a pleasing sight is this!

[*CHRIST* to the CHURCH.]

Thence, where thy mother thee did bear,
  beneath the apple-tree,
Where she with pain had brought thee forth,
  ev'n *thence* I raised thee. (2)

[*The* CHURCH.]

6 O set me then as a dear seal
  upon thy very heart;
As a seal fix'd upon thine arm,
  that we may never part!
For heav'nly love's as strong as death;
  and no relenting knows,
No more than the devouring grave;
  like burning coals it glows:

7 It's

(2) Tho' the *Point* at the End of — *Thee* — represents it as *Masculine*; yet *without the Point*, as the *Synagogue Copies* have none, the *Sense* seems rather to lead to the *Royal Princess*, who came from *Egypt*, thro' the *Wilderness*: and may allude, both to *Eve's* eating the forbidden Fruit, and thence bearing all her feeble Race with Anguish; and to the feeble *Church* of *Israel* brought forth, exposed in *Egypt*, and travelling thro' the Wilderness to the Land of Promise.

7 It's flames are like the flames of JAH.*
   which many waters high
   Can never quench, nor flowing floods
   can drown, or ev'r deftroy.
   And if the wealthieft man on earth
   wou'd for thy love of me
   Give all the fubftance of his houfe,
   it quite defpis'd fhou'd be. (3)
8 But we've a little fifter fair,
   whofe breafts are not yet grown . (4)
   The day when fu'd for fhe fhall be,
   what fhall for her be done?
   [*CHRIST.*]
9 Is fhe firm as a wall, we'll build
   on her a filver tow'r :
   Or as an open door expos'd ;
   with cedar boards fecure. (5)
   The CHURCH.
10 Did He not fee me like a wall?
   my breafts as tow'rs to rife? (6)
   O then like one who favour found
   appear'd I in his eyes !
11 A vineyard in a fruitful foil
   had Solomon ; and there
   The vineyard leafed out to them
   who vineyard-keepers were.

   Each one a thoufand filverlings (7)·
   for it's rare fruit repays.
12 My vineyard (8) is before mine eyes
   and in my view always.

Thy

(3) *Heb.* — utterly defpifed. (4) It may mean young, well in-
clined and hopeful Souls, both *Ifraelites* and *Gentiles* ; unripe
in D vine Knowledge, Wifdom, Grace, &c. (5) I' fhe be *firm*
in *Grace*, we'll adorn her as with a *filver Tower* of *fhining*
Majefty : If expos'd as a new Houfe unfinifh'd, with the
Door-way open ; we'll fecure her as fuch Houfes are with
Boards of Cedar. (6) Mature in Wifdom, Grace, &c. (7)
Ifai. vii. 23. i. e. a Thoufand *Shekels* of *Silver*. 2 Sam. xviii.
11, 12. (8) i. e. my Heart.

Thy part, O Solomon, (9) to Thee
   a thousand justly bears;
And they who keep the fruit thereof
   two hundred have for theirs.

13 O Thou who in the gardens dwel'st!
   they who companions are,
To thy delightful voice attend:
   O cause Thou me to hear!
14 Make haste, O my Beloved one,
   like a swift roe to me;
And like a fawn * of harts * upon
   the spicy mountains be! (10)

ISAIAH II. 2—5.
[*The glorious Reign of CHRIST.*]

2 IN latter days JEHOVAH's mount,
   His sacred house shall rise
Above the mountains and the hills,
   and strike the wond'ring eyes.
To this the joyful nations round
   all tribes and tongues shall flow:
3 ' Up to JEHOVAH's mount, they'll say,
   ' to Jacob's God we'll go.

' To us He'll point his way of truth:
   ' his sacred path's we'll tread:
' From Salem and from Zion shall
   ' *Jehovah*'s law proceed,'
4 Among the nations and the isles
   as Judge supreme He'll sit;
And vested with unbounded pow'r
   will punish or acquit.

No strife shall rage, no angry feuds
   disturb those peaceful years:
To plowshares then they'll beat their swords,
   to pruning hooks their spears.

No

---

(9) i. e. CHRIST the *typified* SOLOMON. (10) The *Church* earnestly longs and prays for CHRIST's *glorious Coming*; and in the mean while for his *gracious* and happy *Visits* by his HOLY SPIRIT.

ISAIAH v.

No nation againſt nation riſe,
  and ſlaughter'd hoſts deplore:
They'll lay the martial trumpet by,
  and ſtudy war no more.

5 O come ye then, of Jacob's houſe,
  our hearts now let us join;
And walking in JEHOVAH's light,
  with holy beauties ſhine.

ISAIAH V.

1 *Now will I ſing to my* BELOVED, *a Song of my* BELOVED *touching his* VINEYARD. ‖

MY moſt Belov'd a Vineyard owns,
  Which on a fruitful hill is ſeen;
2 Around it a ſafe fence He made,
  And clear'd of all the ſtones therein.
He planted there a beauteous vine,
  And in the midſt He built a tow'r,
A wine-preſs made, then look'd for grapes;
But grapes it yeilded wild and ſow'r.

3 And now, O ye inhabitants
  Ev'n of Jeruſalem, and ye
Of Judah, tho' ye parties are,
  Between my vineyard judge and Me.
4 What for my vineyard could be done
  Which I have not perform'd with care?
Why, when I look'd for pleaſant grapes,
  Did theſe degen'rate grapes appear?

5 And now I'll tell you what I'll do:
  My vineyard's hedge remove will I
To be devour'd; and I'll throw down
  It's wall; and it trod down ſhall lie.

6 I'll

‖ This *Song* is plainly in the Style of *Solomon's Song*: where, in Verſes 1, 2, 7, the Pious Part of the viſible *Church* of the MESSIAH ſpeaks; calling Him her BELOVED *three times* in *ver.* 1. and *the LORD of Hoſts*, in *ver.* 7. But in *ver.* 3, 4, 5, 6, the MESSIAH ſpeaks as a final Judge.

ISAIAH ix.

6 I'll lay it waste and desolate;
Unprun'd, undig'd, with brambles spread,
And thorns: yea, to the clouds I'll say,
That on it they no rain should shed.

7 Because the house of Israel,
The LORD of hosts his vineyard is,
The men who dwell in Judah's tribe,
Are that most pleasant plant of his:
And when He judgment did expect,
Lo! there was an oppressing wound;
And when He look'd for righteousness,
Then lo! a bitter cry He found.

ISAIAH ix. 2---7. [CHRIST *described*.]

2 PEOPLE that long in darkness walk'd
Now see a great and wondrous light;
On them who dwelt in shades of death
The light hath shin'd exceeding bright. †

3 The nations thou hast multiply'd,
And now their joys increased are;
As in the harvest they rejoice,
Like conqu'rers when the spoil they share.

4 For Thou the burthen of their yoke,
The staff which on their shoulders lay,
And their oppressors rod hast broke,
As once they were in Midian's day.

5 For all the warriours battles were
Throughout the earth from times of old,
With noise confus'd of shouts and groans,
In reeking blood their garments roll'd.

But now this great, decisive blow,
Whereby thy people will be free,
Shall be by all devouring FIRE,
Wherein their foes shall fuel be. ‡

---

† Expresly apply'd to CHRIST, *Matt.* ii. 14—16.
‡ Tho' *this Salvation* eminently *Began* at the *Beginning* of the *Ministry* of CHRIST; yet the inspired Prophet seems to extend his View to the *compleat Fulfilment* at the *universal Conversion* of *Israel*, just before the *Conflagration*, and in the *glorious Reign* of CHRIST in the *New Heavens* and *New Earth* immediately after it.

ISAIAH xii.

6 For lo! the virgin's child is born,
  To us thine only Son is giv'n;
  Upon his shoulders shall be laid
  The government of earth and heav'n:
  His name is called Wonderful,
  The Councellor, the mighty God,
  Eternal Father, Prince of Peace,
  Peace over-all the earth abroad.
7 His government shall ever grow,
  And far and wide o'er all extend;
  And universal peace, the fruit
  Of his just reign, shall know no end.
  O'er David's kingdom and his throne
  To rule, and them establish sure,
  With judgment right and justice clear,
  His reign for ever shall endure. ‖

ISAIAH XII.

1 (*And in that Day thou shalt say—*)
  O LORD, tho' with me Thou wast wroth
      I'll praises give to Thee;
  For now thy wrath is turn'd away,
  and Thou dost comfort me.
2 Behold! God my salvation is;
      trust, and not fear, will I;
  Because our JAH, * JEHOVAH * is
  my strength and melody.
  He is my full salvation too:
3 so waters plenteously
  Out of salvation's living wells
  shall ye draw forth with joy.
4 Praise ye the LORD, call on his name;
      and to the people show
  His doings: that his name's extoll'd,
  declare abroad also.
5 O sing ye to the LORD, for He
      things excellent has done;
  Yea thro' the universal earth
      the fame is fully known.

6 Cry

‖ *These two Verses* are expresly applied to CHRIST, *Luk.* i. 31—33.

6 Cry out and shout aloud O ye
    who on mount Zion dwell ;
  For mighty is THE HOLY ONE,
    in Thee, O Israel.

ISAIAH XXV. 1---9.

1 LORD, Thou my God ! I'll Thee extol,
    I will thy name confess ;
  Who wonders dost, thy counsels old
    are truth and faithfulness.
2 For Thou a city mad'st an heap;
    its wall in ruin lies ;
  The strangers palace hast eras'd ;
    nor ever shall it rise.
3 Therefore the mighty people shall
    great glory to Thee bear ;
  The city of the terrible
    of nations shall Thee fear.
4 Because Thou to the poor hast been
    their strength, as they confess ;
  A happy strength to helpless ones,
    in times of their distress.
  Thou art a refuge from the storm,
    a shadow from the heat;
  When blasts of dreadful ones like storms
    on walls in fury beat ;
  And like fierce heat in places dry:
5   but Thou shalt quell their noise.
  And, as the heat by shady cloud,
    suppress their dreadful voice.
6 The LORD of hosts moreover will
    upon this mountain make
  A sumptuous feast of fat things for
    all people to partake :
  A feast of wines preserv'd on lees,
    for them He will prepare ;
  Of fat and marrow-things, of wines
    that most refined are. †   7 And

---

† Heb.—*Drawn from the Lees* : and so the *ancient Latin, Montanus, Buxtorff,* and all the *Lexicons* : the *Heb. Root* signifying —*poured out*, and the *Heb. Præposition* signifying—*From*.

ISAIAH XXVI.

7 And in this mountain He deſtroy
   the face of cov'ring ſhall,
Caſt o'er all people, and the vail
   ſpread over natious all.
8 For ever He will ſwallow up
   death into victory.
The Lord JEHOVAH tears ſhall wipe
   from ev'ry face and eye.
His people's whole reproach from all
   the earth He'll take away.
9 Lo this our God ! who will us ſave ;
   for Him we waiting ſtay !
This is the LORD on whom we have
   our expectation had ;
In his ſalvation we'll rejoice,
   and be exceeding glad.

ISAIAH XXVI.

1 A City of exceeding ſtrength
     Doth happily to us belong ;
   And the decreed ſalvation ſhall
   Like walls and bulwarks keep it ſtrong.
2 Set open then the city-gates,
   That ſo the righteous nation, who
   Immoveably maintains the truth,
   May gladly enter thereinto.
3 In perfect peace Thou ſuch a one
   Wilt ever ſurely cauſe to be,
   Whoſe mind on Thee ſecurely ſtays ;
   Becauſe he hopes alone on Thee.
4 Repoſe then ever in the LORD,
   The lively hope of all your mind !
   Becauſe in JAH, * JEHOVAH, * ſure,
   A rock eternal ye ſhall find.
5 He'll bring down thoſe who dwell on high,
   He'll lay the haughty city low,
   He'll lay it level with the ground,
   And down into the duſt will throw.

6 The feet of the afflicted shall
  In triumph tread it wholly down;
  And it shall lie beneath the feet
  Of him that was a helpless one.

[2 *Part.*]

7 The way of ev'ry righteous man
  Is universal righteousness;
  And Thou, O Righteous One, dost weigh
  In righteousness each path of his.
8 Moreover in thy judgments way,
  LORD, Thee we longing look to see;
  Our souls desire is to thy name,
  And to the memory of Thee.

9 In the dark seasons of the night,
  My soul Thee earnestly desires:
  My wakeful spirit in my breast
  For Thee at early dawn inquires.
  For when thy judgments are display'd
  On earth, the world's inhabitants
  Shou'd lay to heart thy righteous works,
  And learn the righteousness of saints.

10 Tho'-for a wicked man there should
   Bowels of heav'nly pity yearn,
   Yet he the way of righteousness
   Will not perswaded be to learn:
   Yea, in the land of righteousness
   He'll work perverse iniquity;
   Nor will he ev'n so much as see *
   JEHOVAH's glorious majesty.

11 LORD, when thine hand is lifted up,
   In thy most awful judgments, high;
   Yet left they see thine hand therein,
   Perversely they will shut their eye.
   But with confusion they shall see
   The zeal * Thou for thy people hast,
   And the consuming fire that shall
   Thine adversaries wholly waste.

[3 *Part.*]

ISAIAH xxvi.

[3 *Part.*]

12 JEHOVAH, certainly Thou wilt
Safety and peace for us ordain:
For our affairs Thou manage doft,
And for us, all our works maintain.

13 O LORD our God, tho' other *Lords*
Have reigned over us, we own;
Yet hence, thy name we mention will,
And by Thee none but thine alone.

14 They'r dead, and fhall not live again;
Deceas'd, and never fhall arife;
Thy judgments have deftroy'd them quite,
Yea caus'd that all their mem'ry dies.

15 The nation, Lord, increafeft Thou,
Our nation greatly haft increas'd;
And Thou haft glorify'd thy felf,
And thro' the earth defpers'd them haft.

16 O LORD, when they were in diftrefs,
They Thee then vifited with cries;
And pray'r in fecret poured out,
When Thou didft forely them chaftize.

17 Like as a pregnant woman when
Approaching travail comes apace,
Is pain'd, and in her pangs cries out;
So were we, LORD, before thy face.

18 We trouble have conceiv'd, are pain'd,
But bring forth vanity, and wind;
Nor do the world's difturbers fall:
Nor we on earth deliverance find.

[4 *Part.*]

19 Thy dead fhall furely live again,
With my dead body rife they muft:
Awake out of the fleep of death,
And fing ye who dwell in the duft!
Becaufe the dew that falls on thee,
Is like the dew that makes herbs grow:
But out abroad with violence,
The earth the wicked ones ‡ fhall throw.

O 20 Come

‡ So the *Sept, Chaldee, Arab,* and fo *Vitab,* in *Pool's Synop.*

20 Come then my people enter in
 To chambers that moſt ſecret are;
 And after thee ſhut thou the doors,
 And make them faſt with utmoſt care.
 There do thou hide thy ſelf a while;
 It ſhall but as a moment be,
 And all the indignation ſhall
 Be paſs'd for ever over thee.

21 For lo, the LORD is coming forth,
 Out of his dwelling place on high,
 Upon the earth's inhabitants,
 To puniſh their iniquity.
 The earth ſhall then diſcloſe and ſhow
 The bloods * within her buried;
 Her ſlain ſhall be brought forth to view,
 And be no longer covered.

ISAIAH XXXVIII. 10—20.

The Song of Hezekiah, after his Recovery from Sickneſs.

10 MY days I ſaid are now cut off,
 And going to the grave am I,
 And of my hop'd for coming years
 I am deprived utterly.

11 I ſaid, that JAH I ſhall not ſee,
 JAH in the land of life behold;
 And man mine eyes ſhall ſee no more,
 Nor any dwellers in the world.

12 My dwelling here is paſs'd away,
 Removed as a ſhepherd's tent;
 My life as threads by weavers cut,
 He cut me off by languiſhment.
 From day to night Thou doſt me waſte,
 An end of me wilt quickly make.

13 I in the morn look; but by night
 My bones He'll as a lion break.

14 Like cranes or ſwallows chatter'd I,
 Like doves I mourn'd thro' pain and grief,
 Mine eyes with looking upwards fail'd.
 LORD, I'm oppreſs'd; O give relief.

15 What

15 What shall I say? but humbly own,
   He well hath spoke and done to me,
   And I in bitterness of soul
   Will all my years repenting be.

16 As, LORD, Thou art the life of men,
   Life to my spirit Thou dost give;
   Thou fully wilt recover me,
   And Thou wilt make me still to live.

17 Lo, I for peace great trouble found,
   But to my soul in love, Thou hast
   From the corrupting pit me sav'd,
   My sins behind thy back hast cast.

18 For graves cannot shew forth thy praise,
   Neither can death Thee celebrate,
   Such as go down into the pit
   To see thy truth no more can wait.

19 The living *does*, the living *will*,
   Thee praise, ev'n as I do this day;
   The father to the children shall
   Thy acts of faithfulness display.

20 Ready to save me was the LORD:
   Therefore we will my songs of praise
   Sing in JEHOVAH's house with joy,
   Throughout our lives, ev'n all our days.

ISAIAH XLV. 21—25.

21 FROM ancient times I have declar'd,
   I am JEHOVAH, GOD alone,
   A righteous God, and Me besides
   A saviour is, or can be none.

22 Then look to me ye fainting souls,
   In ev'ry place, in ev'ry land;
   And ye shall joyfully receive
   Salvation at my mighty hand.

23 For I am God, and none besides,
   I even by My self have sworn
   In righteousness: and now the word
   Gone from my mouth, shall not return;

ISAIAH liii.

It is, 'that every knee to Me
  'Shall bow, and ev'ry tongue shall swear,
24 'And say, that in the LORD alone
  'My strength and righteousnesses * are:'

Yea all who feel their wretchedness
With humble joy shall come to Him:
But those who with Him are displeas'd,
Shall be distress'd with endless shame.
25 In Thee, JEHOVAH, Isr'el's race,
All fully justify'd shall be;
In Thee shall triumph o'er their foes,
And all be glorify'd in Thee.

ISAIAH LIII.
[*The Abasement & Exaltation of* CHRIST; *Acts* viii.]

1 O Who has our report believ'd?
    And who JEHOVAH's arm doth know?
2 For as a tender plant and root
Before Him, from dry ground He'll grow.
He has no form, nor comeliness;
And when his troubled face we see,
No beauty in Him we discern,
That by us He desir'd should be.

3 He slighted and rejected is
Ev'n of the men He came to save:
A man of constant sorrows full,
And intimate with heavy grief.
Yet we, while He was thus abus'd,
Our faces turn'd and hid from Him;
By others round He was despis'd,
Nor did we Him at all esteem.

4. Tho' sure they were our griefs He bore,
Our sinking sorrows bear did He;
Yet strook, and smote, and scourg'd by GOD,
We judg'd Him righteously to be.
5 But ah! 'twas only for our sins
That He did all his wounds receive:
For our iniquities was bruis'd,
That He might us from them relieve.

Our

ISAIAH liii.

Our chaſtiſement on Him was laid,
To purchaſe our eternal peace:
And by his ſtripes it is that we
Are heal'd with wondrous pow'r and grace.

6 We all like ſheep aſtray have gone,
Each turn'd to his own ſinful way:
And yet the treſpaſs of us all
The LORD on Him alone did lay.

7 Oppreſs'd, abus'd, He ſilent was,
As the meek lamb to ſlaughter brought;
Or ſheep, before her ſhearers dumb,
His guiltleſs mouth He op'ned not.

8 From judgment and from priſ'n [the grave]
Soon rais'd and took away was He;
And of his generation who
Shall tell the wondrous hiſtory?
For from the land of living ones
In early age was He deſtroy'd;
And for my people's ſins the ſtroke
Of vi'lent death was on Him laid.

9 With criminals He dy'd; and yet
Among the rich He made his grave;
Becauſe He did no injury,
Nor ever with his mouth deceive.

10 Yet it JEHOVAH pleas'd to bruiſe
And put Him to extreme diſtreſs,
When Thou ſhalt offer up his ſoul
Only for others treſpaſſes:
When this is doue, then He ſhall riſe,
Live ever, and his offspring ſee;
JEHOVAH's pleaſure in his hand
Shall proſper to eternity:

11 The multiply'd and happy fruit,
Of the vaſt travel of his ſoul,
He ſhall ſurvey, and with the view
He ſhall be pleaſed to the full:
By knowledge of the way of life,
My righteous ſervant ſhall appear
Vaſt multitudes to juſtify;
For He their ſins will fully bear.

ISAIAH lv.

12 Therefore a portion with the great
   To Him, as due, divide I will;
   And with the mighty ones shall He
   Divide and share the glorious spoil.
   Because He pour'd his soul to death,
   And with transgressors numbred was:
   The sin of many bore; and He
   For helpless sinners pleads the cause.

ISAIAH LV.
[*The Call of GOD in* CHRIST *to perishing Sinners.*]

1 HO! ev'ry thirsty, longing soul!
   Come where the living waters flow;
   Come, buy, eat, drink my wine and milk;
   Tho' nothing ye, of worth, can show.

2 Why do ye spend your cost and toil,
   For what cannot content the soul?
   Hear Me, and feed on solid good,
   Your souls with fatness shall be full.

3 Incline your ear and come to Me,
   Hear, and your soul shall ever live;
   I'll an eternal covenant
   And DAVID's certain mercies give.

4 Lo! I have HIM a witness giv'n,
   For all the people to observe;
   A leader and commander made,
   That all the people should HIM serve.∥

5 The gentile nations Thou shalt call;
   And they shall run to Thee with joy;
   The LORD thy God, the HOLY ONE
   Of Isr'el Thee will glorify.

6 O seek ye for the LORD, while ye
   To your great joy may find Him here;
   And call upon Him earnestly,
   While in his mercy He is near.

7 Let wicked men forsake their ways,
   Their thoughts let the unrighteous leave;
   And to the LORD let them return;
   And mercy on them He will have.   Let

∥ *David* being now dead about 300 Year, 'tis plain that CHRIST, the promised Seed of *David*, must be here intended: so CHRIST is called *David*, Jer. xxx. 9. Ezek. xxiv. 23, 24. Hos. iii. 5.

Let them remember He's our God,
So wondrous for benignity;
O let them then return to Him,
And He'll forgive abundantly.

LAMENTATIONS III.

1 I Am the man who by his rod
   Of wrath see dismal scenes of woes;
2 He hath me into darkness brought,
   And not a gleam of light He shows.
3 He surely is against me turn'd
   His hand all day He turns on me.
4 My flesh and skin He old hath made
   My bones to pieces broke hath He.

5 He built around me: and with gall
   And travel me encompassed:
6 He hath me set in places dark,
   As those who long ago were dead.
7 So hedg'd me in, I can't get out;
   Makes me his heavy chain to bear;
8 And when I earnest cry aloud,
   He grievously shuts out my pray'r.

9 He with hewn stones enclos'd my path,
   And intricate hath made my way:
10 He as a bear lays wait for me,
   A lion in a hidden place.
11 He turned hath my ways aside:
   He hath to pieces pulled me:
   Of all my comforts hath bereav'd
   And made me desolate to be.

12 He bent his bow; and me a mark
   Did for his sharp'ned arrows place;
13 The arrows of his quiver caus'd
   Into my tender reins to pass.
14 To all my people I'm a scoff,
   And all the day their jeering song;
15 He made me full of bitterness,
   And even drunk with wormwood strong.

16 Yea He my teeth with gravel break,
  And all in ashes rolled me.
17 Thou put'st my soul far off from peace,
  And I forgot prosperity.
18 Yea I did say, my strength and hope
  Are wholly perish'd from the LORD.
19 My grief and pain, wormwood and gall,
  I in my troubled mind record.
20 My soul doth still remember them,
  And in me low abas'd, doth lie:
21 Yet to my mind I this recall,
  And thence a glimpse of hope have I;
22 It's of the mercies of the LORD,
  We are not quite consum'd away;
  Because the pity of his heart
  Nor *does*, nor ever *will* decay,
23 They ev'ry morning are renew'd:
  Thy changeless faithfulness is great.
24 The LORD's my portion, saith my soul;
  And thence my hope I'll on Him set.
25 To them who wait for Him, the soul
  Who seeks Him, gracious is the LORD;
26 'Tis best in quietness * to wait
  Till He salvation will afford.
27 Good for a man it is in youth
  That he should bear the humbling yoke:
28 He sits alone, and silence keeps,
  Because he bears thy holy stroke.
29 He puts his mouth into the dust,
  If so there any hope may be:
30 His cheek to him who smites he gives,
  Tho' filled with reproach is he.
31 Ever the *Lord* will not cast off:
  But tho' He causes pungent grief;
32 Yet in his mercies great He will
  Compassion have, and give relief.
33 For He's not willing to afflict
  Or grieve the sons of men 'tis known:
34 To crush the pris'ners of the earth,
  Or under feet to tread them down.   35 To

LAMENTATIONS iii.

35 To turn aside the right of man
   Before the face of THE MOST HIGH;
36 Or to subvert his righteous cause;
   The *Lord* abhors eternally.
37 Who's he that saith, and then performs,
   Unless it be the *Lord's* good will.
38 Out of the mouth of THE MOST HIGH,
   Proceed all good and penal ill.
39 Why for the punishment of sins
   Doth any living man complain?
40 O let us search and try our ways,
   And to the LORD now turn again.
41 O let us lift our hearts and hands
   Up to the mighty God in heav'n:
42 We all have trespass'd and rebell'd,
   Nor hast Thou yet our sins forgiv'n.
43 Thy wrath us covers and pursues;
   Thou slay'st, and dost not pity show.
44 Thou so with clouds dost hide thy self
   That our loud cries cannot pass through,
45 Amidst the people hast us made
   Th' off-scouring, refuse, and the jeer.
46 And the wide mouths of all our foes,
   Against and round us op'ned are.
47 Fear and a snare are come on us;
   And all in desolation lies:
48 For daughters of my people's waste
   Rivers of tears run down mine eyes.
49 Mine eyes with tears flow down apace;
   And will no intermission know,
50 Until the LORD from heav'n look down,
   And see us in our dismal woe.
51 Mine eye affects my soul * with grief,
   To see my city's daughters case:
52 My foes pursue me unprovok'd,
   The harmless birds as fowlers chase.
53 My life they in the dungeon sunk,
   And on me heavy stones they cast.
54 The waters flowing o'er my head,
   I said, "I'm gone, all hope is past!"
55

55 O LORD, I call'd upon thy name,
   In the deep dungeon, like to die:
56 Thou heardſt my voice, hide not thine ear,
   From my ſhort panting and my cry.
57 Then Thou drew'ſt near, and ſaidſt, "FEAR NOT!"
   Ev'n in the day I call'd on Thee:
58 *Lord*, my ſoul's cauſes Thou did plead,
   And my expiring life ſet free.
59 JEHOVAH judge the cauſe for me,
   As Thou my wrongs haſt always ſeen.
60 As their revenge and all their plots
   Before thine eyes have ever been.
61 All their reproach, Thou LORD, haſt heard;
   Thou feeſt the ſnares they for me lay,
62 Their lips who up againſt me riſe,
   And all their plottings all the day.
63 See, when they ſit, and when they riſe,
   The muſick of their ſongs am I:
64 But LORD, as are their handy works
   A juſt reward Thou wilt apply.
65 Sorrow of heart Thou wilt them give,
   Thy grievous curſe wilt make them bear;
66 In wrath them chace and from beneath
   JEHOVAH's heav'ns waſte ev'ry where.

JONAH II.

[*The Song of* Jonah *upon his great Deliverance.*]

2 To the LORD in my diſtreſs
   I Cry'd earneſtly, and He gave ear;
   Out from hell's belly then I cry'd,
   And He my voice did kindly hear.
3 For down into the hideous deeps,
   And midſt of ſeas, Thou didſt me caſt;
   The floods encompaſs'd me, and all
   Thy waves and billows o'er me paſs'd.
4 I then ſaid, I was caſt away
   Quite from the ſight of thy bleſt eyes, *
   Yet tow'rds thy temple I will look,
   And to Thee there direct my cries.

5 The

HABAKKUK iii.

5 The waters to my finking foul
Pierc'd and encompas'd me around;
The depths all round enclofed me,
The weeds about my head were bound.
6 To mountains bottoms I went down,
Earth's bars for ever me befet;
Yet LORD my God, Thou haft my life
Brought up out of the horrid pit.
7 When my funk foul fainted in me,
JEHOVAH then remember'd I;
And then my pray'r rofe up to Thee,
Into thy holy place on high.
8 They their own mercies fadly leave,
Who look to lying vanities:
But with the voice of giving thanks,
To Thee I'll praifes facrifice.
9 Whatever I in trouble vow'd,
To pay I readily accord;
For all falvation ever comes
From the moft kind and fov'reign LORD.

HABAKKUK III.
The Prayer of HABAKKUK *the Phrophet.*

2 THY fpeech, O LORD, I heard with fear:
In midft of years thy work declin'd
Revive, O LORD, and make it * known:
In wrath thy tender mercies mind.
3 The mighty God from Teman came,
THE HOLY ONE from Paran-hill: (*Selah.*)
His glory cover'd all the fkies,
And all the earth his praife did fill.
4 His brightnefs as the light appear'd,
And beams of fplendor † from Him ‡ flow'd;
Where was the hiding of his pow'r,
There then it blazed all abroad ‖

5 Before

† The Word fignifies both *Horns* and *Beams*; derives from a Root which fignifies *beaming forth:* ‡ and the Word commonly rendered *Hands*, fignifies alfo *Sides:* See *Avenarius, Buxtorf, Schindler, Pagnine* and *Mercer, Caftellus,* and *Martin Albert.*
‖ *Chaldee.*

5 Before Him went the pestilence :
  Coals glowing at his feet were spread :
6 When he stood up, the earth was mov'd : †
  He look'd, and all the nations fled ;

  Th' eternal mountains were dispers'd ;
  The hills of perpetuity,
  Bow'd lowly down before his feet :
  His ways abide eternally.
7 The tents of Ethiopia then
  In great affliction I did see :
  The curtains thro' all Midian's land,
  Shook at the dreadful sight of THEE !

8 Against the rivers, floods or seas,
  Did then JEHOVAH anger bear,
  That on his troops of horses rode ;
  HIS CHARIOTS OF SALVATION WERE.
9 As to thy tribes, to save them, THOU
  Thy solemn word and oath didst give ;
  Made wholly naked was thy bow, (*Selah.*)
  The earth with rivers THOU didst cleave.

10 Thee saw, and shook the mountains great ;
  The floods of waters rolled by ;
  His voice loud utter did the deep,
  And lifted up his hands on high.
11 The sun and moon, when Thee they saw,
  Stood still amaz'd in their high Sphere :
  But quick mov'd at thine arrows light,
  And brighter glitt'ring of thy spear.

12 Thou marchest thro' the land in wrath,
  The heathen threshest as in rage :
13 In flames of zeal Thou goest forth,
  To save thy sinking heritage.
  With thy MESSIAH ‡ them to save :
  Thou from the wicked's house, the head
  Hast quite cut off ; § and from his feet ‖
  Up to his neck, all bare hast laid. (*Selah.*)
              14 Thou

† *Septuagint, Chaldee, Arabick.* ‡ *Heb. Sept. Chald, Syriack.*
   § *Syriack.*   ‖ *Menochius in Pol. Synop.*

14 Thou haſt with his [Messiah's] rods
   Struck thro' the univerſal head,
   Of all their num'rous villages,
   And all in deſolation ſpread.
   They, as tempeſtuous whirlwinds, roſe
   And ruſhed on, to ſcatter me:
   Their joyful hope was to devour
   The poor afflicted ſecretly.
15 But when I ſaw Thee walk along,
   And with thy horſes thro' the ſea,
   Thro' all the waters mighty heaps,
   Againſt the dreadful enemy.
16 I heard! my belly trembled through;
   At thy loud voice my lips did quake:
   A rott'nneſs ſeized all my bones;
   I thro' my ſelf did greatly ſhake:
   That in this day of trouble I
   Might in ſafe quietneſs repoſe;
   While for his people He aſcends,
   And with his troops invades their foes.
17 Tho' figtrees ſhould no bloſſoms yield,
   Nor any fruit on vines appear,
   The labours of the olive fail,
   And tho' the fields no food ſhould bear;
   Tho' from the folds the flocks ſhould ceaſe,
   In ſtalls no cattle have abode;
18 Yet in the LORD I will exult,
   And joy in my ſalvation's God.
   JEHOVAH is my *Lord* and ſtrength:
   He makes my feet ſwift as the roe:
   He leads me to my places high,
   And makes me ſafe on them to go.

LUKE I. 46—55.

The Song of the bleſſed Virgin Mary, *at her meeting* Elizabeth.

46 MY ſoul doth magnify the LORD:
47 My ſpirit greatly doth rejoice
   In GOD my ſaviour; whom I praiſe
   With joyful and exulting voice.

48 For

48 For greatly He regarded hath
His handmaid in her low eſtate:
And hence all ages of the world
Shall me as bleſſed celebrate.

49 Th' Almighty wondrous things hath done,
To me: and holy is his name:

50 To them who fear Him mercies flow;
From race to race they ever ſtream.

51 He with his arm hath ſhewed ſtrength;
The great and proud hath ſcattered
In the devices of their hearts
They vainly had imagined.

52 Down from their ſeats of dignity
The high and mighty put hath He;
And has exalted thoſe on high
Who were before of low degree.

53 The hungry hath with good things fill'd,
The rich has empty ſent away;

54 His ſervant Iſr'el greatly help'd,
His mercy minds, and will diſplay.

55 As what He to our fathers ſpake,
So wondrouſly perform *dzth* He
To Abraham and to his race,
And *will* ev'n to eternity.

LUKE I. 68—79.

The Song of Zacharias *at the Circumciſion of* John *the Baptiſt.*

68 THE LORD, the GOD of Iſrael
be greatly bleſs'd! for He
Hath now his people viſited,
redeem'd, and made them free.

69 Who our ſalvation's mighty Horn,
foretold in ancient days,
Out of his ſervant David's houſe,
hath now been pleas'd to raiſe.

70 According to his promiſes
proclaim'd by holy men,
Who ever ſince the world began
by Him inſpir'd have been. 71 That

LUKE ii. 14.

71 That we from all our enemies
by Him may saved be;
And from the cruel hands of all
who hate us may be free.

72 To grant the mercy promised
our fathers; and to mind
His holy covenant, (73) His oath
to Abraham his friend.

74 That us from fear and foes hand freed,
to serve Him He would give;
75 In holiness and righteousness,
before Him, while we live.

76 And with his prophets, THE MOST HIGH,
dear Child, will number thee;
Before the LORD, to clear his way,
thou shalt employed be.

77 The doctrine of salvation thou
shalt make his people know:
And how He will forgive their sins
thou shalt them clearly show.

78 Thro' tender mercies of our GOD;
whereby the springing day
Begins to rise and visit us,
and chase the night away.

79 To light those who in darkness sit,
and in death's shade reside;
And in the way to endless peace
our foot-steps safely guide.

LUKE ii. 14.
The Song of the heavenly Hosts at the Birth of CHRIST.

ALL glory to the most high GOD,
on high let glory be:
On earth be glorious peace abroad,
and men his favour see.

[*Long Metre.*]

GLORY be to *The most High GOD*,
On high the highest Glory be!
And peace on all the earth abroad,
To men his boundless favour free.

LUKE II. 29, 30.

The Song of Simeon, *upon taking the Child* JESUS *into his Arms in the Temple.*

29 LORD, let me now depart in peace,
　　Who have thy waiting servant been,
　According to thy word ! for now
30 Mine eyes have thy salvation seen !
31 Which Thou hast wondrously prepar'd,
　And shown before all people's face ;
32 A light to all the Gentile world,
　The glory of thine Isr'el's race !

MATTHEW VI. 9—13.
The LORD's *Prayer.*

9 OUR FATHER, who in heav'n art seen,
　　In brightest love and majesty ;
　Let all the universe conspire
　Thy glorious name to sanctify.
10 O let thy promis'd kingdom come
　Of grace and glory from above :
　And let thy will be done on earth
　As 'tis in heav'n with joy and love.

11 Give us this day our daily bread :
12 Our debts to thee forgive and blot,
　As we our debtors free forgive :
13 Into temptation lead us not,
　But us from ev'ry evil save :
　For thine the universal reign,
　The pow'r and glory always was,
　Is, and shall ever be : AMEN.

REVELATIONS IV. 8, 9.
The Song of the FOUR *glorious* LIVING CREATURES *before the Throne.*

8 O Holy ! holy ! holy LORD !
　　th' Almighty GOD alone !
　Who was, and is, and art to come:
9 　who sittest on the throne :
　And who for ever, ever liv'st !
　　we render thanks to Thee :
　To Thee all honour, glory yield:
　　nor ever cease shall we.   *Ver.* 11.

Ver. 11.
The Responsive Song of the Twenty four Elders,
casting down their Crowns before the Throne.

11 LORD, Thou all honour, glory, pow'r,
  art worthy to receive,
From ev'ry creature; for to all
 Thou didst their Being give.
Yea all things thro' the Universe
 at first created were
For thine own pleasure, and for this
 they all continued are.

R E V. V. 9. 10.
To the LORD JESUS, *the* LAMB *of* GOD, *the Song
of the* Universal Church.

9 THOU worthy art to take the Book
  from Him upon the throne,
And open all the seals thereof,
 and none but Thou alone.
For Thou for guilty men wast slain,
 'hast bought us by thy blood;
From ev'ry people, nation, tongue,
 redeem'd us all to GOD.

10 Yea Thou hast made and raised us
 ev'n kings and priests to be,
To minister before our GOD:
 and reign on earth shall we.

Ver. 12.
The Responsive Song of the Four Living Creatures,
The Twenty four Elders, *and Multitudes of* Angels.

THE *Lamb* is worthy that was slain,
  all might and wealth to have,
And wisdom, honour, glory, pow'r,
 and praises to receive.

Ver. 13.
The closing Song of all the Creatures *in Heaven,
on Earth, under the Earth, and in the Sea, together.*

TO Him who sits upon the throne,
  and to the *Lamb* therefore,
Be blessing, honour, glory, pow'r,
 ever and evermore.   *R E V.*

REV. VII. 10.

The grateful Song of the innumerable Multitudes *of* Saints *before the* Throne *& the* Lamb.

TO our moſt glorious GOD on high,
  who ſits upon the throne,
And to the *Lamb*, ſalvation, we
  aſcribe, as due, alone !

Ver. 12. *The Reſponſive Song of all the* Angels, Elders, *and* Living Creatures, *together.*

AMEN ! pow'r, wiſdom, might and thanks,
  all bleſſing, honour then,
And glory ever be aſcrib'd
  to our great GOD, AMEN.

REV. XV. 3, 4. *The Song of* Moſes *& of the* LAMB, *ſung by the Saints in Triumph.*

3 O LORD, Almighty GOD ! thy works
    both great and wondrous are:
Juſt king of ſaints, and true thy way:
4 who ſhall not Thee revere !
And glorify thy name, O LORD !
  who holy art alone:
For nations all ſhall worſhip Thee ;
  whoſe judgments now are known.

XIX. 1, 2. *The Song of the* Multitudes *in* Heaven.

1 O HALLELUJAH ! honour, pow'r,
    Salvation and all glory give,
Give to the LORD our GOD alone,
That all his dues he may receive.

2 For true and juſt his judgments are:
On the great whore hath judgment wrought,
Who with her fornication had
On all the earth corruption brought.

Of all who ſerv'd Him to the death
The blood ſhe ſhed aveng'd hath He ;
Aveng'd on *her,* and crowned *them.*
AMEN ! ſing HALLELUJAH ye !

HYMNS.

HYMNS

Which are not Versions of the Scriptures, but
Pious Songs *derived from them.*
By Dr. WATTS *and* Others.

I. *The Fall of Angels and Men.*

1 WHEN the Great Builder arch'd the Skies,
    And form'd all Nature with a word,
    The joyful Cherubs tun'd his Praise,
    And ev'ry bending Throne ador'd.
High in the midst of all the Throng
Satan a *tall* Arch-Angel sate,
Amongst the Morning Stars he sung,
'Till Sin destroy'd his Heav'nly State.

2 'Twas Sin that hurl'd him from his Throne;
Grov'ling in Fire the Rebel lies:
How art thou sunk in darkness down,
Son of the Morning from the Skies!
And thus *our two first Parents* stood,
'Till S'n defil'd the happy Place;
They lost their Garden and their God,
And ruin'd all their unborn race.

3 So sprung the Plague from *Adam*'s Bow'r,
And spread Destruction all abroad,
Sin, the curs'd Name, that in one Hour
Spoil'd six Days Labour of a God.
Tremble, my Soul, and mourn for Grief,
That such a Foe should seize thy Breast;
Fly to thy Lord for quick Relief:
Oh! may he slay this treach'rous Guest.

4 Then to thy Throne, Victorious King,
Then to thy Throne our Shouts shall rise,
Thine everlasting Arm we sing,
For Sin, the Monster, bleeds and dies.

II. *The*

II. *The* First *and* Second Adam.

1 BACKWARD with humble Shame we look
  on our Original;
How is our Nature dash'd and broke
  in our first Father's Fall!
To all that's Good averse and blind,
  but prone to all that's ill;
What dreadful Darkness veils our Mind!
  how obstinate our Will!

2 Conceiv'd in Sin (O wretched State!)
  before we draw our Breath;
The first young Pulse begins to beat
  iniquity and Death.
How strong in our degen'rate Blood
  the old Corruption reigns,
And mingling with the crooked Flood,
  wanders through all our Veins!

3 Wild and unwholesome as the Root
  will all the Branches be;
How can we hope for living Fruit
  from such a deadly Tree?
What mortal Pow'r from Things unclean
  can pure Productions bring?
Who can command a vital stream
  from an infected Spring?

4 Yet mighty God, thy wond'rous Love
  can make our Nature clean,
While *Christ* and Grace prevail above
  the Tempter, Death and Sin.
The Second *Adam* shall restore
  the Ruins of the First;
Hosanna to that Sov'reign Pow'r,
  that new creates our Dust!

III. *The Deity and Humanity of* CHRIST

5 E'ER the blue Heav'ns were stretch'd abroad,
  From Everlasting was the Word;
With God He was; the word was God,
  And must divinely be ador'd.

By

HYMN IV.

By His own Pow'r were all Things made,
By Him supported all Things stand;
He is the whole Creation's Head,
And Angels fly at his Command.

2 E'er Sin was born or Satan fell,
He led the Host of Morning Stars;
(Thy Generation who can tell,
Or count the Number of thy Years?)
But lo, He leaves those heavenly Forms,
The Word descends and dwells in Clay,
That He may hold Converse with Worms,
Dress'd in such feeble Flesh as they.

3 Mortals with joy beheld his Face,
Th' Eternal Father's only Son;
How full of Truth! how full of Grace!
When thro' his Eyes the God-head shone!
Arch-Angels leave their high Abode,
To learn new Myst'ries here and tell
The Loves of our descending God,
The Glories of *Emanuel*.

IV. *The Nativity of* CHRIST.

1 BEHOLD the Grace appears,
the Promise is fulfill'd;
Mary, the wond'rous Virgin bears,
and *Jesus* is the Child.
The Lord, the Highest God,
calls him his only Son;
He bids Him rule the Lands abroad,
and gives Him *David*'s Throne.

2 O'er *Jacob* shall he reign
with a peculiar Sway;
The Nations shall his Grace obtain,
His Kingdom ne'er decay.
To bring the glorious News,
a heavenly Form appears:
He tells the Shepherds of their Joys,
and banishes their Fears.

HYMN V.

3 *Go humble Swains* said he,
   to David's *City fly;*
The promis'd Infant, born To-Day,
   doth in a Manger lie.
With Looks and Hearts serene
   go *visit* Christ *your* King;
And strait a flaming Troop was seen:
   the Shepherds heard them sing,

4 *Glory to God on High!*
   and heav'nly Peace on Earth,
Good-will to Men, to Angels Joy,
   at the Redeemer's Birth;
In Worship so Divine
   let Saints employ their Tongues,
With the Celestial Host we join,
   and loud repeat their Songs.

5 *Glory to God on High!*
   and heav'nly Peace on Earth,
Good-will to Men, to Angels Joy,
   at the Redeemer's Birth!

V. *The Humiliation and Exaltation of* CHRIST.

1 WHAT equal Honours shall we bring
       To thee, O Lord our God, the Lamb,
When all the Notes that Angels sing
Are far inferior to thy Name?
Worthy is He that once was slain,
The Prince of Peace that groan'd and dy'd,
Worthy to rise, and live and reign
At his Almighty Father's Side.

2 Pow'r and Dominion are his due,
Who stood condemn'd at *Pilate's* Bar:
Wisdom belongs to *Jesus* too,
Tho' he was charg'd with Madness here,
All Riches are his native Right,
Yet he sustain'd amazing Loss;
To him ascribe Eternal Might,
Who left his Weakness on the Cross.

3 Honour

3 Honour immortal muſt be paid,
Inſtead of Scandal and of Scorn;
While Glory ſhines around his Head,
And a bright Crown without a Thorn.
Bleſſings for ever on the Lamb,
Who bore the Curſe for wretched Men;
Let Angels ſound his ſacred Name,
And ev'ry Creature ſay, *Amen.*

VI. *The Offices of* CHRIST.

1 JOIN all the Names of Love and Pow'r
That ever Men or Angels bore,
All are too mean to ſpeak his Worth,
Or ſet *Immanuel's* Glory forth.
But O what condeſcending Ways
He takes to teach his heav'nly Grace !
My Eyes with Joy and Wonder ſee
What Forms of Love he bears for me.

2 The *Angel of the Cov'nant* ſtands
With his Commiſſion in his Hands,
Sent from his Father's milder Throne
To make the great Salvation known.
Great *Prophet*, let me bleſs thy Name ;
By thee the joyful Tidings came,
Of Wrath appeas'd, of Sins forgiv'n,
Of Hell ſubdu'd, and Peace with Heav'n.

3 My bright *Example*, and my *Guide*,
I would be walking near thy Side:
O let me never run aſtray,
Nor follow the forbidden Way !
I love my *Shepherd*, he ſhall keep
My wand'ring Soul among his Sheep;
He feeds his Flock, he calls their Names,
And in his Boſom bears the Lambs.

4 My *Surety* undertakes the Cauſe,
Anſw'ring his Father's broken Laws ;
Behold my Soul at Freedom ſet,
My Surety paid the dreadful Debt.

Jeſus

HYMN VII.

Jesus my Great *High Priest* has dy'd,
I seek no Sacrifice beside;
His Blood did once for all atone,
And now it pleads before the Throne.

5 My *Advocate* appears on high,
The Father lays his Thunder by;
Not all that Earth or Hell can say
Shall turn my Father's Heart away.
My *Lord*, my *Conqu'ror*, and my *King*,
Thy Scepter and thy Sword I sing;
Thine is the Vict'ry, and I sit
A joyful Subject at thy Feet.

6 Aspire, my Soul, to glorious Deeds,
The *Captain of Salvation* leads:
March on, nor fear to win the Day,
Tho' Death and Hell obstruct the way.
Should Death and Hell, and Pow'rs unknown,
Put all their Forms of Mischief on,
I shall be safe; for *Christ* displays
Salvation in more Sov'reign Ways.

VII. *The Offices of the* HOLY SPIRIT.

1 ETERNAL Spirit! we confess,
And sing the Wonders of thy Grace;
Thy Pow'r conveys our Blessings down
From God the Father and the Son.
Inlighten'd by thine heav'nly Ray,
Our Shades and Darkness turn to Day;
Thine inward Teachings make us know
Our Danger, and our Refuge too.

2 Thy Pow'r and Glory works within,
And breaks the Chains of reigning Sin;
Doth our imperious Lusts subdue,
And forms our wretched Hearts anew.
The troubled Conscience knows thy voice,
Thy chearing Words awake our Joys,
Thy Words allay the stormy Wind,
And calm the Surges of the Mind.

HYMN VIII. IX. X.

VIII. *Regeneration necessary.*

1 NOT all the outward Forms on Earth,
   nor Rites that God has giv'n,
Nor Will of Man, nor Blood, nor Birth,
   can raise a Soul to Heav'n.
The sov'reign Will of God alone
   creates us Heirs of Grace:
Born in the Image of his Son,
   a new peculiar Race.

2 The Spirit, like some heav'nly Wind,
   blows on the Sons of Flesh,
New-models all the carnal Mind,
   and forms the Man afresh.
Our quicken'd Souls awake, and rise,
   from the long Sleep of Death;
On heav'nly Things we fix our Eyes,
   and praise employs our Breath.

IX. *Repentance and Faith necessary.*

LIFE and immortal Joys are giv'n
   To Souls that mourn the Sins they've done;
Children of Wrath made Heirs of Heav'n,
By Faith in God's eternal Son.
Wo to the Wretch that never felt
   The inward Pangs of pious Grief,
But adds to all his crying Guilt
   The stubborn Sin of Unbelief.

2 The Law condemns the Rebel dead,
   Under the Wrath of God he lies:
He feals the Curse on his own Head,
   And with a double Vengeance dies.

X. *Difficulty of sincere Conversion.*

1 STRAIT is the Way, the Door is strait,
   that leads to Joys on high;
'Tis but a few that find the Gate,
   while Crowds mistake and die.
Beloved Self must be deny'd,
   the Mind and Will renew'd,
Passion suppress'd, and Patience try'd,
   and vain Desires subdu'd.

P   2 Flesh

HYMN XI. XII.

2 Flesh is a dang'rous Foe to Grace,
    where it prevails and rules ;
Flesh must be humbl'd, Pride abas'd,
    lest they destroy our Souls.
The Love of Gold be banish'd hence,
    (that vile Idolatry)
And ev'ry Member, ev'ry Sense,
    in sweet Subjection lie.

3 The Tongue, that most unruly Pow'r,
    requires a strong Restraint :
We must be watchful ev'ry Hour,
    and pray, but never faint.
Lord ! can a feeble, helpless Worm
    fulfil a Task so hard ?
Thy Grace must all my Work perform,
    and give the free Reward.

XI. *Believe and be saved.*

1 NOT to condemn the Sons of Men
    Did *Christ* the Son of God appear :
No Weapons in his Hands are seen,
No flaming Sword, nor Thunder there.
Such was the Pity of our God,
    He lov'd the Race of Man so well,
He sent his Son to bear our Load
    Of Sins, and save our Souls from Hell.

2 Sinners, believe the Saviour's Word,
    Trust in his mighty Name, and live ;
A thousand Joys his lips afford,
    His Hands a thousand Blessings give;
But Vengeance and Damnation lies
    On Rebels, who refuse the Grace ;
Who God's eternal Son despise,
    The hottest Hell shall be their Place.

XII. *Faith in* CHRIST *for Pardon & Sanctification.*

1 HOW sad our State by Nature is !
    our Sin, how deep it stains !
And *Satan* binds our captive Minds
    fast in his slavish Chains. But

HYMN XIII.

But there's a Voice of Sov'reign Grace
 sounds from the sacred Word;
Ho! ye despairing Sinners come,
 and trust upon the Lord.

2 My Soul obeys th' Almighty Call,
 and runs to this Relief;
I would believe thy Promise, Lord;
 oh! help my Unbelief.
To the dear Fountain of thy Blood,
 incarnate God I fly;
Here let me wash my spotted soul
 from Crimes of deepest Dye.

3 Stretch out thine Arm, victorious King,
 my reigning Sins subdue;
Drive the old Dragon from his Seat,
 with all his hellish Crew.
A guilty, weak, and helpless Worm
 on thy kind Arms I fall:
Be thou my Strength and Righteousness,
 my *Jesus*, and my All.

XIII. *Justification by Faith, not by Works.*

1 VAIN are the Hopes the Sons of Men
 on their own Works have built;
Their Hearts by Nature all unclean,
 and all their Actions Guilt.
Let *Jew* and *Gentile* stop their Mouths,
 without a murm'ring Word,
And the whole Race of *Adam* stand
 guilty before the Lord.

2 In vain we ask God's righteous Law
 to justify us now.
Since to convince and to condemn
 is all the Law can do.
Jesus, how glorious is thy Grace,
 when in thy Name we trust!
Our Faith receives Thy Righteousness,
 which makes the Sinner just.

XIV. *Adoption.*

1 BEHOLD what wond'rous Grace
   the Father hath beſtow'd
On Sinners of a Mortal Race,
   to call them Sons of God!
'Tis no ſurprizing Thing,
   that we ſhould be unknown;
The *Jewiſh* World knew not their King,
   God's everlaſting Son:

2 Nor doth it yet appear
   how great we muſt be made;
But when we ſee our Saviour here,
   we ſhall be like our Head.
A Hope ſo much divine
   may Trials well endure,
May purge our Souls from Senſe and Sin,
   as Chriſt the Lord is pure.

3 If in my Father's Love
   I ſhare a filial Part,
Send down thy Spirit, like a Dove,
   to reſt upon my Heart.
We would no longer lie
   like Slaves beneath the Throne;
My Faith ſhall *Abba* Father cry,
   and thou the Kindred own.

XV. *Baptiſm of grown Perſons.*

1 'TWAS the Commiſſion of our Lord,
   Go, teach the Nations, and Baptize.
The Nations have receiv'd the Word,
Since he aſcended to the Skies.
He ſits upon th' eternal Hills,
With Grace and Pardon in his Hands,
And ſends his Cov'nant, with the Seals,
To bleſs the People of all Lands.

2 *Repent, and be baptiz'd,* he ſaith,
For the Remiſſion of your Sins;
And thus our Senſe aſſiſts our Faith
And ſhows us what his Goſpel means.

HYMN XVI.

Our Souls he washes in his Blood,
   As Water makes the Body clean;
And the good Spirit from our God
   Descends like purifying Rain.

3 Thus we engage our selves to thee,
   And seal our Cov'nant with the Lord;
O may the Great Eternal Three
   In Heav'n our solemn Vows record!

XVI. *Baptism of Children.*

1 HOW large Thy Covenant of Grace
   to *Abr'am* and *his Seed*!
' I'll be a GOD to *Thee* and *Those*
' who from thy Loins proceed.'
JESUS the ancient Word confirms,
   show'd wond'rous Tenderness;
He took young Children in his Arms,
   and them did kindly bless.

2 *Gentiles* by Nature, we belong'd
   to the wild Olive Wood,
Grace took us from the barren Tree
   and grafts us on the Good.
With the same Blessing Grace endows
   the *Gentile* as the *Jew*;
That still if holy be the Root,
   such are the Branches too.

3 The Words of Thy extensive Love
   from Age to Age endure;
The ANGEL of the *Cov'nant* came,
   and seal'd the Blessing sure:
O GOD! how constant are Thy Ways,
   thy Love endures the same;
Thy Promise is to *us* and *our's*;
   we mark them with Thy Name.

4 O dear REDEEMER! take them then,
   and wash them in Thy *Blood*;
O pour Thy SPIRIT out on them,
   and make them pure for GOD.

Then if they live, they'l ſerve thy Cauſe,
  and Glory to Thee bring;
And when they die, to Heav'n they'l riſe,
  and endleſs Praiſes ſing.

XVII. *A Living and a Dead Faith.*

1 Miſtaken Souls! that dream of Heav'n,
    and make their empty Boaſt
Of inward Joys, and Sins forgiv'n,
    while they are Slaves to Luſt.
Vain are our Fancies, airy Flights,
    if Faith be cold and dead,
None but a living Pow'r unites
    to *Chriſt* the living Head.

2 'Tis Faith that changes all the Heart,
    'tis Faith that works by Love;
That bids all ſinful Joys depart,
    and lifts the Thoughts above.
'Tis Faith that conquers Earth and Hell,
    by a celeſtial Pow'r;
This is the Grace that ſhall prevail
    in the deciſive Hour.

3 Faith muſt obey her Father's Will,
    as well as truſt his Grace;
A pard'ning God is jealous ſtill
    for his own Holineſs.
When from the Curſe he ſets us free,
    he makes our Natures clean,
Nor would He ſend his Son to be
    the Miniſter of Sin.

4 His Spirit purifies our Frame,
    and ſeals our Peace with God;
Jeſus, and his Salvation came
    by Water and by Blood.

XVIII. *Example of* Christ.

1 My dear Redeemer, and my Lord,
    I read my Duty in thy Word;
But in thy Life the Law appears,
Drawn out in living Characters.   Such

HYMN XIX. XX.

Such was thy Truth, and such thy Zeal,
Such Def'rence to thy Father's Will,
Such Love, and Meekness so divine,
I would transcribe, and make them mine.

2 Cold Mountains, and the Midnight Air,
Witness'd the Fervour of thy Pray'r;
The Desart thy Temptations knew,
Thy Conflict, and thy Vict'ry too.

Be thou my Pattern; make me bear
More of thy gracious Image here;
Then God the Judge shall own my Name
Amongst the Foll'wers of the Lamb.

XIX. *Love to GOD and our Neighbour.*

1 THUS saith the first, the great Command,
 " Let all thy inward Pow'rs unite
" To love thy Maker, and thy God,
" With utmost Vigour and Delight.
" Then shall thy Neighbour next in Place
" Share thine Affections and Esteem,
" And let thy Kindness to thy self
" Measure and rule thy Love to him."

2 This is the Sense that *Moses* spoke,
This did the Prophets preach and prove:
For want of this the Law is broke,
And the whole Law's fulfill'd by Love.

But Oh! how base our Passions are!
How cold our Charity and Zeal!
Lord, fill our Souls with heav'nly Fire,
Or we shall ne'er perform thy Will.

XX. *Love and Charity.*

1 LET Pharisees of high Esteem
 their Faith and Zeal declare,
All their Religion is a Dream,
 if Love be wanting there.

Love suffers long with patient Eye,
 nor is provok'd in haste,
She let's the present Injury die,
 and long forgets the pass'd.

2 Malice and Rage, thofe Fires of Hell,
  fhe quenches with her tongue;
  Hopes, and believes, and thinks no Ill,
  tho' fhe endures the Wrong.
  She nor defires nor feeks to know
  the Scandals of the Time;
  Nor looks with Pride on thofe below,
  nor envies thofe that climb.

3 She lays her own Advantage by
  to feek her Neighbour's Good;
  So God's own Son came down to die,
  and bought our Lives with Blood.
  Love is the Grace that keeps her Pow'r,
  in all the Realms above;
  There Faith and Hope are known no more,
  but Saints for ever love.

XXI. *The Beatitudes.*

1 BLEST are the humble Souls that fee
  Their Emptinefs and Poverty;
  Treafures of Grace to them are giv'n,
  And Crowns of Joy laid up in Heav'n.
  Bleft are the Men of broken Heart,
  Who mourn for Sin with inward Smart;
  The Blood of *Chrift* divinely flows;
  A healing Balm for all their Woes.

2 Bleft are the Meek, who ftand afar
  From Rage and Paffion, Noife and War;
  God will fecure their happy State,
  And plead their Caufe againft the Great.
  Bleft are the Souls that thirft for Grace,
  Hunger and long for Righteoufnefs;
  They fhall be well fupply'd and fed
  With living Streams and living Bread.

3 Bleft are the Men whofe Bowels move
  And melt with Sympathy and Love;
  From *Chrift* the Lord fhall they obtain
  Like Sympathy and Love again.

Bleft

HYMN XXII. XXIII.

Bleſt are the pure, whoſe Hearts are clean
From the defiling Pow'rs of Sin;
With endleſs Pleaſure they ſhall ſee
A God of ſpotleſs Purity.

4 Bleſt are the Men of peaceful Life,
Who quench the Coals of growing Strife;
They ſhall be call'd the Heirs of Bliſs,
The Sons of God, the God of Peace.
Bleſt are the Suff'rers who partake
Of Pain and Shame for *Jeſus*' ſake;
Their Souls ſhall triumph in the Lord,
Glory and Joy are their Reward.

XXII. *Grace and Holineſs.*

1 SO let our Lips and Lives expreſs
The holy Goſpel we profeſs;
So let our Works and Virtues ſhine,
To prove the Doctrine all Divine.
Thus ſhall we beſt proclaim abroad
The Honours of our Saviour God;
When the Salvation reigns within,
And Grace ſubdues the Pow'r of Sin.

2 Our Fleſh and Senſe muſt be deny'd,
Paſſion and Envy, Luſt and Pride;
While Juſtice, Temp'rance, Truth and Love,
Our inward Piety approve.
Religion bears our Spirits up,
While we expect that bleſſed Hope,
The bright Appearance of the Lord,
And Faith ſtands leaning on his Word.

XXIII. *Submiſſion to Afflictive Providences.*

1 NAKED as from the Earth we came,
    and crept to Life at firſt,
We to the Earth return again,
    and mingle with our Duſt.
The dear Delights we here enjoy,
    and fondly call our own,
Are but ſhort Favours borrow'd Now,
    to be repaid Anon.

2 'Tis God that lifts our Comforts high,
    or sinks them in the Grave,
He gives, and (blessed be his Name!)
    he takes but what he gave.
Peace, all our angry Passions then,
    let each rebellious Sigh
Be silent at his Sov'reign Will,
    and ev'ry Murmur die.

3 If smiling Mercy crown our Lives,
    it's Praises shall be spread,
And we'll adore the Justice too
    that strikes our Comforts dead.

XXIV. *The* Lord's Supper *Instituted.*

1 'TWAS on that dark, that doleful Night,
    When Pow'rs of Earth and Hell arose
Against the Son of God's Delight,
And Friends betray'd him to his Foes.
Before the mournful Scene began,
He took the Bread, and bless'd and brake:
What Love thro' all his Actions ran!
What wond'rous Words of Grace he spake?

2 *This is my Body, broke for Sin,*
Receive and eat the living Food:
Then took the Cup, and bless'd the Wine;
'Tis the New Cov'nant in my Blood.
For us his Flesh with Nails was torn,
He bore the Scourge, he felt the Thorn:
And Justice pour'd upon his Head
It's heavy Vengeance in our Stead.

3 For us his vital Blood he spilt,
To buy the Pardon of our Guilt;
When, for black Crimes of biggest Size,
He gave his Soul a Sacrifice.
Do this, he cry'd, *'till Time shall end,*
In Mem'ry of your dying Friend;
Meet at my Table and record
The Love of your departed Lord.

4 *Jesus,*

4 *Jesus*, thy Feast we celebrate,
We shew thy Death, we sing thy Name,
'Till thou return and we shall eat
The Marriage Supper of the Lamb.

XXV. *The bitter Sufferings of* CHRIST.

1 COME let us all who here have seen,
   And tasted of our Saviour's grace,
From his bless'd table to his cross,
In thought, his weary footsteps trace.
Into the garden first he goes,
Where mortal fears beset him round;
Sin's pressing weight o'erwhelms his soul,
And sinks his body to the ground.

2 Here, prostrate as he lies, he groans,
Pouring out Pray'rs with fervent Cries,
'Till he sweats drops of Blood, to mix
With Floods that issue from his Eyes,
Yet are his Sorrows but begun;
By one Disciple He's betray'd,
Another Him with Oaths denies,
The rest all run like sheep afraid.

3 Falsly accus'd, He's doom'd to die;
Loaded with blasphemy and scorn,
He's rudely buffeted and bound,
His naked flesh with scourges torn.
His temples wear a wreath of thorns,
Vile Spitting his pure face profanes;
His weary shoulders bear a cross,
On which He suffers mortal pains.

4 Between two thieves He ling'ring dies,
While thousand tortures on Him meet;
His heart's dissolv'd within; his blood
Flows out in streams from hands and feet.
These streams, join'd with the other flood
That gush'd out from his wounded side,
Compose a sov'reign bath, wherein
The leprous Soul is purify'd.

HYMN XXVI. XXVII.

XXVI. *The Loveliness of a suffering* JESUS.

1 THOU art all Love, my dearest Lord,
    thou art all lovely too:
Thy Love I at thy Table taste,
    thy Loveliness I view.
But Thou more lovely art to me
    for all that thou hast born:
Each Cloud sets off thy Lustre more;
    thee all thy Scars adorn.

2 Thy Garments tinctur'd with thy Blood,
    the best and noblest Dye,
Out-shine the Robes that Princes wear;
    thy Thorns their Gems out-vie.
That I may be all Love to thee,
    and lovely like thee too,
O cleanse me with thy precious Blood,
    and me thy Beauty shew.

3 My former Vows I now renew:
    O Lord, as thou art mine;
I freely give my Heart to thee,
    for ever I'll be thine.

XXVII. CHRIST *finishing his Purchase of Redemption.*

1 'TIS finish'd the Redeemer cries;
    Then lowly bows his fainting Head;
And soon th' expiring Sacrifice
Sinks to the Regions of the Dead.
'Tis done—the mighty Work is done!
For Men and Angels much too great;
Which none, but God's eternal Son,
Or would attempt, or could complete.

2 'Tis done,—his Tears, his Groans and Wounds,
His Sweat and Blood, his Pains and Toils,
Vict'ry with deathless Glory crowns
With Trophies, and triumphant Spoils.
The Conqu'ror falls a Sacrifice,
Heav'n's just Resentments to appease:
Justice with Mercy now complies,
Both with the Sinner's Pardon pleas'd.

3 Once he was dead; now lives and reigns
  Where Angels his great Deeds proclaim:
  Let's tell our Joys in pious Strains,
  And spread the Glory of his Name.

XXVIII. *The New Covenant in the Blood of* CHRIST.

1 THE Promise of my Father's Love
    shall stand for ever good:
  He said, and gave his Soul to Death,
    and seal'd the Grace with Blood.
  To this dear Cov'nant of thy Word
    I set my worthless Name;
  I seal th' Engagement to my Lord,
    and make my humble Claim.

2 Thy Light, and Strength, and pard'ning Grace
    and Glory shall be mine;
  My Life and Soul, my Heart and Flesh,
    and all my Pow'rs are thine.
  I call that Legacy my own
    which *Jesus* did bequeath;
  'Twas purchas'd with a dying Groan,
    and ratify'd in Death.

3 Sweet is the Mem'ry of his Name
    who bless'd us in his Will,
  And to his Testament of Love
    made his own Life the Seal.

XXIX. *The Grace of the divine* FATHER, *and Fulness of* CHRIST.

1 JEHOVAH, we in Hymns of Praise
    thy matchless Grace adore,
  That Grace that gave thy only Son:
    what could'st thou give us more?
  He's all in all: His Saints in Him
    divine Perfection view:
  'Tis of his Fulness they receive
    all Grace and Glory too.

2 He

2 He freely gave his Blood, the Price
   of our eternal Blifs ;
Since no lefs could atone for Sin,
   his Love could give no lefs.
He in the Wine-prefs of thy Wrath
   for guilty men was crufh'd ;
Humbled himfelf to die, and laid
   his Honour in the Duft.

3 That we might at his Table fit,
   and be replenifh'd there,
With thefe dear Pledges of his Grace,
   'till we his Glory fhare.

XXX. *The Memorial of our abfent* LORD.

1 JESUS is gone above the Skies,
   Where our weak Senfes reach him not;
And carnal Objects court our Eyes,
To thruft our Saviour from our Thought.
He knows what wand'ring Hearts we have,
Apt to forget his lovely Face;
And, to refrefh our Minds, he gave
Thefe kind Memorials of his Grace.

2 The Lord of Life this Table fpread,
With his own Flefh and dying Blood,
We on the rich Provifion feed,
And tafte the Wine and blefs the God.
Let finful Sweets be all forgot,
And Earth grow lefs in our Efteem;
Chrift and his Love fill ev'ry Thought,
And Faith and Hope be fix'd on Him.

3 While He is abfent from our Sight,
'Tis to prepare our Souls a Place,
That we may dwell in heav'nly Light,
And live for ever near his Face.
Our Eyes look upwards to the Hills,
Whence our returning Lord fhall come;
We wait thy Chariot's haft'ning Wheels,
To fetch our longing Spirits home.

HYMN XXXI. XXXII.

XXXI. *Divine Love making a Feast and calling in the Guests.*

1 HOW sweet and awful is the Place
   with *Christ* within the Doors,
While everlasting Love displays
   the choicest of her Stores!
Here ev'ry Bowel of our God
   with soft Compassion rolls;
Here Peace and Pardon bought with Blood,
   is Food for dying Souls.

2 While all our Hearts and all our Songs
   join to admire the Feast,
Each of us cry, with thankful Tongues,
   " Lord, why was I a Guest?
" Why was I made to hear thy Voice,
" and enter while there's Room;
" When Thousands make a wretched Choice,
" and rather starve than come?"

3 'Twas the same Love that spread the Feast,
   that sweetly forc'd us in;
Else we had still refus'd to taste,
   and perish'd in our Sin.
Pity the Nations, O our God!
   constrain the Earth to come;
Send thy victorious Word abroad,
   and bring the Strangers home.

4 We long to see thy Churches full,
   that all the chosen Race
May with one Voice, and Heart, and Soul,
   sing thy redeeming Grace.

XXXII. *Feasting on* CHRIST *at his Table.*

1 HOW glorious is the holy Place,
   where Bread of Life is giv'n!
This surely is the House of God!
   this is the Gate of Heav'n!
Jesus, the Master of the Feast,
   vouchsafes his Presence here;
The Cup of Blessing passes round,
   the pious Guests to chear.

2 Hence faithless Doubts, desponding Fears,
  no more our joys molest:
Hence all vain Thoughts, and vile Desires
  no more our Souls infest.
Can Sinners doubt their Pardon, when
  their Judge upon them smiles?
Can they ungratefully rebel,
  whom *Jesus* reconciles?

3 The Merit of his Blood can calm
  the Soul with Guilt opprest:
The Torments of his Cross can make
  the Soul all Sin detest.
O may our Sins, that made thee bleed,
  all on thy Cross expire!
O may the Joys thy Banquet gives,
  equal our warm Desire!

4 So shall we mount upon the Wings
  of chearful Hope and Love;
And here begin the Songs that we
  shall better sing above.

XXXIII. *Communion with* CHRIST *and Saints.*

1 *JESUS* invites his Saints
    to meet around his Board;
Here pardon'd Rebels sit and hold
  Communion with their Lord.
For Food he gives his Flesh;
  he bids us drink his Blood:
Amazing Favour! matchless Grace
  of our descending God!

2 This holy Bread and Wine
    maintains our fainting Breath,
By Union with our living Lord,
  and Int'rest in his Death.
Our heav'nly Father calls
  Christ and his Members one;
We the young Children of his Love,
  and he the first-born Son.

HYMN XXXIV.

3 We are but sev'ral Parts
of the same broken Bread;
One Body hath it's sev'ral Limbs,
but *Jesus* is the Head.
Let all our Pow'rs be join'd,
his glorious Name to raise;
Pleasure and Love fill ev'ry Mind,
and ev'ry Voice be Praise.

XXXIV. *The Death of* CHRIST *is the Death of Sin.*

1 COME let us go and die with him,
  Who was content to die for us;
Let's wound and crucify those Sins
That nail'd our Saviour to his Cross.
May holy Indignation raise
A just Revenge in ev'ry Breast!
May ev'ry Soul that JESUS loves
The very Thought of Sin detest!

2 Hence all ye viprous Brood of Vice,
That bring a Train of endless Woes;
O how I hate you mortally,
As mine, and as my Saviour's Foes!
Hence all your vain deluding Arts,
Which the unwary Soul beguile;
These have no Charms for one that sees
Redeeming Mercy on him smile.

3 My Robes, when wash'd in sacred Blood,
Shall I again with Blots deface?
My Soul, by Grace advanc'd to Heav'n,
Shall I again to Hell debase?
Prevent me O almighty Grace!
Nor let me e'er so treacherous prove,
To crucify my Lord afresh,
And render Hate for all his Love!

4 His Life the Model be of mine;
His Word the Rule to guide my Way;
His Cross the Death of all my Crimes;
His Love the Subject of my Praise.

XXXV.

HYMN XXXV. XXXVI.

XXXV. *Crucifixion to the World by the Death of* CHRIST.

1 WHEN I survey the wond'rous Cross
On which the Prince of Glory dy'd,
My richest Gain I count but Loss,
And pour Contempt on all my Pride.
Forbid it, Lord, that I should boast
Save in the Death of *Christ* my God:
All the vain Things that charm me most,
I sacrifice them to his Blood.

2 See from his Head, his Hands, his Feet,
Sorrow and Love flow mingled down!
Did e'er such Love and Sorrow meet?
Or Thorns compose so rich a Crown?
His dying Crimson, like a Robe,
Spreads o'er his Body on the Tree;
Then am I dead to all the Globe,
And all the Globe is dead to me.

3 Were the whole Realm of Nature mine,
That were a Present far too small:
Love so amazing, so divine,
Demands my Soul, my Life, my All.

XXXVI. *Pardon and Strength from* CHRIST.

1 FATHER, we wait to feel thy Grace,
to see thy Glories shine;
The Lord will his own Table bless,
and make the Feast divine.
We touch, we taste the heav'nly Bread,
we drink the sacred Cup;
With outward Forms our Sense is fed,
our Souls rejoice in Hope.

2 We shall appear before the Throne
of our forgiving God,
Dress'd in the Garments of his Son,
and sprinkled with his Blood.
We shall be strong to run the Race,
and climb the upper Sky;
Christ will provide our Souls with Grace,
He bought a large Supply.

3 Let

3 Let us indulge a chearful Frame,
   for Joy becomes a Feast;
We love the Mem'ry of his Name,
   more than the Wine we taste.

XXXVII. *Grace and Glory by the Death of* CHRIST.

1 SITTING around our Father's Board,
   we raise our tuneful Breath;
Our Faith beholds her dying Lord,
   and dooms our Sins to Death.
We see the Blood of *Jesus* shed,
   whence all our Pardons rise;
The Sinner views th' Atonement made,
   and loves the Sacrifice.

2 Thy cruel Thorns, thy shameful Cross,
   procure us heav'nly Crowns:
Our-highest Gain springs from thy Loss;
   our Healing from thy Wounds.
Oh! 'tis impossible that we
   who dwell in feeble Clay,
Should equal Suff'rings bear for Thee,
   or equal Thanks repay.

XXXVIII. *The View of Divine Glories excite our Graces.*

1 HOW are thy Glories here display'd,
   Great God! how bright they shine,
While, at thy Word, we eat the Bread,
   and drink the fragrant Wine!
Here thy revenging Justice stands,
   and pleads it's dreadful Cause;
Here saving Mercy spreads her Hands,
   like *Jesus* on the Cross.

2 Thy Saints attend with ev'ry Grace,
   on this great Sacrifice;
And love appears with chearful Face,
   and Faith with fixed Eyes.
Our Hope in waiting Posture sits,
   to Heav'n directs her Sight;
Here ev'ry warmer Passion meets,
   and warmer Pow'rs unite.

HYMN XXXIX.

3 Zeal and Revenge perform their Part,
   and rising Sin destroy;
Repentance comes with aching Heart,
   and yet excites the Joy.
Dear Saviour, change our Faith to Sight,
   let Sin for ever die;
Then shall our Souls be all Delight,
   and ev'ry Tear be dry.

XXXIX. *A new Song to the* LAMB *slain.*

1 BEHOLD the Glories of the Lamb,
      amidst his Father's Throne:
   Prepare new Honours for his Name,
      and Songs before unknown.
   Let Elders worship at his Feet,
      the Church adore around,
   With Vials full of Odours sweet,
      and Harps of sweeter Sound.

2 Those are the Prayers of the Saints,
      and these the Hymns they raise:
   Jesus is kind to our Complaints,
      he loves to hear our Praise.
   Eternal Father, who shall look
      into thy secret Will?
   Who but the Son should take that Book,
      and open ev'ry Seal?

3 He shall fulfil thy great Decrees,
      the Son deserves it well;
   Lo in his Hand the Sov'reign Keys
      of Heav'n, and Death, and Hell!
   Now to the Lamb, that once was slain,
      be endless Blessings paid;
   Salvation, Glory, Joy remain
      for ever on thy Head.

4 Thou hast redeem'd our Souls with Blood,
      hast set the Pris'ners free,
   Hast made us Kings and Priests to God,
      and we shall reign with thee.

The

HYMN XL. XLI.

The Worlds of Nature and of Grace
are put beneath thy Pow'r;
Then shorten these delaying Days,
and bring the promis'd Hour.

XL. CHRIST's *Compassion to the Weak and Tempted.*

1 WITH Joy we meditate the Grace
　　of our High Priest above;
His Heart is made of Tenderness,
　his Bowels melt with Love.
Touch'd with a Sympathy within
　he knows our feeble Frame;
He knows what sore Temptations mean,
　for he has felt the same.

2 But spotless, innocent and pure
　the great Redeemer stood,
While *Satan*'s fiery Darts he bore,
　and did resist to Blood.
He in the Days of feeble Flesh
　pour'd out his Cries and Tears,
And in his Measure feels afresh
　what ev'ry Member bears.

3 He'll never quench the smoaking Flax,
　but raise it to a Flame;
The bruised Reed he never breaks,
　nor scorns the meanest Name.
Then let our humble Faith address
　his Mercy and his Pow'r,
We shall obtain deliv'ring Grace
　in the distressing Hour.

XLI. *The Christian Race.*

1 AWAKE our Souls (away our Fears,
　　Let ev'ry trembling Thought be gone,)
Awake, and run the Heav'nly Race,
And put a chearful Courage on,
True, 'tis a strait and thorny Road,
And mortal Spirits tire and faint;
But they forget the mighty God,
That feeds the Strength of ev'ry Saint.

2 The

2 The Mighty God whose matchless Pow'r
  Is ever new and ever young,
  And firm endures, while endless Years
  Their everlasting Circles run.
  From Thee, the overflowing Spring,
  Our Souls shall drink a fresh Supply
  While such as trust their native Strength
  Shall melt away, and drop, and die.

3 Swift as an Eagle cuts the Air,
  We'll mount aloft to thine Abode;
  On Wings of Love our Souls shall fly,
  Nor tire amidst the heav'nly Road.

XLII. *The Christian Warfare.*

1 STAND up, my Soul, shake off thy Fears,
  And gird the Gospel Armour on;
  March to the Gates of endless Joy,
  Where thy great Captain Saviour's gone.
  Hell and thy Sins resist thy Course,
  But Hell and Sin are vanquish'd Foes;
  Thy *Jesus* nail'd 'em to the Cross,
  And sung the Triumph when he rose.

2 What tho' thine inward Lusts rebel?
  'Tis but a struggling Gasp for Life;
  The Weapons of victorious Grace,
  Shall slay thy Sins, and end the Strife.
  Then let my Soul march boldly on
  Press forward to the heav'nly Gate,
  There Peace and Joy eternal reign,
  And glitt'ring Robes for Conqu'rors wait.

3 There shall I wear a starry Crown,
  And triumph in Almighty Grace,
  While all the Armies of the Skies
  Join in my Glorious Leader's Praise.

XLIII. *Death and Burial of Saints.*

1 WHY do we mourn departing Friends;
    or shake at Death's Alarms?
  'Tis but the Voice that *Jesus* sends
    to call them to his Arms.   Are

Are we not tending upward too,
    as faſt as Time can move?
Nor would we wiſh the Hours more ſlow,
    to keep us from our Love.

2 Why ſhould we tremble to convey
    their Bodies to the Tomb?
There the dear Fleſh of *Jeſus* lay,
    and left a long Perfume.
The Graves of all his Saints he bleſs'd,
    and ſoftned every Bed:
Where ſhould the dying Members reſt,
    but with the dying Head?

3 Thence he aroſe, aſcending high,
    and ſhew'd our Feet the Way:
Up to the Lord our Fleſh ſhall fly
    at the Great riſing Day.
Then let the laſt loud Trumpet ſound,
    and bid our Kindred riſe;
Awake, ye Nations under Ground,
    ye Saints aſcend the Skies.

XLIV. *The beatifick Sight of* Chriſt.

1 FROM Thee, my God, my Joys ſhall riſe,
    and run eternal Rounds
Beyond the Limits of the Skies,
    and all created Bounds.
The holy Triumphs of my Soul
    ſhall Death itſelf out brave,
Leave dull Mortality behind,
    and fly beyond the Grave.

2 There where my bleſſed *Jeſus* reigns,
    in Heav'n's unmeaſur'd Space,
I'll ſpend a long Eternity
    in Pleaſure and in Praiſe.
Millions of Years my wond'ring Eyes
    ſhall o'er thy Beauties rove,
And endleſs Ages I'll adore
    the Glories of thy Love.

3 Sweet *Jesus*, ev'ry Smile of thine
  shall fresh Endearments bring,
And thousand Tastes of new Delight
  from all thy Graces spring.
Haste, my Beloved, fetch my Soul
  up to thy bless'd Abode;
Fly, for my Spirit longs to see
  my Saviour and my God.

XLV. *The humble Worship of Heaven.*

1 FATHER, I long, I faint to see
   the Place of thine Abode;
I'd leave thy earthly Courts, and flee
  up to thy Seat, my God!
Here I behold thy distant Face,
  and 'tis a pleasing Sight;
But to abide in thine Embrace,
  is Infinite Delight.

2 I'd part with all the Joys of Sense,
  to gaze upon thy Throne;
Pleasure springs fresh for ever thence,
  unspeakable, unknown.
There all the heav'nly Hosts are seen,
  in shining Ranks they move,
And drink immortal Vigour in,
  with Wonder, and with Love.

3 Then at thy Feet with awful Fear
  th' adoring Armies fall;
With Joy they shrink to NOTHING there,
  before th' Eternal ALL.
There I would vie with all the Host
  in Duty and in Bliss;
While LESS THAN NOTHING I could boast,
  and Vanity confess.

4 The more thy Glorie strike mine Eyes,
  the humbler I shall lie;
Thus while I sink, my Joys shall rise
  unmeasurably high.

HYMN XLVI. XLVII.

XLVI. *Resurrection of the Saints.*

1 AND muſt this Body die?
    this mortal Frame decay?
And muſt theſe active Limbs of mine
lie mould'ring in the Clay?
God my Redeemer lives,
   and conſtant from the Skies
Looks down and watches all my Duſt,
   'till he ſhall bid it riſe.

2 Array'd in glorious Grace,
   ſhall theſe vile Bodies ſhine,
And ev'ry Shape, and ev'ry Face,
   look heav'nly and divine.
Theſe lively Hopes we owe
   to *Jeſus'* dying Love;
We would adore his Grace below,
   and ſing his Pow'r above.

3 Dear Lord, accept the Praiſe
   of theſe our humble Songs,
'Till Tunes of nobler Sound we raiſe
   with our immortal Tongues.

XLVII. *The glorious Reign of* CHRIST *on Earth.*

1 LO, what a glorious Sight appears
   to our believing Eyes!
The Earth and Seas are paſs'd away,
   and the old rolling Skies.
From the third Heav'n where God reſides,
   that holy, happy Place,
The *New Jeruſalem* comes down,
   adorn'd with ſhining Grace.

2 Attending Angels ſhout for Joy,
   and the bright Armies ſing,
Mortals, behold the ſacred Seat
   of your deſcending King,

The God of Glory down to Men
removes his bless'd Abode;
Men the dear Objects of his Grace,
and He the loving God.

3 *His own soft Hand shall wipe the Tears*
from ev'ry weeping Eye,
And Pains and Groans, and Griefs and Fears,
and Death itself shall die.
How long, dear Saviour, O how long!
shall this bright Hour delay?
Fly swifter round, ye Wheels of Time,
and bring the welcome Day.

XLVIII. *The Last Judgment.*

1 SEE where the great incarnate God
fills a majestic Throne,
While from the Skies his awful Voice
bears the last Judgment down.
" I am the First, and I the Last,
" thro' endless Years the same;
" *I AM* is my Memorial still,
" and my eternal Name.

2 " Such Favours as a God can give,
" my Royal Grace bestows;
" Ye thirsty Souls, come taste the Streams
" where Life and Pleasure flows.
" The Saint that triumphs o'er his Sins,
" I'll own him for a Son;
" The whole Creation shall reward
" the Conquests he has won.

3 " But bloody Hands, and Hearts unclean,
" and all the lying Race;
" The faithless and the scoffing Crew,
" that spurn at offer'd Grace:
" They shall be taken from my Sight,
" bound fast in Iron Chains,
" And headlong plung'd into the Lake
" where Fire and Darkness reigns."

HYMN XLIX. L.

4 O may I stand before the Lamb,
   when Earth and Seas are fled !
And hear the Judge pronounce my Name,
   with Blessings on my Head !
May I with those for ever dwell,
   who here were my Delight,
While Sinners, banish'd down to Hell,
   no more offend my Sight.

XLIX. Heaven *after the General Judgment.*

1 WITH Christ and all his shining Trains
    Of Saints and Angels, we shall rise,
And pass the glitt'ring Worlds around,
While Heav'n wide opens to our Eyes.
There to the FATHER He'll resign
The vast Dominion He hath bought,
Hath by his SPIRIT form'd and rul'd,
And then to full Perfection brought.

2 There glorious Services we'll do;
And He'll unvail his wond'rous Ways,
His Love and Glories ever show;
And fill'd with Joy, we'll ever praise.

L. *Praise to God the* FATHER, SON *and* SPIRIT.

1 BLESS'D be the Father, and his Love,
   To whose celestial Source we owe
Rivers of endless Joys above,
And Rills of Comfort here below.
Glory to Thee, Great Son of God,
From whose dear wounded Body rolls
A precious Stream of vital Blood,
Pardon and Life for dying Souls.

2 We give Thee, Sacred Sp'rit, Praise,
Who in our Hearts of Sin and Woe,
Makes living Springs of Grace arise,
And into boundless Glory flow.
Thus God the Father, God the Son,
And God the Spirit we adore,
That Sea of Life and Love unknown,
Without a Bottom or a Shore.

340 HYMNS, &c.

Glory to the Divine Trinity.

TO FATHER, SON and HOLY GHOST,
 One GOD, all Glory be,
As ever was, and as now is,
So to Eternity.

Long Metre.

TO FATHER, SON and HOLY GHOST,
 One GOD of universal Reign,
All Glory, as it ever was,
And is, so ever be. *Amen.*

THE END.

N.tt.—The Corrections and Amendments, which were *annexed* to the *First Edition*, are in *this* attended to and made in their *proper Places*.——

www.ingramcontent.com/pod-product-compliance
Lightning Source LLC
Chambersburg PA
CBHW030314240426
43673CB00040B/1159